BOOKS BY ROBERT DALEY

Nonfiction:

Treasure
Target Blue
A Star in the Family
Cars at Speed
The World Beneath the City

Fiction:

To Kill a Cop
Strong Wine Red as Blood
A Priest and a Girl
Only a Game
The Whole Truth

Text and photos:

The Swords of Spain
The Cruel Sport
The Bizarre World of European Sport

TREASURE

TREASURE

ROBERT DALEY

RANDOM HOUSE NEW YORK

All rights reserved under International and Pan-American
Conventions. Published in the United States
by Random House, Inc., New York, and simultaneously
in Canada by Random House of Canada
Limited, Toronto.

Library of Congress Cataloging in Publication Data

Daley, Robert.
Treasure.

1. Nuestra Señora de Atocha (Ship)
2. Treasure-trove—Florida.   I.   Title.
G530.N83D34   975.9′41   76-53478
ISBN 0-394-41271-0

Manufactured in the United States of America

2 4 6 8 9 7 5 3

FIRST EDITION

To Those Who Search
and especially for
Eugene Lyon–Mel Fisher–John Lewis

CONTENTS

1: *The Wreck Site*   3

2: *Last Cruise of the* Atocha   19

3: *Treasure Hunters—1622*   30

4: *The World's Greatest Treasure Hunter*   41

5: *Fisher's Obsession*   59

6: *The Documents*   71

7: *A New Start*   100

8: *The Night-and-Day Search*   108

9: *Swimming the Minefield*   117

10: *Gold Fever*   129

11: *Raising and Spending Money*   138

12: *Back to the Archives*   147

13: *Bouncy John*   164

14: *The Silver Bars*   172

15: *The Bank of Spain*   180

16: *Fisher Accused*   190

17: *Expert Testimony*   199

18: *The Vindication of Eugene Lyon*   213

19: *All Precautions Taken*   233

20: *Sharks*   238

21: *The Cannons*   251

22: *Mysticism*   271

23: *The Curse of the* Atocha   279

24: *Survivors*   297

25: *Aftermath*   307

26: *The Deep-Water Hypothesis*   312

27: *Winter Dreams*   327

28: *More Silver Bars*   335

TREASURE

1

The Wreck Site

He was a treasure hunter—
proud words in Florida and the Caribbean. He belonged
to that handful of men whose life it was to scour the floors
of the seas for the remains of wrecked Spanish galleons
and to bring to the surface after a lapse of centuries the
fabulous gold and silver they had once started out with,
under sail, across oceans. He was the most famous treasure
hunter of his time, certainly, and, some said, the best of
them. Some others called him a charlatan.

His name was Mel Fisher, he was fifty-two years old,
and his problems, that 1975 summer afternoon, were numerous. Though he stood on the edge of the greatest
treasure lode that had ever dazzled the eyes of a man—a
sunken galleon worth $600 million if he could find it, so
he claimed—yet all his boats were in port and there was
some doubt they would ever sail again. These last terrible
weeks had drained Fisher. His son and daughter-in-law
were dead. A new action just filed against him in Washington claimed that the federal government, not Fisher,
owned the wrecked galleon into which he had already
poured so many years, so much money, and such anguish.

In addition, he was out of money yet again. He had nothing left with which to fight this lawsuit or any of the others that had been filed against him, or to recondition his dive boats, or to pay his divers to go out and dive again.

He had been seeking a galleon called *Nuestra Señora de Atocha,* part of Spain's 1622 plate fleet and one of the richest vessels that ever sailed, for most of the previous ten years; but today it was possible to speculate that he would not be able to resume his search. However tantalizingly close the *Atocha's* treasure lode might be, Fisher himself looked beaten. However valuable the many bits and pieces of that treasure he had brought up so far, however much proof he held that the rest was near, still Fisher himself would lack both the cash and spirit to go on—or so one imagined.

Even his office was sinking beneath his desk.

His offices were, and had been for some years, aboard a somewhat spurious vessel moored to a Key West pier. This vessel was a modern replica not only of the *Atocha,* but of all the other treasure galleons which, for 250 years, had plied the *Carrera de Indias,* Spain's Highway to the Indies, bringing tools and manufactured goods to the New World and returning with all that seemed exotic to Spaniards: spices; indigo and cochineal dyes; jewels, especially emeralds and pearls; and tobacco. But most important of all, these ships carried gold and silver: tons and tons of freshly minted doubloons and pieces of eight and tons and tons of gold and silver bullion. This treasure had been mined by slaves out of those amazing New World mountains, the richest ever discovered.

Scrawled on the bow of Fisher's office galleon were the words *"Pirates' Treasure Ship,"* a name designed to lure tourists aboard at $1.50 a head; the galleon had nothing to do with pirates, and neither did Fisher. The king of Spain's treasure was what Fisher had always sought, and in the past he had most often found it. He had dived on around 110 galleons by his own estimate, and even rival treasure hunters, who envied or hated him and who slandered him when they could, considered this figure fairly accurate. He and his divers had brought up millions of dollars worth of treasure and artifacts, but the IRS, the state of Florida, and Fisher's backers had each time taken their cuts, and Fisher had always poured what was left into the next search. So he was almost always chronically short of money. His galleon replica had seemed a solution for a time. Its hull had been built in Finland in 1949 to haul timber, and its eighteenth-century masts, rigging, and superstructure had been added in a Fort Pierce, Florida, boatyard in 1966 and 1967. Thereafter this galleon had moved up and down the east coast of Florida, roughly following in the wake of Fisher's diving vessels. He had kept the sterncastle for himself for office space and had outfitted the rest of the galleon as a treasure museum.

This was an ingenious solution—and Fisher was nothing if not wildly ingenious—for with one stroke he had gained mobility, solved his office problem, and cut down on overhead. Most important, the museum brought in small sums of money every day; sometimes this was the only liquid cash Fisher had, and at night he would dip into the cash register so that he and his divers might eat. Most of the galleon replica's real treasure had long since been removed; the few tourists each day saw mostly more replicas—the "gold" discs, for instance, were cast iron sprayed with gold paint, and they were displayed in showcases whose glass had not been cleaned in some time.

But this galleon was vital to Fisher. It was the nerve center of his empire, if you could call it an empire, and it was a continuing promise that no matter how bad things got there would always be small change to scoop out at dinnertime. But the galleon's rigging was slack, its masts had warped away from true, and it was sinking—literally—beneath Fisher's desk from rot and neglect.

On deck this afternoon a small knot of people waited to be shown through the galleon by Fisher's fifteen-year-old daughter Taffy and the other child guides. Several of the tourists stared down at the two bronze cannons—the fatal cannons—that Fisher's dead son Dirk had found at the bottom of the sea scarcely three weeks before. None of the tourists could have had any idea of these cannons represented to Fisher, or what the *Atocha* represented to him, either. Probably not one had ever heard of the *Atocha* before today or knew the work and doubt and heartbreak that had gone into finding part of it and into raising and identifying these two cannons. Probably not one had ever heard of Dirk Fisher, dead at twenty-one.

At the moment the cannons lay hidden under wet rags and sopping old mattresses; only their muzzles could be discerned. Fisher's men threw buckets of seawater onto the wretched rags and mattresses every hour or so to keep them soaked lest, after 350 years on the bottom of the sea, they begin to flake apart on contact wtih fresh air. To most of the tourists the mattress-draped cannons must have seemed mere rubbish—rubbish that interfered with the romantic spell that the tourists had hoped to find on Fisher's deck. The black cannons at the galleon's gunports looked far more interesting; one couldn't even tell they were made of concrete. Of course, Fisher might have done something else with his glorious bronze cannons, rendered these rare relics attractive in some way, but then he was not a man who cared about appearances. He did not care that his galleon had become shabby, any more than he cared that his diving vessels were in a similar deplorable state. Fisher had one obsession and one only, finding the *Atocha*'s gold.

At the moment he stood on the pier, dressed in Bermuda shorts and a sports shirt opened two-thirds of the way down his chest. A gold doubloon, glinting in the sun, hung from his neck, and the inevitable cigarette dangled from his mouth. He was watching his divers drag a huge rubber tarpaulin under the galleon's hull. The tarpaulin was more than 140 feet long and more than 50 wide. It weighed tons. Again Fisher's solution to a problem had been ingenious, even brilliant, but its principal merit was price. It was the only solution he could afford. Henceforth the galleon would wear this vast rubber diaper—diaper was what Fisher, grinning proudly, called it—tacked to its sides. Never mind that is was unsightly. The bilge pumps would remove the water trapped between diaper and hull, and after that the galleon would no longer sink.

A reporter had come down from New York, and now Fisher led the way into his office in the galleon's sterncastle, and there he described how he had raised and spent $2.5 million so far in his search for the *Atocha*. It would all pay off, he said confidently. The main treasure hold could not be far from where Dirk had found the cannons.

It was hot in the low-ceilinged windowless office; like much of Fisher's gear, the single air-conditioning unit above his head was never designed for the job he put it to. It could not cool the galleon all by itself. Fisher had removed his shirt; he often conducted business at his desk shirtless. Sweat ran down his breastbone under the hanging gold doubloon. He was a big man, six feet two, 201 pounds. He wore glasses. He seemed relaxed and cheerful. He was baldish and myopic, and he spoke with the drawl of the Midwestern chicken farmer he once had been. In somewhat technical language he explained how he had searched some 120,000 miles of ocean floor, mostly in water fifty feet deep, and at last had found a huge galleon anchor. Its shank was sixteen feet long. Each fluke was wider than a diver's armspread, and it had a ring that a man with a tank on his back could swim through. The day of this find had been a joyous one for Fisher, who was certain he would have the entire galleon soon. He did not know then how much expense and suffering lay ahead, nor that today more than four years later, he would still not be very much closer to his goal.

In response to questions, he began to speak with considerable enthusiasm of other treasure he had found and brought up in the past and of other wrecks he might move to after this one. Probably he would work on the *Atocha* for about another year, he said. By this time next year he would have taken out her treasure and he would move on.

These past few weeks must have been agony for Fisher, but his voice was firm, and he spoke of the *Atocha*'s gold and silver as if his divers were about to come in and drop it on his desk. He made it clear that he did not intend to abandon his search; the idea simply had never occurred to him. One way or another, he would go on.

His new dive vessel would be ready to put to sea soon, Fisher said. It was three times the size of any of his past vessels, meaning that his divers would be able to stay at sea even through bad weather. They would be able to work even all next winter if that proved necessary. The new vessel would be able to carry more divers, more provisions, more gear and even a nearly complete machine shop. It would be possible at last to repair compressors, winches, and other such contraptions without returning to port. The new vessel would make all the difference to his search, Fisher was sure. Of course, it had no engines—this was a 187-foot derelict hulk he was refitting. It would have to be towed to the wreck site by tugs and anchored there. If a sudden hurricane came up it would not be able to move.

He had been spending $50,000 a year on reasearch into gold detectors, Fisher said. But this research was about to bear fruit. Two different inventors were due in with their gadgets—detectors that really worked—next week. Within two weeks, three at the most, these detectors would lead him, Fisher felt sure, to the *Atocha's* main treasure hold.

The best gold detector in existence at that time had a range of six feet or less. The *Atocha's* gold and silver bullion was not only under fifty feet of water, it was probably covered by many feet of sand, and no one in Fisher's entourage believed the new gold detectors would work any better than past ones. One of Fisher's divers had said privately, "Mel's the softest touch in the world. All you have to do is give him a sob story, and he'll finance your project. One of those inventors has been stringing him along for three years now."

In any case, Fisher said, he was confident he would find the bulk of the *Atocha's* treasure soon.

Fisher's most serious problem that day was not legal or financial, but personal, and he did not talk about it. His wife Dolores, who had once set the women's underwater endurance record—more than fifty-five hours without coming up—had stuck by Fisher through all of his adventures, but now, mourning her first-born son, she was on the edge of hysteria all the time. Fisher was forever having to take her aside and put his arms around her.

Just then a man entered the office carrying a life ring that bore the name *Northwind.* The *Northwind,* captained by Dirk Fisher, had been Mel Fisher's principal diving vessel. Now, like the *Atocha,* it lay on the bottom of the Gulf of Mexico.

"The Coast Guard just brought this in, Mel," the man

said. "It washed up on Loggerhead Key in the Tortugas. Hell, that's thirty miles from where she went down."

Fisher stared at the unhappy souvenir. But all he said was, "Man, those currents are something."

"Do you want to keep it here, Mel?"

"Too many bad memories. Take the *Northwind* name off it, and put it on one of the other vessels. Maybe it will save somebody's life some day."

When the man had gone out, Fisher brought forth a photo of a two-year-old boy wearing mask and wet suit. "This is Dirk when he was a baby," Fisher said. "I remember when I bought him his first snorkel. He couldn't get the mouthpiece in his mouth. His mouth was too small. So I took the fitting off and cut the end off the nipple of a baby bottle and put that on, and it worked fine, and he took to it right away."

Fisher stared at the photo of his dead son, and perhaps his eyes misted over. He said, "Dirk was the most fanatical and gung ho diver you ever saw, and he was so experienced. I used to go out to the site every day by seaplane or motorboat and talk to him for twenty minutes. But he was the one who ran the search. I don't see how this terrible thing ever happened."

In a few minutes Fisher was leaving for Tampa to talk to some potential investors about a new influx of capital, his most pressing need. From there he would fly to Washington to argue with the Justice Department over ownership of the *Atocha* and whatever treasure it might contain. His divers had been working in international waters, forty miles west of Key West and almost eleven miles from the nearest uninhabited atoll—in the middle of the open sea. And so the government's claim seemed preposterous to Fisher. But proving this was going to cost him much energy and some stiff legal fees.

He was packing a briefcase on his desk. "But come back next week, he told his visitor. "We'll have the new vessel out and the new detectors working. We should break into the main treasure hold next week or the week after. That's where the gold will be. I'm sure you'll want to be here when we start bringing up the gold. Why don't you plan on coming back in about a week." There was no twinkle in his eye, no tremor in his voice. He was not making a joke, or pretending to a bravery he did not feel. Apparently, he believed every word he spoke, though how could he after all that had happened so far?

Even as Fisher's scheduled flight disappeared into the north, his company's seaplane carrying four men climbed into the sky for a flight down over the wreck site, for Fisher's only fear seemed to be that someone else would find the *Atocha*'s treasure in his absence. Fisher, after all, held no legal title to that section of the sea or any other.

None of his men had been out there for days, and perhaps even now some rival treasure hunter was anchored amid Fisher's buoys. They all knew where the site was, and it was no trick for a diver to swim down a buoy line and attach a cable to whatever he found there. Perhaps the pirates were even now hauling Dirk Fisher's remaining cannons to the surface. In the past Fisher had always sought to maintain physical presence at the site—a kind of squatter's rights over the wreck—as if this would have some legal weight if it came to a court test, or to shooting. But it had been impossible to maintain this physical presence in the days following the tragedy. Fisher believed so absolutely in the *Atocha*'s treasure that he imagined all other treasure hunters did also, and by now they might have swarmed there.

At the seaplane's controls was Bob Moran, forty-six, one of the many curious figures clustered around Fisher. Moran was what used to be called a soldier of fortune. At one time or another he had been a charter boat captain, sports car driver, photographer, dance teacher, advertising executive, and treasure diver; he had once spent sixty-two days in one of Castro's prisons, most of them in solitary confinement; and, of course, he was also a pilot. A vice-president and stockholder of Treasure Salvors, Inc., Fisher's principal company, Moran was said to be the only man in Fisher's entourage capable of administrating an operation as big as this one had become, and he was assuming an even larger role. Fisher now owned three ocean-going vessels, not including the *Northwind* at the bottom of the sea, plus a number of smaller ones, and he held leases on still others. He owned tens of thousands of dollars worth of pumps, compressors, and other such gear, most of which was in poor condition, and additional tens of thousands of dollars worth of electronic detection instruments, each piece of which either did or did not work with pinpoint accuracy. There were about forty full-time employees, about a hundred stockholders, and about thirty-five people who had invested specifically in the *Atocha* project—to the tune of $2.5 million, according to Fisher—for which investments they would reap half of all eventual profits, if any. Fisher was not the man to manage a business as vast as this; and he had always needed Bob Moran, or someone like him, around.

Moran was now pointing down at the last of the Florida Keys spread out below the plane.

Moran's earliest view of the Keys had surprised him. He grew up near Buffalo, New York, and like most Americans had imagined that Key West was the last of the Keys. Moran had supposed that there were only a dozen or so keys in all, but this was wrong, too. There must be ten thousand keys in all, he had decided, perhaps more, and from two thousand feet above Key West his eye could discern at least a hundred of them. Most were uninhabited. A good many did not even have names, and they dribbled westward for seventy miles as far as the Dry Tortugas. There was an almost unbroken line of reefs for most of that distance, too, and on the other side of the reefs ran the deep unending river that was the Gulf Stream. It was this river that had carried home each year the high, wooden treasure galleons of the greatest seaborne empire the world had known up to that time. The Carrera de Indias had been just that, a highway. The galleons' route, Moran had learned, was as inflexible as if committed to concrete. The Spaniards would sail north out of Havana until they came in sight of the low-lying Florida islands, at which point they would head dead east, riding the Gulf Stream, the multitude of islands floating steadily backward off the port beam. The Spaniards knew that the reef line was there, close to their hulls, but the risks presented by it, and by the atolls and islands it guarded, were preferable to riding the deeper water of the central Gulf Stream. They did not like to be out of sight of land. Their

instruments could fix latitude well enough but they had
no means of telling longitude at all, for the necessary
chronometer would not be invented until after the galleons stopped sailing. To the Spaniards the Florida Keys
archipelago was a series of checkpoints, neither more nor
less, and they needed each one to know precisely where
they were. Of course the barometer hadn't been invented
yet either. They had no scientific aid in forecasting
weather whatsoever, and so each time a tropical storm or
hurricane caught them close to the shoals and islands,
they were helpless. The galleons could not be put into reverse or stopped dead in the water. And so for centuries
individual ships and even entire fleets merely plowed forward toward destruction. It was probable that every single
key beneath Moran's wings had exacted Spanish tribute at
one time or another, however calm or peaceful their waters looked today.

The scenery below was indeed beautiful. It seemed to
Moran that he was gazing down on a vast, submerged desert. The myriad colors testified to the shallow depth
soundings in far more subtle detail than the chart spread
open on his knees. The water, for mile after mile, was
sometimes only a foot deep. It was also exceptionally
transparent, and the sand was white, though here and
there patches of coarse sea grass moved gently as the endless currents combed their way through. Deep water val-
leys showed dark off some islands; off others solid stony
plateaus showed orange or red in the shallows. Wherever the submerged desert gave way to submerged
meadows the sea grass was scarred with dozens of white
sand paths where pleasure boats had run aground and
then, apparently, been dragged off.

A few miles to the south was the unseen barrier reef;
beyond it the Gulf Stream was gun-metal blue. Out there
was safety; in here, for any galleon blown this way, was
death. Death amid such apparent peace. Each tragedy,
when it happened, would have rocked not only the Empire, but individual families as well. All that grief was in-
gored today. It was as if no widow, no mother, no child
had ever wept over what happened here, as if the men
who died here had never existed at all. Time dimmed pain

above all else; treasure buried in the sea it did not dim at all, and nothing counted this year except the *Atocha's* bullion.

Moran at the controls shouted and pointed down at the Marquesas Keys. Aboard the seaplane were Tim March, twenty-four, from York, Pennsylvania, and Canadian-born Spencer Wickens, twenty-three. Young as they were, these two were among Fisher's oldest and most experienced divers, and over the past long months they had dived hundreds of times on the bones of the *Atocha*, bringing up many items of treasure; it had also been their sad job only three weeks before to bring up the bodies of their friends. Now, viewing the Marquesas from the air for the first time, they were excited. The Marquesas atoll was lower and more vast than they had thought. They had never before had a clear picture of what it looked like, even though they had spent countless hours and even days anchored in its lee, waiting for the weather to moderate enough so that they could return to the wreck site to dive again on the *Atocha*. Nor were they the first divers to use the Marquesas as a base camp, they remarked to Moran. The Spaniards, searching for the *Atocha* three and a half centuries ago, had kept a camp there too, perhaps off the same beach they used, for from the air there was clearly no other as attractive.

The plane droned steadily on. West of the Marquesas the water deepened sharply. From the controls Moran shouted back that he hoped he would be able to find the wreck site. When the seas were rough he sometimes couldn't. The wreck site, after all, was no more than a dozen floating spar buoys.

Having found the remains of a wrecked destroyer named the *Patricia*, which had served navy gunners for years as a target ship, Moran sought to get his bearings, but in the open sea there was no other point on which to fix a cross reference. Flying low over the choppy water he spied a wreck site buoy at last, and after that he was able to point out a line of them. They were white plastic sewer pipes sealed at both ends, they must have been twelve or more feet long each, and the top four or five feet rode above the waves. Each buoy was anchored to some known underwater feature: one to the reef that was believed to have sunk the *Atocha*, another to the galleon anchor, a third to Dirk Fisher's remaining cannons, and so on. The buoys were vital. They pinpointed what had been found so far, and allowed Fisher and all who worked for him to believe the rest was nearby. But from the plane they resembled nothing so much as a handful of white pencils bobbing in the sea. It was difficult to believe that they pointed the way towards anything.

There were no pirates on the scene. The treasure, if it was there at all, was still safe.

The water here was deep enough so that the bottom was not visible. The water was black, and the waves were rough for an afternoon as placid as this one. The wreck site looked to be what it was, a particularly malevolent corner of the ocean, perpetually storm tossed, for the prevailing currents here were permanently at war with the tides. But at this spot fifty feet down lay the fulfillment or the destruction of Fisher's dream.

The surface of the choppy sea, however long one stared down at it, gave back no clues as to where the mass of treasure might be, much less whether Fisher would ever find it.

A wooden sailing vessel like the *Atocha* did not simply sink to the bottom in one piece. The reef that destroyed it—presumably the one back there under Fisher's buoy—would have torn the galleon's bottom open. Perhaps the mighty waves lifted the ship and dropped it onto the reef several times. After that it would have staggered on in the direction of the winds, spilling people and treasure into the sea all the way. The body of the ship might have broken into several big pieces and numerous small ones, all of which would have settled to the bottom in a scattered pattern maybe a mile square. Maybe more. Eventually the bulk of each of these pieces would have settled through the sand to bedrock. Any part of the ship's timbers that projected above the sand would have been devoured by teredo worms. After 350 years it was possible that even timbers totally buried in sand would have been devoured. Only metal, porcelain, and precious stones would remain, plus ballast. How much sand would this stuff be under by now? Five feet? Ten feet? Twenty? How had Fisher come close enough even to fix these buoys? And what would he do next? If the overburden of sand was thick enough none of Fisher's gold detectors was going to find the treasure for him. There were tools for moving this much sand; if Fisher could get a reading he could possibly bore straight down to the treasure, but as yet he had obtained no useful reading, and perhaps he never would. Lacking a reading, he could only go on boring random holes in the ocean floor, hoping to stumble on the ballast pile. The *Atocha,* like all galleons, had carried two hundred tons of stones in its hull to counterweight the enormous leverage of its masts. Those stones should lie there somewhere, still conforming in shape to the *Atocha's* hull. The gold and silver bullion, in theory at least, would repose atop the aft section of this pile. But it was also possible that the ballast had leaked out of the breached hull stone by stone and did not exist as a pile anywhere; conceivably the gold and silver bullion, which would have filled a locked and guarded cabin, might have done the same. The *Atocha's* treasure could be strewn in as many directions as there had been bars. Or the cabin might have become detached from the hull, and this cabin, or what was left of it, might now lie somewhere else.

So far Fisher and his divers had brought up a good many interesting items: some gold and silver bars; a gold chalice; encrusted spoons and plates; Dirk Fisher's cannons, of course; a bosun's gold whistle that was like a penknife, for it opened up into a toothpick, nail cleaner, and earwax scoop; a bronze astrolabe that still worked; dozens and then thousands of pieces of eight; a box of 1622 firearms; some random gold and silver—loose change out of people's pockets, so to speak. All of this stuff might indeed be worth $6 million, as Fisher had once claimed; even so, its cost was unacceptable. It was simply too high, both in money and in lives. Only the main treasure lode, which he had searched for in vain in this spot for five years, could restore some measure of sanity to Fisher's search. Not that money can pay for lives, but the attainment of some great goal sometimes can, a successful crusade can—or at least so people have believed since history began. But where was this mother lode? Would Fisher ever find it? Below Moran's slowly circling seaplane, the sea, endlessly struggling with itself, gave no answer. The sea looked cold, uninviting, implacable. It shared its secrets with no man. Fisher could dream all he wanted. The sea would not be impressed.

Now Moran added power and when the seaplane had gained some height he pointed obliquely down toward a spot that lay about a thousand yards north of where the unseen reef must be. "The Quicksands," Moran shouted. The water was clearer there and also slightly less deep, and from aloft it was possible to discern a pattern of interlocking craters in the open floor. Most of Fisher's finds to date had come out of those craters. His ships' propellers had been fitted with elbow-shaped ducts that he himself had invented (another of his ingenious solutions); the ducts had forced the prop wash straight down, creating those craters, each time blowing sand away until bedrock lay exposed. In each hole divers had hovered, ready to grab any item that came to light. There were years of craters down there.

From the air the interlocking craters resembled the craters of the moon, except that there were more of them in a smaller space. It was impossible to determine the size of the area that those craters covered—distances are immeasurable at sea. The eye must relate to something before it can make even a guess, and there was nothing to relate to here except Fisher's tiny buoys. But certainly the craters covered several football fields' worth of ocean floor, and they represented hundreds of tons of sand moved. The work already done here, most of it useless, seemed in retrospect as heartbreaking as the tragedies to which it had led.

Presently Moran steered the seaplane back toward Key West, leaving Fisher's insubstantial, pencil-thin buoys bobbing amid the wave tops, like individual points of hope. No, there had been no pirates. That would be something pleasant to report. In a few minutes the Marquesas atoll began to pass beneath the wings, and then the low mangrove keys. One looked down again on the multicolored shallows and shoals. At Key West airport the silent

Moran tied his plane down and perhaps he too brooded. A small cabin filled from floor to ceiling with bars of bullion—that's what Fisher was hoping to find. Fisher was searching for something no greater in size than a dozen suitcases lost somewhere on or under the immense floor of the sea. Would he ever find them?

It seemed hopeless.

2

Last Cruise of the Atocha

It was the Spaniards' practice for two and a half centuries to dispatch two fleets a year to the New World. One sailed to northern South America and was called the *Flota de Tierra Firme*—the Mainland Fleet. In 1622 the *Atocha* was vice-flagship of this fleet. The other went to Veracruz, Mexico, and was called the *Flota de Nueva España*—the New Spain Fleet; New Spain to the Spaniards was all of North America north of Honduras, though principally it meant Mexico. Some years the two fleets sailed from Spain separately, one in the spring, the other in the fall. Often they sailed together, driving south toward the Canary Islands, off the northwest coast of Africa, to catch the westbound trade winds, then crossing the Atlantic on the latitude of Guadeloupe. Once the chain of Caribbean islands was reached, the combined fleet would split up. The New Spain Fleet would head northwest, pass between Cuba and Yucatan and drop anchor at last in the harbor at Veracruz. The voyage of the Mainland Fleet was slightly shorter, for after Guadeloupe it made for Cartagena on the coast of what is now Colombia, the first of its several stops.

The 1622 fleet which was commanded by the Marqués de Cadereita and which included the *Atocha* had sailed out of the Bay of Cadiz on April 23. "The weather was so good," Cadereita later wrote to the king, "that on May 3 Grand Canary was seen; and at the end of May, the islands of Dominica." Cadereita's good luck was almost over for the year. Off Huza Key adverse winds held him up seven days, so that he entered the port of Cartagena on June 14, having been at sea a total of fifty-three days. The king's tobacco was not ready, so after eight days in port he sailed for Portobelo, Panama, a distance on the map of only about three hundred miles. Galleons were not speed boats. This voyage took him seven additional days, meaning sixty at sea so far. Well, he had known in advance that it would be seven to nine months before he ever saw Spain again. If he returned at all.

There was a third fleet, the Pacific one, which sailed each year to Panama City from Callao, the port for Lima. This fleet carried principally silver from the Potosí mine, which in 1545 had been discovered thirteen thousand feet up in the Andes in what is today Bolivia, and which has proven to be the richest silver mine in history. Tons of Potosí silver bars, loaded onto pack trains of llamas, had come down out of the mountains to Callao, where the silver was loaded onto the waiting Pacific galleons. The distance between the Potosí mine and the sea at Callao is 950 miles by air, much more over the stony mountain trails of that day, but treasure, to the Spaniards, was treasure. Once loaded, the Pacific treasure galleons would sail up the west coast of South America to Panama City, where the silver had to be off-loaded again and carried by mules across the Panamanian Isthmus to the waiting Mainland Fleet—Cadereita's fleet in 1622—at Portobelo.

It was all beautifully regulated. The timetables were all in sync. The bureaucrats were in full control at all times, or at least they pretended to be.

The *Casa de Contratación*—the House of Trade—had been established in Seville on February 14, 1503, to regulate the riches and the commerce that the Indies would surely produce. At the time there had been no riches or commerce yet. Columbus was still out there somewhere on his fourth voyage, cruising around. Although Columbus cannot be overpraised, of equal significance was the fact that Spain was ready to exploit him and his discoveries almost at once. Spain had only a vague idea of what Columbus had found. Even Columbus had only a vague idea of what Columbus had found, but the House of Trade was already hiring scribes and laying down rules. These rules would govern everything having to do with the New World, from the size and armament of the ships that were permitted to sail, to the cargo they would carry, to the diet at sea. Decades before most of the men were born who would sail aboard the *Atocha* in 1622, the House of Trade had already decided what they would eat. A common sailor that year would be entitled each day to a quart of wine, two pounds of biscuits, an ounce and a half of olive oil, half a quart of vinegar, and a small piece of cheese. He was entitled to eat two ounces of peas or beans four days a week, eight ounces of salt pork and one and a half ounces of rice three days a week. This diet sounds healthful enough. The trouble was that each voyage lasted too long; weeks before the New World was sighted, the drinking water turned green, the wine became vinegar, the oil and cheese turned rancid, and the biscuits, salted meat, and dried vegetables crawled with maggots and weevils.

The galleon as a type was developing even as Columbus returned home for the last time, and by 1510 the first of them was in service. The design lasted until 1750. The galleon was the principal tool by which Spain conquered, exploited, and colonized the New World, and as early as 1555 both Mexico City and Lima boasted populations of over one hundred thousand persons each, larger than Seville and Toledo, the two greatest cities in Spain. By the time the *Atocha* sailed on its final voyage there were seventy thousand churches in the New World, five hundred monasteries and convents, six archbishoprics, thirty-two bishoprics, three inquisitions, two universities, two viceroys (Mexico and Peru), and over two hundred cities. The whole world was changing in what must have seemed to Spaniards inconceivable ways, but their habits and methods remained the same for centuries and their captial ships did not change significantly either, except to grow bigger. A hundred years might pass without even a change in the rigging. The Spaniards counted a ship's tonnage by the amount of cargo she could carry. The first galleons weighed about three hundred tons, and the House of Trade stipulated that they could draw no more than nine *codos* (fifteen feet) of water. One hundred years later a major galleon like the *Atocha* was about twice this size, six hundred tons. It had three masts, all mounting square sails except the furthest aft, and it had the traditional forecastle and sterncastle, though these tended to make it, and all other galleons, top heavy. It had two main decks, and four decks at the sterncastle. Spaniards must have considered the *Atocha* enormous, and it was, if you compared it to Magellen's ship, ninety tons, that had first circumnavigated the globe, or to Columbus' *Santa Maria*, which probably had been even smaller. The *Niña* and the *Pinta* had been smaller still. By comparison the largest passenger liner ever built, the *Queen Elizabeth*, displaced eighty three thousand tons.

It has been estimated that in two and a half centuries Spain looted the New World of some $14 billion worth of gold and silver, all of which was transported back to Spain aboard the galleon fleets. The dollar figure is only a guess. Currencies do not relate to each other over the centuries. The House of Trade kept records in pesos but the value of the peso changed steadily; even its relationship to other units of Spanish currency did not remain constant. But the buying power of a single peso in 1622 may have been the equivalent of two hundred dollars now, and the *Atocha* was carrying about 1.5 million pesos in treasure. When it went down Spain trembled, and individual fortunes were wiped out.

The loss of the *Atocha* made that a bad half decade for Spain. The next half decade was bad too. In 1628 the entire homeward-bound treasure fleet was captured by the Dutch in Matanzas Bay, a harbor scarely fifteen leagues east of Havana, into which the galleons had been driven, and the captain general of the Spanish fleet was later publicly beheaded in a Seville square for his cowardice. Thus less than half as much treasure reached Spain during the years 1621–1630 as during the last decade of the previous century, treasure's peak, and possibly Spain's as well.

The *Atocha's* principal cargo was silver, not gold. When

the highway to the Indies first opened, Spain was experiencing economic stagnation caused by a shortage of money, which at that time was coins, not paper. One couldn't simply print up more coins. Coins had to be precious metal, and there was very little available. Then suddenly Spain had plenty, more than anyone else; it poured in from the New World every year, and before very long Spain was the richest nation on earth. By 1622 about 85 percent of the galleons' return cargo each year was precious metal.

The value of silver in Columbus' time closely approached that of gold. Both metals were extremely rare. But by the middle of the sixteenth century the great Mexican and Bolivian silver mines had been discovered; from then on the value of silver dropped steadily. By the time the *Atocha* sailed in 1622 silver was only one-fifteenth as valuable as gold, and roughly 99 percent of the treasure aboard the *Atocha* and all the other galleons was now silver. The *Atocha*, for instance, carried 901 silver bars weighing roughly 70 pounds each, plus 250,000 pieces of eight freshly minted in the New World for circulation in Spain; she also carried 161 items in registered gold, but their total weight came to only 216.5 pounds. The *Atocha* carried altogether 47 troy tons of registered treasure and possibly as much gain in unregistered treasure—meaning contraband—plus 264 people. She was criminally overloaded.

But then the galleons every year were so low in the water from treasure and other cargo, so jammed to the gunwales with provisions, ships' stores, cannons and cannonballs, chickens, livestock, hawsers, firewood, sailors, artillerymen, slaves, officers, passengers, not to mention personal luggage, that those charged to defend the ship in emergencies, whether from fire, storm, reefs, pirates, or enemy warships, quite literally could not get out of each other's way. That is, not all of the scores of treasure galleons that went to the bottom over the centuries were destroyed by acts of God. A good many were simply so heavily loaded that some minor calamity sank them. The House of Trade knew all about Spanish greed, but there was no way to prove that a sunken galleon had been overloaded. Usually there was no survivor to prosecute anyway. And when an overloaded galleon or fleet did reach Spain safely there was no desire to prosecute. Often a *Te Deum* was sung in the Seville cathedral instead. One pocketed one's profits, and said nothing.

The House of Trade during almost its entire lifetime was a curious mixture of the astute and the corrupt, the venal and the God-fearing, the practical and the superstitious. No ship could sail for the Indies without a license, which required an inspection of the vessel first. But neither could any person sail without a license and this required a certificate of confession and holy communion, signed by a priest and issued within the week. If God were in the heavens searching out a sinner for retribution, let him not seek among the galleons.

Realizing that these galleons, though the mightiest ships afloat, were also extremely fragile, the House of Trade had ordained that four copies of each ship's registry and other vital documents should always be made. One copy would sail on the ship itself, another would go on the fleet's flagship, and a third on the vice-flagship. The fourth copy would stay behind to cross with the next year's fleet. The men who wrote such rules were hard-headed businessmen. They would protect what they could, and once the galleons were at sea they could protect nothing but their accounting ledgers; so that's what they did. One result was that, although the *Atocha's* original papers went to the bottom with her, copies eventually reached Spain. It was these copies that came to light again three and a half centuries later, to fire the imaginations of Fisher and the other treasure hunters.

Although in some years entire fleets returned safely, there were others when every single ship was lost; overall statistics are hard and clear. Galleon losses averaged out to 10 percent. There seemed nothing men could do about such odds in 1622 except pray, and so, by regulation, chaplains sailed with every fleet. When disaster, such as an oncoming hurricane, threatened the priests would pray frantically, for the seas and the gods were mightier than any galleon, and it was thought that only a holy man could save the ships. Sometimes the storm would promptly lift or pass to one side, seemingly miraculously, and when this happened the priests were accorded the credit. They were laughingly pummeled and embraced by passengers and officers alike. Like Christ, they had calmed the very waves. Wine flowed, and each priest was the hero of the moment. Some accepted congratulations modestly, some preened with self-importance. When a ship sank, the names of any priests aboard always led the casualty lists, and fifteen of them went to the bottom in 1622.

The galleons and the merchant ships they guarded always sailed in convoys, but the size of these convoys varied. In 1548 there were seventy-three ships in the combined treasure fleets returning to Spain and in 1715 there were as few as ten. The Marqués de Cadereita's 1622 fleet, as it massed in Havana harbor for the return voyage, numbered twenty-eight sails, eight of them treasure galleons. Missing were the New Spain galleons from Mexico which had reached Havana earlier and which had waited for Cadereita for a time. Having no idea where he was or when he might arrive—it was always possible he had been captured or sunk—the New Spain fleet had started home alone.

Cadereita had been delayed in Panama, for a dispatch had been received; thirty-six Dutch Urcas had been sighted off the South American coast. These enemy warships were even now believed to be cruising the Caribbean. Cadereita promptly called a meeting of every important personage in Panama. Its purpose was to decide what to do, so he later wrote the king. But these personages, however illustrious they may have been, were less illustrious than Cadereita himself and knew no more than he did concerning the whereabouts and intentions of the Dutch. Since there was no way to find out about the Dutch, there was nothing to decide. One could merely sail and hope for the best. But Cadereita appears to have been a very careful politician; he called a lot of meetings, and he always remembered to inform the king that he had done so. The meeting in Panama accomplished one thing—if Cadereita's fleet was later intercepted by the enemy, at least he would have managed to spread the blame a bit in advance.

After that, Cadereita's flagship, *Nuestra Señora de Candelaria,* was careened and its bottom scraped. One big new merchant vessel, *Nuestra Señora del Rosario* was armed with cannons, and thus was transformed into a fighting galleon. The king's Peruvian silver was then loaded, and Cadereita sailed back to Cartagena. Although it had taken seven days to come from there, it took only five to sail back to pick up the king's tobacco, and the emeralds, pearls, and gold. Packed in bales, barrels, and chests, and weighing many tons, this cargo had to be ferried out to the anchored ships and then lifted aboard, and the job took a full week. So it was August 3 before Cadereita set sail for Havana, a distance of about a thousand miles. This next-to-last leg of his journey home took nineteen days—his average speed was about four miles an hour. He watched somewhat fearfully for the Dutch ships all the way, but did not see any.

In Havana more cargo came aboard the twenty-eight ships of his fleet, principally copper from Cuban mines. Cadereita called another meeting whose purpose was twofold. First of all, a *cédula* had arrived from the king ordering that no treasure go aboard the very two ships that Cadereita considered his strongest, the *Rosario* and the *Candelaria*. This *cédula* was dated May 23, and it reached Havana on August 25, three months and two days after the king had signed it with the words "*Yo El Rey.*" Cadereita had no idea why the king was trying to shift his cargo around from three thousand miles away. Perhaps the king, or some advisor, was having visions again. The king, who would prove himself over the years to be somewhat dimwitted, was Philip IV, and he was at this time seventeen years old. Apparently Cadereita immediately determined to ignore the king's order, but he was careful to call a meeting first. Again he needed backing in case anything should go wrong later.

The second purpose of the conference was to fix a sailing date. All of Cadereita's admirals, as well as Don Francisco Vanegas, who was governor and captain-general of Cuba, were present. The date of the conference was August 26; the decision was made to set sail at dawn on September 4 because the weather was expected to be good that day, and everybody got up from the table pleased. Cadereita had, in effect, consulted the local weather bureau. The weather bureau had consisted of these men sitting around a table. That was it. There was no other. There were no meteorological instruments. There were no ships that could travel faster than storms could travel, thus bringing reports of oncoming weather fronts. Nor were there in operation methods of conveying weather information overland. A system of smoke signals along Cuba's seven-hundred-mile length did exist, but its purpose was to bring news of enemy ships. No one had yet thought to use it to signal changes in weather.

September 4 had been chosen as the sailing date because it was one day before the day that the moon and the sun conjoined, as the Spaniards put it. The conjunction of the moon was the phase exactly opposite full moon, and the Spaniards believed that whatever weather occurred during the conjunction would last until three days before the next full moon, which was called the opposition of the moon. In other words weather tended to stick around. If there was good weather during the conjunction, there was supposed to be continued good weather, and if the weather was vile, it supposedly would stay that way. This passed for sophisticated weather lore in 1622.

Cadereita now decided to split his fleet into two parts, and he divided up responsibility at sea among his admirals. He himself would sail aboard the *Candelaria* at the head of the column. At night the only light allowed in the convoy would be the great stern lantern of this lead galleon. The blackout must be absolute. It was not enemy submarines that men feared in 1622, nor even enemy galleons, but disaster far more terrible than either: fire.

Cadereita ordered five other galleons and three smaller warships called *pataches* to remain under his direct command out front; perhaps he planned to range far forward, searching out any lurking enemy vessels before they could strike. Whatever his reason, this decision to lead the convoy saved his life. He also ordered the seventeen slow and unruly merchantmen to remain intact; and to the *Rosario* as flagship and the *Atocha* as vice-flagship he assigned the job of direct supervision over the merchantmen. The vice-flagship, as always, would bring up the rear of the convoy, which meant in this case that the *Atocha* was doomed.

And so just after dawn on September 4, 1622, under a serene sky, the fleet set sail. All aboard must have expected to sight the Spanish coast at the beginning of November.

The convoy headed north-northwest all day under a fair wind. Ahead, glittering in the sun, waited the coral necklace that Florida wore beneath its island beard. Cadereita knew the reefs were there; so did all his captains. The Casa de Contratación, in addition to regulating all traffic in the Indies, had also been collecting for over a century all data that hundreds of captains had sent back. By 1550 most New World bays and headlands, and even many Pacific islands, had been mapped. The latitudes in each case were fairly accurately designated, but the longitudes, like Spanish navigation as a whole, were guesswork. Maps of the period show the Florida peninsula ending in a point as sharp as an arrowhead. From this arrowhead the islands straggled west, an area Spaniards called Caveza de los Mártires—Martyrs' Head—because so many ships had been lost there. Three and a half centuries later such unsophisticated and dangerously inexact maps might appear quaint and almost comical, but Cadereita no doubt considered them the most modern navigational aids ever devised. He was grateful to have them, for predecessors within living memory had sailed without any notion at all of what was ahead. Their charts had been completely blank. Cadereita's ships were the latest type too, and the *Atocha* was the newest of them, only two years old. Every modern convenience had been built into her and into a good many of Cadereita's other galleons as well. Those subjects and the slaves who sailed out of Havana would have thought these galleons enormous, rather marvelous, the greatest, swiftest, most modern vessels ever built. They were the 1622 equivalent of the Boeing 747, and passengers' reactions could only have been similar—it was incredible, if one paused to think about it, that such a huge creation actually existed, actually floated, could actually transport so many people so fast to the other side of the world. What a wonder man was to have managed to construct such a thing at all!

There were about as many people—264—jammed into the *Atocha* as a 747 might carry, and they were jammed in just as tightly, even though their trip was expected to be not of several hours duration, but of two or more months.

All day under a brilliant sun the fleet sailed north toward the Caveza de los Mártires, tacking only once, at three in the afternoon. At sunset, according to later reports, Cadereita looked over his fleet and found it in good order. He judged his position to be ten leagues from Havana, which could no longer be seen, for it did not cast any glow against the night sky in 1622, and would not for several hundred more years. It is known that, before darkness fell, Cadereita signaled a final change in course to due north. The combined fleet was ordered to run on this heading all night.

3

Treasure Hunters—1622

The first treasure hunters to scavenge galleons were black and Indian slaves owned by Spanish salvors. These forerunners of Mel Fisher dove stark naked. Some may have been women. They were elite teams, the most skilled professional divers then available.

They moved out to wreck sites fast, before divers working for pirates or the enemy could get there, before seas and storms had broken up the wreck so that it could no longer be found. They were on top of the *Atocha* within nine days.

Such speed was possible because in Havana, as in all major New World ports, salvage vessels were kept fully provisioned, in a state of permanent alert. They were prepared, once over a wreck, to stay there for months, and sometimes years. Salvaging a major galleon was no quick job, and, in the case of the *Atocha,* divers were to remain on the scene almost continuously for the next two decades.

These original treasure divers, both black and red, were spiritual descendants of those Indians the Spaniards had found diving for pearls when they first touched Santa Margarita Island. The Spaniards had watched them go down wearing net bags around their necks, clutching rocks to their bellies, and they came up with pearls in great profusion. The Spaniards thought this so marvelous that they promptly enslaved the whole tribe. Such divers, unaided by any device, were supposed to have been able to go down 150 feet, a considerable depth but one still attained by the naked female pearl divers of modern Japan (the world record seems to be 212 feet). The Spanish historian Oviedo, an eyewitness writing in 1535, claimed they could stay under for fifteen minutes. Some of today's Japanese women have managed five minutes, and the current world's record is thirteen minutes set by a man keeping absolutely motionless on the bottom of a swimming pool. Presumably Oviedo's timepiece was lying to him, although six later historians also wrote of fifteen-minute dives.

The Spaniards drove their pearl divers so hard and communicated to them so many European diseases, that the entire tribe died out. So from other Caribbean islands other Indians were imported to Santa Margarita, and these adapted perfectly, with no discernible reduction in the quality or quantity of pearls recoverd. However, the second tribe soon became extinct also, and for the same reasons. From Africa the Spaniards then imported blacks, most of whom, before their enslavement, had never seen water deeper than a swamp. Amazingly these black slaves adapted to pearl diving, too.

So there was a long tradition of skilled diving in the Caribbean, and soon enough there was a long tradition of sunken galleons to match. The wealth contained in some of them was incredible, and often this wealth was not under very much water. Salvage concerns came into existence, and they purchased their human diving machines from the pearl fisheries.

There were easy wrecks to salvage, and hard ones.

Most galleons went down in fairly shallow water, having been flung against reefs or shoals, or even up onto beaches. Often entire superstructures were awash, and wrecks like these were salvaged of treasure and artillery almost completely. The technique was to burn the ship to the water line. This opened it up to the divers, who glided down amid the entrails knowing exactly what they were looking for and where.

The hard wrecks were those so deep that only a stub of mast showed. However remarkable their lung capacity, the naked divers had an extremely short bottom time, and even a single bar of silver was too heavy for a diver to swim up with alone.

Nearly every wreck, hard or easy, was scavenged over for years, Meticulous records were always kept, because, although the divers legally did not even exist, the salvors were official. They were assigned contracts by the civil authorities. A king's accountant was on board at the wreck site, and the salvor got paid a percentage of whatever his divers recovered. These records were sent back to the House of Trade, and most of them eventually wound up in the Archive of the Indies in Seville.

After those first divers departed, the *Atocha* waited for oblivion, motionless on the bottom of the sea. The decades and centuries passed over her. Those who had watched her sail proudly out of Havana died, one by one, as did each of the salvage contractors, each of the divers. Cadereita died, and all his captains. New kings ruled Spain. Newer treasure ships sank and engaged men's interest, until no one spoke of the *Atocha* any more, or even remembered her. There was still a good deal left of her below the sea, and would be for a long time, but above the sea a handful of handwritten documents was all that remained, a few sheets of paper moldering on shelves in Seville. No one knew which ones they were.

Gradually, Spain's treasure fleets diminished in size and at last stopped altogether. In 1763 the British took Florida and implanted a different language there, and a different culture in which the golden galleons played no part. Early in the next century Spain lost most of the rest of her colonies. The former highway to the Indies, now totally disused, ceased to be even a memory in Florida.

But below the surface of Florida waters, the route was still delimited by wrecked ships, many of which still contained vast wealth. A man swimming along the bottom from the Keys to Miami and then up the East Coast might have come upon a rotting galleon every quarter mile—or so Mel Fisher decided after he had located scores of them and marked them on his charts. But for more than three hundred years there was no such swimmer. In many cases the wrecks were only just offshore, and only just beneath the surface. Generations of Florida schoolboys sometimes swam and frolicked directly above ballast piles and the mouths of protruding cannons, the same cannons Florida fishermen sometimes snagged their nets on without knowing or caring what they were.

Nor did suitable salvage gear exist.

Over the centuries a number of diving engines had been conceived; but those that were actually built did not work, until at last the modern air compressor and the first deepsea diving rigs were invented. During the early decades of the twentieth century a good many salvage operations were carried out by so-called deep-sea divers who wore heavy, rubberized canvas suits, surmounted by brass screw-on helmets that weighed sixty pounds. They also wore eighty-pound lead belts, and they clomped about the bottom in forty-pound elevator boots. Such rigs were so heavy that divers usually had to be lifted in and out of the water on platforms, and even on the bottom they were nearly immobile. Deep-sea divers were useful for repairing the footings of river bridges, and they became celebrated when they attempted to get trapped crews out of early sunken submarines; books about their exploits made exciting reading for the youth of those years, Mel Fisher among them. But deep-sea gear was not suitable for treasure hunting. It was too heavy, too cumbersome, and too expensive. It was also very dangerous. In addition, hard-hat diving was singularly unappealing to what would prove to be the secretive, treasure hunter mentality: the hard-hat diver was tied to too many other people topside.

Not until Jacques Yves Cousteau and Emile Gagnan in France invented the Self-Contained Underwater Breathing Apparatus (scuba) in 1943 did modern treasure hunting become feasible. Scuba gear suddenly made every shallow-water wreck accessible and opened up what at first appeared to be a new sport.

It did not stay a sport for long. It proved as addictive as heroin. It soon became no more a sport than betting on horses. "We don't call treasure hunting a profession," Fisher's wife Dolores said once, "we call it a disease."

Most treasure hunters were lone-wolf, free-lance adventurers. A good many had failed at a number of other jobs already.

Modern treasure hunting might have begun anywhere that treasure-laden, homeward-bound galleons had sunk. In fact it began, and this was only fitting, in those waters where galleons had sunk in the greatest abundance: off Florida. A single man invented it there, a hard-hat diver from Delaware Bay named Art McKee.

In 1934 McKee had migrated to Homestead, Florida, where he took the only job available, town recreation director. McKee was twenty-two.

(Fisher, then a twelve-year-old seventh grader in Gary, Indiana, had already made his first dive in Lake Michigan wearing a helmet he had fashioned himself from a five-gallon paint can. Air came down from a bicycle pump that a pal worked topside. Fisher had been mired in mud and unable to free his feet, when his view plate, which was held in place by melted-down lead soldiers, popped out because his pal had been pumping too hard. That was the first time Fisher almost drowned in a contraption of his own invention, though not the last.)

In 1937, diving on a "pile of stones with corroded pipes on its top" pointed out to him by a fisherman, McKee found a single coin dated 1721. What wreck could this be? he wondered. McKee was so tantalized that he wrote to the Archive of the Indies in Seville for information.

Incredibly, a bulging package reached McKee from Spain. It contained hundreds of pages of photocopied records about Spain's 1733 treasure fleet, which, according to the documents, had numbered twenty-two sails. As it passed the northern keys the fleet had been engulfed by a hurricane of such force that all twenty-two vessels went to the bottom. McKee had never heard of any such fleet. The photocopy of an old map was in the same package. McKee grabbed it up. It showed the supposed locations of all twenty-two wrecks. McKee became consumed with a desire to find and loot them all.

Many other treasure hunters, in the decades since McKee's request, have written to Seville for information. Some letters were not answered. Others were answered briefly. No one ever received a package like McKee's, and

McKee never knew why some nameless Spaniard had gone to so much trouble on his behalf. Spain in the late 1930s was embroiled in a savage civil war. There were mass executions, bodies in the streets and not enough to eat, but the Archive of the Indies was working nonetheless.

And so the golden galleons of long ago reentered Florida's cultural heritage. Because of Art McKee, schoolchildren would grow up knowing about them. Because of McKee, fishermen and charter-boat captains would peer down through gin-clear waters with increased interest, spy cannon muzzles pointing up at them, and pause to delimit the awesome ballast mounds—each of which, from above, resembled nothing so much as the neatly tended grave of some gigantic prehistoric creature. The talk would spread, and there would be rival treasure hunters.

McKee decided he had found the flagship of the 1733 fleet, and he began to work it. Crouched in his hard-hat rig, he fanned the bottom by hand. Sand blew away. Not much, but some. He was going to have to find sand-dredging tools. The best of them was called an airlift, which was a kind of underwater vacuum cleaner. The diver held a length of pipe upright in the water and injected compressed air into it at the bottom. As the air rushed up the pipe it created a vacuum behind it. Sand, stones, shells, and whatever else was under the pipe—possibly even treasure—immediately filled the vacuum, spewing out the top of the pipe in a dense spray. The diver could fill a barge with it. Or it could be spewed into a more or less neat pile beside the hole, where a confederate could extract from it any goodies. The greater the diameter and length of the pipe, and the greater the pressure of compressed air injected into it, then the better it worked. McKee's airlift was homemade. He was the first ever to use one on an old shipwreck, and until Fisher came along, the airlift was virtually the only tool treasure hunters had.

By 1949 McKee had gathered enough encrusted cannons and decayed artifacts to open a sunken treasure museum on Plantation Key. He also rebuilt the ballast mound of his 1733 flagship to its 1937 appearance and began selling tickets to tourists, whom he would take out in his glass bottom boat to stare down at, and perhaps even dive on "his" wreck.

The state of Florida had evinced no interest whatsoever in its offshore shipwrecks. Nonetheless, McKee applied for and received a ten-year exclusive lease to waters extending out to six miles offshore. According to this lease, the 1733 flagship was his exclusively. So was nearly every other 1733 wreck, found or not. No one could go near them without his permission.

The Keys were a sleepy place in the early 1950s (Mel Fisher was a poultry farmer in California then), and men respected what they took to be McKee's personal property. But when the first face masks, swim fins, and snorkels reached southern Florida, with Cousteau's scuba equipment not far behind, McKee's wrecks suddenly became fantastically attractive. They weren't even deep. A number, including the flagship, were more than three miles offshore, but a diver could almost walk there. The flagship was in twenty feet of water, the *Tres Puentes* was in fifteen feet, and the *Chaves* only ten feet. The *El Sueco* was not only in shallow water, it was only a thousand yards offshore. For a while gentlemanly rules still prevailed. Men asked McKee's permission to dive on McKee's wreck, and McKee was usually generous. He had worked all these wrecks for years, and believed, wrongly, that nothing of value was left. McKee had searched only the central portions. He had known nothing about what marine archeologists now call the scatter pattern. The divers he allowed onto his wrecks began to spread out and to find things. The gentlemanly era of treasure diving ended almost as soon as it had begun.

Of the earliest treasure hunters, one was a chiropractor, another a house painter, a third a building contractor. The Roberts brothers had a seafood restaurant and also a light plane in which they used to scout for schools of fish. But from aloft, they sometimes spotted ballast piles. There was a treasure hunter known as Julius the Frenchman, and a former tugboat sailor named Tim Watkins who in 1954 picked a gold shoe buckle off a wreck near Tavernier Key. Immediately he bought a sixty-foot boat, anchored over the galleon he had found (one of McKee's) and brought up some eighteen tons of relics while McKee screamed. Watkins was the first treasure-hunting buccaneer, and *Buccaneer* was also the name of his boat. He anchored it over

McKee's original flagship and grabbed all the cannons McKee had left there to show tourists. McKee went to court, flashing the lease for which he had paid the state a hundred dollars a year for seven years. But the court ruled the lease invalid.

The treasure-hunting rage spread. Treasure hunters interrogated every fisherman whose path they crossed, listened for rumors in every restaurant, and visited other treasure hunters unexpectedly and at odd hours, hoping to find the competition cleaning or studying new treasure—which might mean that a new galleon had been found.

Every gas-pump operator in the Keys could recognize a treasure hunter: the treasure hunter's hands would be scraped, cut, and black, for the conglomerate—metal objects fused together over the centuries—worked its way under the skin and would not come off. There was also the inevitable question: "Say, have you heard anything about any new wrecks being found?"

These men had no charts, no bearings. They found wrecks by rumor, and by eye.

Watkins had a relatively big boat, Marty Meylach a small one. When he gave up working and went into treasure hunting full time, Meylach built himself an 18-foot catamaran by hand. To Meylach a treasure boat had to be small enough to tow behind a car. News of a strike might come at any end of the Keys, and the first boats to the scene would get the pickings.

The treasure hunter's code kept changing. At first men spoke of "my wreck," but very soon it became "my side," then, "my hole." Soon even this rule no longer held. If a man found anything, then inevitably competitors would jump into the hole beside him. Treasure hunters became like packs of sharks all tearing bites out of the same carcass. It was no longer possible to leave heavy items— cannonballs or cannons, for instance—behind overnight. They'd be gone by morning. Soon it was not possible to leave anything at all unattended; it would simply disappear.

Bigger and bigger airlifts, some six inches in diameter, were brought into use, and they bit deeply into sand, mud, and timbers. Someone tunneled completely underneath McKee's flagship until all that supported the tons of ballast stone was the galleon's rotted hull. The hull collapsed into the hole in a great cloud of mud, and the 1733 flagship was destroyed at last. Another wreck was blown apart by dynamite.

Not that anybody made much money. Meylach was happy to get a pair of 1733 cuticle scissors. Other divers found pewter plates, which were seldom intact, and went home to clean them lovingly by hand with muriatic acid. The huge galleon anchors could occasionally be sold to seafood restaurants as patio decorations.

But the mood got darker. Boats mysteriously sank at their moorings. Treasure hunters, meeting over the same galleon, sometimes threatened each other with guns. Once, a portable air compressor was apparently booby-trapped one night. The next morning it exploded, ripping off a diver's foot and injuring some bystanders.

McKee's documents had opened up only the waters of the Keys. So far treasure hunting had not spread beyond there. But now in Vero Beach, two hundred miles farther north, a building contractor named Kip Wagner, who was not even a diver, had begun to wonder why he sometimes found pieces of eight lying on the beach after severe northeast storms. None were dated later than 1715. Where had they come from?

Wagner began to ask around: another "scientific" treasure hunt had begun.

Obsessed with discovering the provenance of his coins, Wagner sent a friend to do research in the Library of Congress. Some hard answers came back. The entire 1715 plate fleet had sunk off Vero Beach, ten galleons, or perhaps twelve. The emissary even had a copy of a chart, dated 1774, that placed the fleet's graveyard between the Sebastian and Fort Pierce inlets.

So Wagner built a surfboard with a glass view port and went paddling about looking for one or another of these wrecks. Weeks passed. All Wagner had to show for his obsession was a sunburned back.

But through his view port one fine day he peered down through nine feet of clear water and counted portions of five cannons jutting from the sand.

Wagner was thrilled, and so was the small group of friends he told about it. Their imaginations were fired.

Together they formed the Real Eight Company with Wagner as president. Wagner bought exploration and salvage leases from the State of Florida; these gave him exclusive title to fifty miles of coastline. The company bought a dilapidated old launch and renovated it, but none of the men quit their other jobs. For the next three years they dove regularly on weekends if the weather was fine, though only during the four-month diving season. They did make a few finds: clumps of silver coins fused together by time and salt water, and some more or less ruined artifacts similar to those even then being removed by Meylach, Watkins, and the others from units of the 1733 fleet two hundred miles to the south. But after three years Wagner and his friends had not yet cleared expenses.

Surely there was gold down there. Why hadn't they been able to find it?

It was time for Mel Fisher to step out onto the stage. Without even knowing it, the treasure-hunting world awaited him eagerly. Fisher, now a shopkeeper, still lived in California. He had a wife and four kids. He had never heard of the Real Eight company or the 1715 plate fleet. He knew nothing about the waters off Vero Beach, Florida.

But it was Fisher who would show Real Eight and all the other treasure hunters how to find gold. He would revolutionize the little game they all played, raise the stakes to levels they had not dreamed of. His appetite would be huge. He would risk more, find more, suffer more.

Even now he was on his way east, his wife beside him, all of his kids stuffed into the back seat. His battered car pulled a trailer containing all their earthly belongings. In a sense he was on his way to tilt at windmills, so it was only fitting that he was followed by his own personal Sancho Panza, a black man named Demostines Molinar, in a second battered car pulling a second trailer. Fisher had sold everything and was en route to Florida not so much to save treasure hunting as an industry as to save a dream, one of the oldest and most abiding of all men's dreams, unchanged since the dawn of history: Eldorado, vast treasure at the end of the rainbow, pie in the sky. The dream of gold. Gold for which there was no need to work. Gold that simply lay there waiting for the lucky man. Anyone could find it, even you or me. One need only look in the right place.

Fisher was coming East to find gold for all of us.

4

The World's Greatest Treasure Hunter

Who was Mel Fisher? He was an Indiana carpenter's son, born August 12, 1922, in Hobart, a Gary suburb. He went to Purdue, then Alabama. He was trained as an engineer. World War II yanked him out of junior year. Reverting to carpenter, he moved through Europe behind the armies, helping rebuild what had been destroyed. When the war ended Fisher was twenty-three. College interested him no longer. He did not know where he wanted to go. He tried Chicago, then Denver, then Tampa. In the early 1950's he went to California to work with his father, a chicken rancher, and for four years the world's greatest treasure-hunter-to-be watched ten thousand chickens lay ten thousand eggs a day. At night school the future dreamer of gold took a course in animal husbandry. He was like St. Paul waiting for the call.

He already knew scuba diving. He had first seen it on the Riviera while still in the army. He had first tried it in Tampa. One afternoon, while fishing off the Bay bridge there, Fisher had watched a man in mask and swim fins plunge in with a spear gun. The skin-diver surfaced for breath. "You're wasting your time," Fisher informed him cheerfully. "I've been here all day and there ain't no fish in the ocean."

But the skin-diver, thirty seconds later, surfaced with a grouper impaled on his spear. Fisher was amazed.

Would the skin-diver meet him there tomorrow and teach him how to use such gear? Sure, said the skin-diver. Fisher bought the fins and mask, and waited at that spot all the next day. The skin-diver didn't show up. At last Fisher plunged in by himself. He found the new sport tougher than he had imagined: "I was trying to hold my breath and go down seventy feet and there was about a five-knot current. The current knocked me against the bridge piling. I got all cut up with barnacles. I was bleeding. I didn't know how to clear my ears and they were hurting. My eyes were going cross-eyed from the pressure pushing the mask in against my face."

But the next day he went back again, and this time the skin-diver was there.

"This is no place to learn," the skin-diver said. "Come into the shallow water."

Shortly after the first lesson, Fisher read a Tampa *Tribune* ad for aqualungs signed "Rene Bussoz, Westwood Village, California." The Frenchman had come to the United States with six aqualungs to sell. Fisher jumped into his car, drove three thousand miles to California, and bought one. Fisher also told Bussoz that he wanted the Florida franchise for those aqualungs. But back in Florida, Fisher found aqualungs impossible to sell. There were no ad campaigns and no instructors. There was no way even to refill tanks. Fisher's own aqualung, filled, he used only once. For his first dive he decided to go after a three-hundred-pound sea bass he had noticed near the center of the bridge. He stepped over the side of the skiff and swam to the bottom to spear it. Visiblity was between four and six feet. About ten minutes passed before Fisher realized that the huge bass was right beside him, close enough to eat him, and had been hovering in darkness there all along. There were big fish all around him. He crouched behind a piling: tarpon, drum, sharks, rays. The water was so murky that he couldn't see them, only their shadows swimming over him, when he looked up at the sun.

He swam to the surface, dropped the aqualung to the

bottom of the boat, and didn't use it again until he moved to California six months later.

Skin diving at that time was one of the fastest-growing sports in the United States. In California, Fisher joined a spear-fishing club, and he began to use his scuba tank regularly. Like everyone else he had to drive to Rene Bussoz's place in north Los Angeles to get it filled. So he bought an air compressor. Soon thousands were driving up to his father's chicken ranch to get their scuba tanks pumped up. Fisher built a machine shop and began manufacturing spear guns. Then he went into masks, fins, and snorkels. His dive shop in one end of one shed was open only from four to six each afternoon, but was the most profitable activity on the ranch. But his father decided to put the ranch up for sale.

The couple who came to buy it had a daughter named Dolores, called Deo, a big girl, very young, with red hair and no knowledge of the sea. Fisher took the girl into the water. She was about to help him earn the money to build a skin-diving shop on the ocean front. Money to Fisher was something a man could always find. All you had to do was think up a method.

This time Fisher's solution was lobsters. They lay on the bottom off Santa Cruz Island.

The water was cold. Fisher and Deo wore dry suits. Fisher would nose along the bottom, and snatch up a lobster. The young girl would snorkel down for the lobster and then swim up to toss it into the skiff. Fisher, meanwhile, would already be holding up the next lobster. Every time a lobster touched one of the dry suits it would snag a hole. Fisher and Deo would start sinking and freezing. Fisher began to dress himself and the girl in long underwear under the dry suits and overalls over them.

Receiving tanks stood in the shallows a quarter of a mile apart. When they were full Fisher had a ton of lobsters, which he sold to restaurant chains for a better price than he could have obtained at the fish market. In Redondo Beach he built the dive shop he wanted, with his own hands, on the profits of lobsters caught the same way—the first skin-diving shop in the world. People wanted scuba instructions. Fisher rented the pool at the Hermosa Biltmore Hotel and began giving courses. So many people came that he had to hire assistant instructors. To promote his shop and lessons, he promoted himself a weekly TV show on a Los Angeles station—underwater films, guest interviews. This show was to last four and a half years.

The girl with the red hair was now seventeen. Fisher, then thirty, married her. For a honeymoon he took her diving off the Florida Keys, choosing by accident, or in fulfillment of some cataclysmic cosmic joke, that same corner of the ocean where the *Atocha* lay, and where their unborn son Dirk, would die. Neither had ever heard of the *Atocha*. It was the wreck of a steel-hulled freighter that had attracted Fisher there, for he knew its romantic story. He and his young bride swam down to the wreck together. The water was warm and sparkling with light. Twenty years afterward Fisher still spoke excitedly of that first glorious honeymoon morning. "I speared eleven jewfish, a hundred-and-fifty pound tarpon, and a huge shark that was twelve feet long or more. I got movies of the whole thing. I had my movie camera bolted right to the barrel of my gas gun, and I would turn on my camera and go down shooting."

So that was their honeymoon.

The wreck whose story Fisher had found so irresistible was the *Barbinero*, which had sailed from Seville to Havana around 1929 with a cargo of wanton women from the Spanish jails, together with all the sour wine the Spaniards could load aboard. Spain was getting rid of its bad wine and its bad women in one fell swoop, Fisher always chortled. But Havana refused to let the *Barbinero* land. It then turned toward Key West, drove into a hurricane, and capsized. It left a trail of junk and people along the bottom that, Fisher claimed, extended for twenty miles. The *Barbinero* during his honeymoon entered deep into Fisher's soul. It would draw him back, for he was a sentimental man. Two decades later, though it wasn't quite in the right place, he would try to make it help him in his search for the *Atocha*.

The honeymoon with Deo lasted many years, for Fisher quickly learned to float expeditions to anywhere he and Deo wished to dive. The man who would later promote the search for the *Atocha* to the tune of $2.5 million had no trouble promoting a trip to Panama or the Virgin Islands. Pan American would hand him air tickets in exchange for possible publicity on his TV show or in his column in *Watersports* magazine. Equipment manufacturers were eager to loan gear for similar publicity. Dolores Fisher wore a swim suit nicely, and Jantzen was happy to pay for film footage that showed Deo drifting past exotic reefs. Fisher came home from one such trip with three thousand feet of 35-mm. movie film, two thousand feet of 16-mm. film, and twenty rolls of stills. He edited most of this himself, broke it into a number of shows, wrote his own voice-over, and as soon as he could, he and Deo took off again. His store, Mel's Aqua Shop, was thriving, but the boss was rarely there, except when his wife was having babies.

Dolores had two by the time she was twenty and would have two more later. She became an extremely skilled diver. Swimming along at Mel's side, she was always as stunned as he by the beauty of the undersea world, though occasionally she was terrified. The first time she was nosed by a barracuda she burst out of the water screaming. Fisher explained to her his theory: barracudas are accustomed to eating only fish, not people. He shoved a 16-mm. underwater camera in her hands and sent her back down for a close-up shot of the barracuda grinding its jaws. Meekly, Dolores did as she was told. Soon she was casual toward sharks too. She believed her husband when he told her they were harmless, though on two terrible occasions later she would change her mind.

Fisher spoke and wrote eloquently about diving: "You just can't imagine how beautiful coral reefs are. There are bright red corals, yellow stag horns, purple fan corals, green brain corals, just about every color in the rainbow. Each reef is a maze of canyons, slots, caves, and each one you drift over has a new surprise for you, a new type of odd-looking fish." Off the Virgin Islands Fisher found water so clear that visibility was a hundred feet or more until a huge school of sardines swam by. The tiny silvery fish were dashing around, swiftly changing directions. Swimming among those sardines was like being in a blinding snow storm, thought Fisher. He could see only a few inches ahead and the silvery blurs whizzing past made him dizzy.

Moving down through the water with his camera bolted to his spear gun, he would watch the colors filter out. Red was the first to go. At thirty-three feet water pressure doubled, a great stillness seemed to come upon the world, and red was gone. At that depth gear weighed nothing. A little deeper and orange and yellow diminished until they too were absorbed, and he was swimming through a serene blueness.

At seventy feet one day off Cozumel he came upon a three-hundred-pound bass. It spied him and darted into a cave. He swam in after it. Ahead the cave branched out in three directions, and this scared him. He could get lost, use up all his air, and fail to find his way out. But he could see, from the dust settling, which corridor the bass had taken, so he followed, swimming along until suddenly the corridor opened up into an enormous room, a cathedral of blue pierced by a shaft of sunlight that entered through a hole in the ceiling. Filming all the while, Fisher moved closer and closer to the giant bass until it panicked and, with a sudden thrash of its tail, pointed itself straight up toward the hole in the ceiling and smashed its way out into the sunlit water. Presently the awed Fisher followed.

The fish stories he filmed became ever more dangerous.

Off the Virgin Islands, Fisher came upon a leopard ray. It had a wing spread of about nine feet and he judged its weight at about nine hundred pounds. Flapping its huge wings, it glided slowly toward him. It was jet black but spotted with white rings about three inches in diameter, and each ring contained a number of white polka dots. When it turned away the ray showed a tail perhaps fifteen feet long. It's five poisonous stingers were located about two feet out.

Fisher handed his camera to Nelson Mathison, the California physician who was diving with him that day, for he wanted footage of whatever would happen next. Swimming after the ray, he sent a spear into it. The monster sounded. Fisher, clinging to his gun, was pulled twenty feet down. The ray then headed straight out to sea at terrific speed. Then it turned and swam toward shallow water; bursts of green blood spurted from its gills each time it breathed.

But Mathison had missed the footage. After resetting the camera and returning it to Mathison, Fisher climbed on the huge ray's back. Avoiding the thrashing tail with its deadly stingers and exercising extreme care, he began to wrestle it. The camera turned. Perhaps ten times the poisoned barbs nearly reached Fisher, but he was being very exact and very careful. He was riding along the surface of the sea, hanging to one wing and grinning at the camera inside his mask, when the ray suddenly nose-dived, swung him in front of the poisonous stingers, and whacked him hard.

The barbs that went into him were eight inches long. Two penetrated the flesh of his upper arm, embedding themselves in the bone. The ray then plunged toward the bottom, dragging Fisher with it, arm first. He had gulped some air—not very much. The rushing water knocked his face mask off. The barbs were stuck fast in his arm. Though he tugged and pulled, they would not come out. The ray dove still deeper. Fisher, out of air, yanked with all his strength, but the barbs were planted in bone. If he couldn't pull them out of his arm, then his only hope, he decided, was to pull them out of the ray. He was trying to get his feet against the wing for leverage, but his fins made him clumsy, and the water was rushing by too fast. At last he got his feet under him, pushed against the wing, and with the last of his strength yanked the barbs loose from their own roots.

Mathison managed to drag Fisher up into their boat and to pull one poisonous barb out with a pair of pliers. The other broke off inside Fisher's arm. They got to shore and to a hospital, where Mathison opened the wound, cleaned it, sewed Fisher back up again, and ordered him to stay at the hospital overnight. But Fisher, by now pumped full of morphine, penicillin, antitetanus serum, and other drugs, announced that he felt fine and was leaving at once. The hero jumped up off the table, took two steps, and fainted.

Running out of fish stories to film for his TV shows, searching for some newer adventure, Fisher turned to treasure hunting, and he started by forming a club called the Treasure Hunters Association, whose membership consisted of about 250 customers of Mel's Aqua Shop. Members' dues and fees paid Fisher's way to every wreck site that interested him along the southern California coast. Each weekend for three years he took a different group out to practice with old maps and ineffective digging equipment. They found no treasure. They did stumble upon a number of nineteenth-century and later wrecks, including two gambling ships that had once anchored out in the channel, and from which they recovered rusty old safes and slot machines.

Presently Fisher constructed an underwater sled that could be towed behind a boat and a somewhat primitive underwater detector to go with it. The diver rode the sled deep, hanging on, and there was a plexiglass dome under his nose which contained the detector's electronics.

Fisher had heard that one of Spain's Pacific galleons, having been blown far off course, had sunk off Cortez Bank, and on his new sled he went looking for it. The search started in about twenty feet of water, but nothing turned up at this depth, so Fisher went deeper—and gradually deeper, and deeper, and deeper. At a depth below one hundred feet the dome under his nose imploded, and it sucked his face mask into it. Shards of shattered glass then whipped back against his face. His first thought was that he had been blinded. Unable to see or breathe, bleeding profusely, he had to get off that sled and up through a hundred feet of water to the surface. Squirming clear, avoiding the sled's various trailing antennae, he began kicking his way up. The swim seemed endless. The sunlight got closer, though too slowly. At last he burst into the clear, where he sucked in great gulps of air. "That was the most dangerous thing, the worst accident that ever happened to me."

From California Fisher jumped to the big leagues: the Caribbean. He took Dolores and nine others to Yucatán. Barely ten miles off the coast was Cozumel Island, which the golden galleons had once rounded regularly. There Fisher found his first galleon, but he recovered only its huge anchor. Cozumel was soon to become one of the Caribbean's most posh resorts, but in the fifties it was a primitive fishing village. Fisher floated the anchor along the mangrove shoreline to where the village basked sleepily in the sun, and began to winch it up onto the village's single pier. A number of Indians watched in silence as Fisher and friends worked. When the great anchor was on the pier and Fisher was satisfied with its placement, he unhooked the chains, and he and his friends sailed sway, leaving behind this curious record of the passage there of Melvin A. Fisher.

The treasure-hunting compulsion was now thriving in Fisher's system. On one expedition, to Portobelo, Panama, the harbor seemed to fill up before his eyes with the anchored galleons of three hundred years ago. Fisher had brought no detection gear with which to find wrecks, but he was determined to find some wrecks anyway. From careful study of his charts, he deduced where the pirate captains would have waited offshore. He also deduced that the galleon captains would have been forced to sail in this direction, though the prevailing winds and currents were wrong, and the reef line here was dangerous. Inevitably, over the centuries, galleons would have shipwrecked precisely here.

When he dove at the spot he had picked out, he found the bottom littered with galleons. He was elated, but he ran out of money before any treasure could be found.

Each expedition was put together on a shoestring. Most times he and his group would charter any vessel they could get, as long as it was cheap. But Fisher was going into debt anyway.

One way to work off debts was to set customers of Mel's Aqua Shop to mining the rivers and streams of California for gold. Fisher, in the grip of gold fever himself, set about instilling it in others. He developed and began marketing an underwater gold vacuum dredge. To help sell it he produced a twenty-four-page magazine called *Mel's Gold Diving Tips*. The inside cover bore a map purporting to show the major gold deposits in California, southern Oregon, and Nevada. "Gold is where you find it!" was the headline over the map. Most of the text was written by Fisher in prose as enticing as any ad agency copywriter would have wished.

To teach potential buyers how to use his dredge, Fisher

began taking groups up to the mountain rivers each weekend. One weekend found him shepherding five hundred families. Hardly anybody found gold, but Fisher sold thousands of dollars worth of dredges.

Each time he paid off his debts, he launched a new expedition to the Caribbean, where he ran up new debts and again found no treasure.

In August 1959 Dolores Fisher decided she wanted to go for the underwater endurance record. She was twenty-three with three small sons at home. To break the record was her own notion, and she took the idea to the Merle Norman Cosmetics firm, which agreed to pay her expenses. A woman named Jones had set the old record earlier that same year: fifty hours, two minutes, and forty-three seconds—more than two days under the surface of the water. Deo plunged into a tank at the Hermosa Ocean Aquarium shortly before noon on a Friday, planning to sit on the bottom all weekend.

The porpoises and other large fish had been moved out of the tank, which was about ten feet deep. A kind of underwater outhouse had been installed on the bottom.

The hours began to pass. They passed exceedingly slowly.

Fisher had arranged for friends in relays to wave at Dolores through the view window. With some of these friends she sometimes played Chinese checkers or chess, using hand signals. There was a television set outside, too. From time to time her air ran out, and Fisher would swim down with a fresh tank.

The second day began to pass. She ate breakfast, then lunch, then dinner, squeezing mush into her mouth out of plastic bottles.

When she had been thirty six hours without sleep she began to doze uncontrollably—whereupon her mouth would relax, the mouthpiece would pop out, and she would wake up choking. Gagging and coughing, her teeth would bite down on her mouthpiece once again, and she would struggle to stay awake.

During the third day she read soggy books and magazines. A message was held up outside the window: Kane, the youngest of her three sons, had just taken his first steps. Behind her mask, the proud young mother beamed.

It was Sunday. At midafternoon she broke the old record, and her oldest son, Dirk, then five years old, swam down and handed her a rose.

She stayed down until sunset, rubbing the old record into the dirt. At last her head broke the surface. Her new record: fifty-five hours, thirty-seven minutes, and eleven seconds. When the welcoming crowd's cheering died down, Dolores was rushed by ambulance to the hospital for "observation," part of the show Fisher had cooked up in advance to improve the drama. Fisher always liked to improve drama. Dolores was perfectly fine, except for her "dish pan hands, dish pan feet, and dish pan all over," as Fisher later proudly reported. "I've got a photograph of the bottom of her feet, and you wouldn't believe it."

Fisher came home from one treasure hunt $25,000 in debt. Another one soon loomed, but Fisher regretfully withdrew—he still owed $4,000.

Unknown to Fisher, Dolores had been squirreling away house money. Into this secret savings account had gone almost exactly $4,000—every dime she didn't spend on food or on her children. To Deo this was their insurance policy, the only security they had as a family, and it meant a lot to her.

She asked her husband, "If you had the $4,000, what would happen?"

"We'd go treasure hunting," answered Mel.

Dolores pulled out her bankbook and said, "Let's go."

In California, Fisher ran into Captain Jacques Cousteau. The great man was there to promote another of his brilliant books, an upcoming TV special, and sales of the diving gear on which he still held original patents. No man in history had ever taken as much money and fame out of the sea, or explored as much of it, either.

But Cousteau had never gone treasure hunting.

The Frenchman listened enthralled as Fisher described a planned expedition to Silver Shoals off the Dominican Republic, where one of the richest of all galleons was to be found.

"Come with us," Fisher urged.

"Alas, I can not," the great man replied, adding with regret, "My life is written on a piece of paper to the end."

Fisher said later, "Isn't that sad? And here I thought he was sitting on top of the world."

Cousteau finally did go treasure hunting, though only once, sailing into the Caribbean at the helm of his converted warship *Calypso*. He and his divers succeeded in locating and partially excavating a galleon wreck. Although this produced another beautiful book, *Diving for Sunken Treasure*, and also another brilliant TV special, Cousteau found no treasure. Indeed, he found little more at the bottom of the sea than a sandal stamped "Mel's Aqua Shop."

Fisher bought a 65-foot boat called the *Golden Doubloon*. It boasted four small bunk rooms, a forecastle that slept four and also held two 14-foot freezers, and a main stateroom containing four bunks. Of the twenty passengers he recruited, all of whom put up money to pay for this most elaborate of all Fisher expeditions, six were women. Two of the passengers had met Fisher when they went into his shop to get change for parking meters. No one ever said Fisher wasn't a great salesman.

The *Golden Doubloon* sailed down the coast of Baja California, through the Panama Canal and into the Caribbean. About halfway between Panama and Jamaica a tropical storm blew up. Seas rose twenty feet high. Walls of water crashed down on deck. The stern windows were smashed in. Gear lashed to the decks broke loose and began smashing the boat to pieces.

The boat began taking on water fast. The hull began to fill. The engine shaft went underwater, then the engine room itself. The bilge pumps short-circuited. Fisher's passengers ran about screaming "We're sinking!" Fisher put out a Mayday call to any ships in the vicinity, but no answer came back.

The bow began to point into the air at an ever-sharper angle. Soon the stern was totally underwater. The engines had run for a while, forcing blue smoke and boiling seawater out the exhaust pipes, but then had cut out entirely. Fisher began throwing weight over the side: food, diving gear, compressors, a spare fifteen-foot skiff. But the storm was still howling, and walls of water still toppled down on top of them. Fisher formed a bucket brigade. Everybody bailed.

At last the tempest passed, but the seas remained high. Anyone trying to work on deck risked being swept overboard. But a cofferdam had to be constructed in the submerged stern, one that would project above the level of the sea. There was no other way that the stern could be pumped out. With help from Demostines Molinar, working at first mostly underwater in still-tumultuous seas, Fisher began to construct the cofferdam. He built it with boards and canvas ripped loose from other parts of the boat. It took him most of six days, during which no other ship answered the *Golden Doubloon's* repeated Mayday calls. Pumping began by hand, and with infinite slowness the stern section of the boat began to rise above the level of the still-angry ocean. Finally one engine was started, and the *Golden Doubloon* limped back to Panama, where repairs were completed. Afterward no one, except possibly Fisher, had the heart to try for Silver Shoals, their original destination, so they dove on a few galleon wrecks off the coast of Panama and then went home.

Again Fisher had failed to find treasure. Again he appeared not in the least discouraged. Incredibly, he seemed to take strength and even confidence from each defeat.

In December of 1962 a Florida man named Lou Ullian passed through Los Angeles. He and Fisher sat drinking and swapping stories. Ullian was a member of Kip Wagner's Real Eight, Inc. He described how Wagner, paddling face down on a surfboard, had discovered the remains of a 1715 galleon off Vero Beach, and how, for the past couple of years, the Real Eight weekend divers had recovered some interesting artifacts from this wreck. Some treasure, too. Why, they had found wedges of silver worth . . .

That night Fisher could not sleep. He paced the floor, smoking furiously.

Fisher flew to Florida to lay a proposal before Wagner. The Real Eight men, Fisher pointed out, were working only one galleon when there were nine—possibly eleven—more out there to be found and looted. And they worked only during the three or four months of each year when the ocean was reasonably warm and reasonably calm. Why, it would be years before they completed the job. But Fisher had a plan: he would form a team of full-time professional divers. They would find the other galleons, dig them, and bring up treasure. The state would get 25 percent of the spoils, by law; the rest would be divided fifty-fifty between Fisher's group and Real Eight.

Fisher sat back and put another Tareyton in his mouth, lighting it off the butt of the one in his fingers. He spoke in his usual lazy drawl, sounding as confident as always. His hands did not tremble. Only the incessant smoking showed what inner tensions Fisher might be feeling.

Wagner told him that Real Eight would take the proposal under advisement.

That was enough for Fisher. The absolute optimist saw life the way he chose to. He flew back to California and persuaded five other men to sign on with him. All agreed to sell their possessions, move to Florida, and hunt treasure there for one year without pay. Fisher himself, though he had never yet found treasure anywhere, promptly sold his house, store, and boat, and started East. He was forty years old.

The men he had selected were Rupert Gates, Dick Williams, Walt Holzworth, Demostines Molinar, and Fay Feild. All had been on at least two past expeditions with Fisher.

Gates was a Stanford graduate and an engineer. Williams had sailed the world aboard commercial vessels as radio operator. Holzworth had worked as a construction superintendent. Molinar, called Mo-Mo, had been a diesel mechanic in Colón, Panama, when the *Golden Doubloon* put in there one year for repairs.

Feild, from Fort Bridger, Wyoming, was an electronics engineer and had once worked as project engineer on ground-controlled approach radar systems. As an avid shell collector, Feild noticed that the rare spiny oyster shell he coveted was most often found clinging to wrecked iron ships. So he invented a magnetometer—a supersensitive underwater detector that would make marks on graph paper when pointed at ferrous metal. Fisher, learning of this gadget, had taken Feild treasure hunting to the Caribbean. Feild had quickly located six old wrecks, more than they could possibly dig during one short expedition. From then on, Feild's place in Fisher's affections was assured, even though Feild sometimes lapsed into scientific jargon that none of the others could understand. He was nearly bald, wore a pencil-thin mustache and smoked cigars; but he was also broad-shouldered, narrow-waisted, heavily muscled.

What Fisher asked of his five men was simple: "Sell what you have and come follow me." Fisher was never one to change a good line that had worked before. If at the end of one year they had not found treasure, the group would disband. They would call themselves Treasure Salvors Incorporated, and would each have a portion of stock in the corporation—it would be worth plenty, Fisher told them eloquently, next year, when they had found gold. As slowly and precisely as a spider, he spun his web of hope. He ensnared them all.

The next thing Kip Wagner knew, the Treasure Salvors were ringing his doorbell in Florida.

Wagner was appalled. There had been no agreement. Reluctantly he made one, and then put the Salvors on a pile of ballast stones that, though it lay within Real Eight's lease, had been public knowledge for years. Hundreds of amateur divers had pawed over the pile. It was believed to contain nothing. That was the start of a long hard year for Treasure Salvors, Inc.

Fisher couldn't afford to invest much money in a diving vessel, so he bought the cheapest hulk he could find, a decrepit fifty-footer. The refitting took months, and by then the best dive season was over. The fall and winter ocean off that part of Florida was almost always too rough for diving, though they tried. Once, Fisher was thrown against a bulkhead and cracked some ribs. Worse, the rough seas churned up the bottom. The divers couldn't see what they were doing. Month after month they dove, and found nothing.

The year of treasure hunting that Fisher and his men had allotted themselves was fast running out. They worked— whenever the seas permitted—with airlifts and other such dredges poking holes in the ocean floor. They were like men working with shovels when the tool that was needed was a bulldozer. But for moving sand underwater no such bulldozer existed. No major tool existed at all.

Fisher was about to invent the device that would revolutionize underwater excavation. It came about by accident while he was trying to invent something quite different.

Fisher had noticed that there was always a patch of clear water near the surface. How helpful it would be if that clear water could be sent down to where the diver worked, in the blinding swirling sands of the bottom.

Since there was no money left in the community till, Fisher took his own money and bought some sheet metal. For the next several nights he worked to hammer it into the shape he wanted.

The result was something that looked like a corner mailbox. He mounted it on rails on the stern of the dive boat so that it could be pushed down into the water and encase the propeller—whose blast would thus be funneled straight down. Sailing out into Fort Pierce inlet, he dropped his "mailbox" into position over a modern wreck from which the Salvors had sometimes, in economic desperation, brought up scrap metal to sell.

Fisher plunged in to see how the mailbox worked. To his amazement, he was able to swim down a column of calm clear water all the way to the bottom. He couldn't believe it. The column became a bubble of clear water, and the bubble kept getting bigger and bigger and bigger. Pretty soon he could see the whole shipwreck, thousands of fish, and all kinds of equipment lying around.

Elated, he moved the boat over a galleon ballast pile and turned the mailbox on again. This time the results were absolutely astonishing. In the shallower water the mailbox blasted or blew away enormous quantities of sand. A crater began to form. It got larger and larger. Rocks became exposed. Shells rose into the water and simply blew away.

The mailbox, it seemed, was the greatest underwater digging tool every invented.

But bad weather forced them back into port. In the next month several members of the team began making plans to return to California. Six men had worked hard for a year, had made magnetometer surveys of vast areas of the sea, moved tons of sand by hand, withstood hours and hours of severe buffeting at sea, not to mention weeks and weeks of anxious waiting on shore. But they had found nothing.

Then the weather moderated. On May 24, 1964, Fisher anchored his boat near a galleon ballast pile and turned on the mailbox. Divers swam down.

They were almost blinded by gold. The bottom of the sea was a carpet of gold. Sand blew away exposing more and more of it.

The first man to the surface screamed, "Gold!"

In an instant everybody was on the bottom. Everybody. The boat floated empty on the surface of the sea. Below, men stuffed gold doubloons into their gloves until the gloves would hold no more, then scooped up a last double handful, kicked to the surface, and dumped the gold out on deck. The bemused Fisher at first hovered to one side. But soon this first reaction to the fulfillment of all his dreams passed, and he began scooping up coins as fast as anybody.

"That was the first day. I took my wet suit off and laid it down, and we covered my complete wet suit with gold coins. The whole thing, the straps and everything, was just solid gold coins, and the sun was coming down on the gold.

"But during the afternoon, about three-thirty or four, I came up and everybody else was still down there. Everybody. And there was a tornado coming. I'd never seen one before in my life. It scared the hell out of me. I went back down and grabbed everybody and got them up. We started to head out to sea and it hit us and started pushing us back toward shore. I couldn't see a thing. It was such torrential rain that if you tried to look at it with your face out in the rain, it hurt your eyes so bad you couldn't keep them open. I put my mask on to try to see. To see where shore was. To see anything to keep us from going up on the beach. I couldn't see with a mask on either.

"But about ten minutes later it just lifted. The tornado went in over the land and tore up parts of orange groves and a few houses. But the ocean got real flat right after that. It was smooth and the sun was shining beautiful, and the gold was all shiny and beautiful. It was a terrific feeling, because I'd been hunting for so many years. I don't know how many years."

The first day they brought up 1,033 gold doubloons, and the next day 900 more. Before the vein petered out they had found more than 2,500. In all likelihood they had come upon the remains of a chest of gold coins. The chest itself, not to mention the ship's cabin around it, had long ago rotted away, and the coins had drifted down through the timbers and sands to bedrock.

The sea bottom carpeted in gold is a sight from which few men would recover. Certainly Fisher did not.

There were other finds that summer: two gold disks weighing over seven pounds each; about six thousand silver coins; some gold chains, medallions, and rings. To test the market Fisher sent certain items north to be auctioned off. One of the gold disks brought $17,500. The best of the gold doubloons went for $3,600—for a single coin. Fisher began to project those first prices onto his total haul; it came to $1.6 million. At night he had dreams in which the ocean floor was literally paved with gold. When awake he seemed at times amused by his success, but there were other times when he was drunk with it, so that when reporters asked him the value of a specific piece of treasure he would assign it any preposterous figure that came into his head. It was the same when asked the value of other galleons that he planned to salvage next. This one was worth $5 million, he would reply, or $10 million, or whatever. Of course, the biggest of all was the *Atocha*, he said. At first he placed its worth at $50 million, but this must have sounded too small to him, because he soon raised it to $300 million. Reporters came away thinking the *Atocha* the richest galleon that ever sank, and perhaps it was, but Fisher didn't know this as he raised his estimate still again. The *Atocha* had carried treasure, he declared, worth $600 million on the open market today.

In any case, by then he had decided to go for it.

5

Fisher's Obsession

Why had he fixed on the
Atocha with such single-mindedness?

Flushed with his Vero Beach success Fisher had run
into Mendel Peterson, curator of the Undersea Hall of History at the Smithsonian Institution. Among treasure hunters Peterson's name was revered, principally because he
was not one of them. He could dive as deep as they could,
and stay down as long, but gold fever was unknown to
him. To identify and date artifacts was what Peterson
loved, and he had written a number of scholarly tracts.

Fisher really ought to look for a deep-water wreck now,
Peterson advised. All galleons stranded in easily accessible
water had been quite thoroughly salvaged by the Spaniards at the time. If Fisher could find a galleon fifty or
sixty feet down, he would also find that its cargo was intact. The *Atocha* would be a good bet, Peterson said.

The *Atocha*?

Fisher went home and looked it up in Potter's *Treasure
Diver's Guide*, which had been published in 1960 and had
by 1964 acquired bible status among treasure hunters.
Potter had gone treasure hunting himself in the mid-
fifties. He had spent several years diving on the 1702

plate fleet—seventeen galleons scuttled by the Spaniards in Vigo Bay, Spain, to "save" them from an English armada—only to discover that the fleet had been stripped by the Spaniards before being sunk. No treasure. Potter then decided there was more money to be earned writing about wrecks. His tome covered 501 pages and listed the "whereabouts" of hundreds of wrecks, including the *Atocha*.

Potter disposed of the *Atocha* in six lines, which cooled Fisher's enthusiasm. Fisher wanted a wreck whose fame matched his own, whose challenge was worthy of him.

"Over two million dollars in gold and silver," wrote Potter, "went to the bottom off Alligator Reef when the New Spain armada's *Almiranta, Nuestra Señora de Atocha* was swamped and sank taking down with her Admiral Pedro Pasquier and nearly her entire crew. She settled at a depth of 'ten fathoms,' then too deep to salvage. Her treasure should still be there, strongly inviting."

Alligator Reef, eh?

Fisher ran into a rival treasure hunter, Captain Bob Jordan. The bonanza, Jordan told him, would be the *Atocha*, if anyone could find her. He himself was looking.

Fisher flew to Los Angeles. By accident he met Art McKee on the plane.

"What do you know about the *Atocha*?" Fisher asked guardedly.

"I've got its complete manifest here," McKee said, flashing it.

It was a list of every gold and silver bar, complete with identifying markings, that the *Atocha* had carried.

So McKee was looking too.

Fisher worked hard to keep his face blank.

At his Vero headquarters, La Pesada Inn, Fisher met still another rival treasure hunter, Roy Vulker. Vulker and some others had come from St. Louis to seek treasure off Florida. Vulker had found nothing yet except a certain document. Would Fisher care to speak confidentially with him? The two men walked out onto the beach under the hot sun, and in a portentous voice, Vulker announced that the document in his hand told where a certain big galleon could be found and that he was willing to exchange it for money or a percentage. The document was of immense value, the only one of its kind. He waved it dramatically in the air.

He waved it too close to Fisher, who grabbed it and sprinted to the other side of a sea grape bush.

"Here it is!" cried Fisher.

"Don't you read that."

"I wouldn't think of reading it," said Fisher, opening the document.

Vulker was chasing Fisher round and round the sea grape bush.

"You wouldn't read that!"

As they ran, both were laughing.

But Fisher, glancing down at the document in his hand, saw that it too spoke of the *Atocha*. Written in seventeenth-century English, it was apparently a narrative translated and published in an English newspaper sometime in 1623. It told a vague story. The *Atocha* had hit bottom in two to three *arms* of water, and had opened up from below. It took on water fast, and had sunk in ten arms of water. Fisher had no idea how much an arm was.

He could barely read the old typeface, but he understood enough: a wooden galleon loaded with treasure had sunk and was still there. If any man could find it, it was his. In that moment the *Atocha* took on historical reality for Fisher. Sobered, he handed the document back to Vulker.

Fisher called a meeting of his partners to discuss the *Atocha*. It should be easy to find, he said. All the evidence suggested it had gone down in fifty feet of water somewhere off the Matecumbes in the upper Keys. That meant it must have struck a reef first. The men now crouched over a chart, searching for the proper depth of water and a nearby likely reef.

There was none.

Well, Potter had said Alligator Reef, remarked Fisher, so that was obviously the place to look.

In time Potter's *Treasure Diver's Guide* would become known in Florida treasure hunting circles as the home wrecker. It would lead to the formation of a hundred or more corporations and the expenditure of tens of thousands of dollars in legal fees and gear purchases. It would separate men from their families during hundreds of weekends, and most divers after consulting it would find nothing. But in 1964 Potter was believed absolutely. Had he not done his research in Seville? To treasure hunters, most of whom had never been there, Seville was a holy place, and Potter was, most likely, a holy man.

The meeting at which Fisher and his partners formally decided to go after the *Atocha* is on film. In those days Fisher filmed almost everything, perhaps because, after one success, he already saw himself as a man of destiny.

The camera shows the chart.

RUPERT GATES: The Matecumbes aren't all that big. If we set up a search from here [jabs at the chart] to here, we should find it right away. In a week or two at most.

WALT HOLZWORTH: A two-week search will cost us about eleven thousand. We'd be gambling eleven grand.

DICK WILLIAMS: We gambled before, we can do it again.

So Fisher moved his boats, gear, and personnel down into the upper Keys. Even the most cutthroat treasure hunter there was terrified of him. He might pretend to be friendly Mel Fisher, but to them he was the Vero Beach Treasure King, with whom no ordinary diver could compete.

Fisher had bought leases from the state of Florida, which was now beginning to exert stringent control over its offshore wrecks. An exploration lease covering eighteen square miles of ocean bottom cost $600, plus $5,000 security bond. Should a galleon be found, a salvage lease would cost an additional $1,200. This didn't bother Fisher—for the moment he could afford such prices. But other treasure hunters could not.

Next the state of Florida had arbitrarily decided that, although forty-seven treasure hunters had applied for exploration leases, only eight would be granted. It came as no surprise to the inbred Florida Keys treasure hunters that four of these, all in their waters, had gone to the Vero Beach Treasure King. Now Fisher, in effect, owned every wreck off the northern Keys. He had virtually put them out of business.

Fisher did not want any of his boats sinking at the pier.

To blunt local hostility, he threw an enormous house-warming party and he did not stint on the booze. Most of the local treasure hunters staggered away liking him, but feeling more outclassed than ever. He had the mysterious magnetometer to find wrecks for him. He had the equally mysterious mailbox to excavate galleons almost instantaneously. He would find all the gold the Spaniards had lost. . . .

Fisher put out to sea, dropped his magnetometer over the boat's transom, and began his electronic search for the *Atocha*.

Believing Potter, he started at Alligator Reef, crisscrossing the surface of the sea, the magnetometer dragging behind. Almost at once it signaled a hit, and Fisher dove. There in a blaze of refracted sunlight lay the galleon wreck that could only, he assumed, be the *Atocha*. It partially protruded from the bottom, exactly where Potter said it should be. Fisher was jubilant.

For almost three weeks he and his men worked the wreck. By then they knew they were wasting their time. It was not the *Atocha*. This wreck wasn't even two hundred years old.

Perhaps it was rich anyway, but Fisher wasn't interested. Over the next several weeks the mag recorded numerous hits, and Fisher sent divers down each time. More than a dozen hits were obviously galleons. Just as obviously they were not the *Atocha*. Fisher marked them with buoys, charted them, and subcontracted each to other salvage groups.

His first headquarters was at Marathon. Later he moved to Islamorada, where he worked out of the marina in front of the Chesapeake Fish House. The months began to pass. And then the years.

Marty Meylach had stumbled on a wreck and sometimes secretly worked it. But, because Fisher was finding wrecks everywhere and would surely find this one tomorrow or next week, Meylach decided to sell it to him first. After agreeing to a percentage of whatever treasure Fisher brought up, Meylach went away.

As soon as Fisher found that Meylach's galleon wasn't the *Atocha* he farmed it out to a man named Tom Gurr. Gurr began to bring up treasure.

Meylach was appalled. He had only a handshake deal
with Fisher, and no deal at all with Gurr. He was sure his
percentage was lost. Weren't all treasure hunters crooks?
And Fisher was no better than the rest of them. Expecting
an ugly argument, he phoned Fisher.

"Where's my percentage?"

"I have it right here," answered Fisher. "Do you want
me to mail it to you, or do you want to come by and get
it?"

Meylach was astonished. Later, at Fisher's house, he
was even more astonished when Fisher let him select his
share from among the best pieces Fisher himself had received from the wreck.

Twice Fisher interrupted his search long enough to fly
with Deo to Spain. The first time they visited the Archives in Madrid and in Simancas, a mountain village near
Valladolid. Fisher knew no one in either place, he spoke
no Spanish, and he had come only because all the other
treasure hunters were now sending to Spain for research—
or claimed they were. Fisher's trip was a failure. He made
a lonely pilgrimage to Seville with no better results, and
then he flew home.

The following year he went again. This time he hired a
girl to do research for him at Simancas, and he hired a
man in the Archives of Madrid. His instructions were
vague. He wanted anything they could find on the 1715
fleet, the 1733 fleet, or the *Atocha*. What he was really
hoping was that someone would discover a map that
would pinpoint exact locations where he could find gold.
In Seville, Fisher met Angeles Flores Rodriguez, a professional researcher who worked in the Archive of the Indies.
The Spanish matron showed Fisher what the documents
looked like. The paper was thick, almost like parchment,
and each sheet measured about eight inches by fourteen;
the Spaniards had somehow managed to standardize their
paper, though little else was standaridzed in that country
in that century, not even the language and certainly not
either the spelling or the script. Fisher gazed down at the
scribblings of some nameless seventeenth-century scribe.
The ink had faded until it was scarcely darker than the
paper itself. The script looked indecipherable to Fisher. It
was like trying to read handwritten Russian or Greek. He

himself could not separate or identify a single word. A few scholars, those who specialized in the period, could read such archaic script, but only with difficulty, Señora Flores Rodriguez told him. And even so it might take all day to read a single page.

This first view of the documents shocked Fisher. Nonetheless, he hired Señora Flores Rodriguez and gave to her the same instructions he had given his researchers in Simancas and Madrid.

In Seville, as previously in Madrid, Fisher stepped into every book store he saw and, in halting Spanish, demanded books pertaining to treasure, or to salvage, or to shipwrecks. Anything presented to him he bought, and he flew back to Florida with a box load of such books, none of which he could read, together with the hope that Señora Flores Rodriguez or one of the others would soon find and send him the incredibly precise treasure map he was counting on.

From time to time in the months and years that followed, one or another researcher did send him documents, and Fisher couldn't read these either. Señora Flores Rodriguez sent the bulk of them, but each one relating to the *Atocha*, once translated, only reaffirmed the same message: it had gone down off "the last Key of the Matecumbes." Every document reported only this. Which was why Fisher had magged off Upper and Lower Matecumbe Keys and why all the other treasure hunters had magged there too, and were still magging there. It was as if all were in possession of the exact same document. Which in fact they were. Though none knew it, Señora Flores Rodriguez was working secretly for all of them.

The useless books from Spain Fisher had stored in his house in Vero Beach. But he must have brooded about what they might contain and about the reports he was receiving from Angeles Flores Rodriguez, and about the fact that all the other treasure hunters were crowded close around him. Fisher was not a suspicious man. He trusted nearly everybody. He was a dreamer, and he was cheerfully optimistic to an incredible degree. But he was also at all times extremely shrewd. Ideas came to him. He heard voices and he listened to what they said. If the *Atocha* did not lie off the Matecumbes, and he had not found it there yet, then it must lie some place else. Perhaps Angeles had found the wrong documents. Perhaps everybody had. His own books that he could not read might provide better clues. Or perhaps all he needed was someone new to lead his search—though who?

He went on magging and finding galleons. On most galleons a single day's excavation was all Fisher did. A scrap of pottery, a single coin bearing the wrong date was all he needed. If it wasn't the *Atocha*, he'd call in the divers.

Fisher began to mag off Delta Shoals. He found seven more wrecks, and on one of them a copper maravedi coin dated 1619. Perhaps this was the *Atocha*. Fisher and his colleagues began to work it. Soon enough they saw that it was not, but by then they were so fascinated that they went on digging.

There was no treasure on this ship, or at least none that Fisher ever found. The only artifact of note was an ancient cannon, the strangest cannon he had ever seen. The barrel was composed of about twenty square rods clamped together and bound with bands. The cannon's cascabel had an arch about two and a half feet high that pointed back toward the muzzle.

Of all the galleons Fisher had found so far, this one intrigued him most, because in excavating it he was able to put together its bizarre story. He had uncovered one of the most curious disasters in the whole history of the Highway to the Indies.

The ship's hull, once Fisher and his divers had excavated around it, was found to be totally intact, and all the ballast was still in place. There was no hole anywhere in the hull. There seemed only one possible explanation: the ship had been swept into the shallow water on a huge tide, probably a hurricane tide. After the storm passed, the tide had dropped and the ship was stranded on the bottom in about ten feet of water. The ship would remain stuck there forever, but those aboard refused to believe it. They went ashore, cut down thousands of mangrove branches, and wove them together into mats. Working in ten feet of water they dug under the hull of their ship, and placed the mats there. They cut down their masts and made rollers out of them, and somehow got the rollers under the hull, too—not only under the hull but in between it and the mats. They cut blocks and tackles from the rigging and fixed them into place, and then tried to roll that ship out to sea again. They had about a mile to go.

As Fisher and his men cut under the hull they found the old mangrove mats, and the cut-off masts, and even the old rope, sloshy to the touch.

Fisher went away wondering what had become of those people who had been cast up on an uninhabited Florida key—a desert island to them—but had refused to give up. No history book, so far as Fisher knew, mentioned them: and but for his discovery their heroism, the dimensions of their struggle, would have gone unrecorded for all time.

Fisher concentrated on the waters off Upper and Lower Matecumbe Keys, steaming back and forth, up and down. One day the mag fixed on a galleon wreck that proved to be the supposedly rich *San Fernando* from the 1733 fleet, a vessel that no other treasure hunter had yet found. Fisher and his partners, aware of its reputation, allowed themselves to be diverted. Most of what treasure they were to find they found quickly: some gold, some silver. There were a great many iron cannons, but it was hardly worth bringing them to the surface. The *San Fernando* quickly dried up on Fisher. Though he persisted for six months, it seemed to contain nothing more. Finally he turned away, claiming he had broken even, that he had spent $60,000 on the *San Fernando* and that it had repaid him almost exactly the same amount.

He had lost only time. If he had been faithful to the *Atocha* he might have her by now, or so he imagined.

He resumed the search. The two weeks he had once allotted to the vice-flagship of the 1622 fleet went into its fourth year, 1968.

During the summer season Fisher still worked off Vero Beach to the north. The rest of each year he was either at sea off the Matecumbes or else away trying to raise money.

By now he had developed a fund-raising technique. Admitted to a prospect's office, he liked to drop a seven-pound gold disk on the man's desk. Next he would take gold coins from his pockets and spill them across the man's blotter. Invariably some spilled onto the floor. Invariably the rich businessman went to his knees scrambling for them, and when he rose to his feet, it was to stare at Fisher with overbright eyes.

"Everybody," rival treasure hunter Robert Marx once remarked, "has got treasure fever."

In his mild, Midwestern drawl, Fisher then began the sales pitch. Basically, he was inarticulate, which only added to his credibility. He was no city slicker, he was the ol' chicken farmer. He knew what he was talking about. All he needed was money to operate next week.

A great many rich men became excited at the idea of returns on the magnitude Fisher projected: maybe forty to one, maybe one hundred to one. Maybe more, who knows? True, the investment was speculative, but . . . Rich men jumped at the chance to hand over the money. Fisher was never surprised.

Investors' identities seldom became public. One was a midrank politician. One was a poultry magnate. One was a thirty-year-old heir to part of the Gulf Oil fortune who liked to buy up old airplanes, repair them, and sell them, just for something to do; treasure hunting was more interesting than that.

Sometimes, to raise money, Fisher sold pieces of treasure, either at auction or across a restaurant table. A single coin could be fantastically valuable to collectors. A royal doubloon from the 1715 fleet sold at aution for $3,000, was resold privately for $6,000, and then resold for $12,000. After that Fisher sold his remaining doubloons for $12,500, until only one was left. Hell, this doubloon is not worth $12,500, he said to himself, it is worth $25,000. And he sold it at that price. So he said.

He carried coins and other treasure in his pockets everywhere he went. He had a gold nose ring, which he would wear in his nose at the slightest provocation, and he liked to flash whatever he had with him unexpectedly in bars and restaurants, because this was a good way to sell it. A Florida citrus grower named Art Jones saw Fisher flash a gold disk one day and bought it on the spot. After that Jones flashed it in bars and restaurants himself.

Inevitably, Fisher attracted thieves.

He had gone to Miami with Deo and Bob Moran to do a TV show. He had shown his coins, worn his nose ring. They spent the night in a motel part way down the Keys.

In the morning Fisher, in his underwear, knocked on Moran's door.

"Somebody stole my pants."

In the night someone had reached inside his room and grabbed both Deo's purse and Fisher's pants, whose pockets contained about $17,000 worth of rare gold coins.

"Come on," said Fisher. "Let's hire a plane and find my pants."

"Hire a plane?"

Surely the thief would've chucked the pants out the car window. "They were orange," Fisher said. "They should be easy to spot from the air, and maybe the thief didn't find the gold coins in the pockets."

As someone once said of Fisher, to be the greatest treasure hunter in the world, you also have to be the greatest optimist in the world.

Though Fisher and Moran flew around for a couple of hours, they did not spot the pants.

Apart from searching for the *Atocha*, and financing that search, Fisher had few interests. He and Deo did not care for sports or music or gracious living. They were not gourmets. Neither read anything but treasure books. They did like movies. Fisher's idea of a hero was Gene Autry or Roy Rogers. The code of the West was something Fisher believed in. His favorite song was "Home on the Range"—it could bring tears to his eyes. His idea of a day off was to pack a picnic lunch and go out in a boat with Deo and the kids, but always heaving the magnetometer over the side, just in case.

By now Fisher had seen additional research. Every document only confirmed the location of the *Atocha*'s grave: the Matecumbes. Besides, all the other treasure hunters were searching the Matecumbes, too. So it must be there. He resolved on a last all-out effort to find the sunken vice-flagship. He would simply mag and remag off the Matecumbes; he would mag as far north as Miami and as far south as Key West. He would mag until he found it.

And so he began. He magged from morning until night; when the weather was fine and in the rain; when the sea was as glossy as an oil slick, and in storms that battered his boat with huge waves. He magged all winter long, without a day off. He located thirteen galleons but none was the *Atocha*. He had a crew working all night to repair whatever broke down during the day. He'd park at the wharf each evening, turn in a list of needed repairs, have a few stiff drinks, and go to bed. When he came down to the pier the next dawn, the boat was ready to go again.

Sometimes he went out with only Deo and his two oldest sons, both were still children, as crews. He needed only three people in all—one to steer, one to watch the instrument, and one to throw buoys over the side if the instrument scored a hit.

He checked every square inch of water off the Upper Keys, and also off the Lower Keys, and the *Atocha* wasn't there. He was so convinced he had missed it that he re-magged all that ocean again. And the *Atocha* still wasn't there.

At the end of 101 days he stopped.

After a while he flew to Spain for the third and last time to talk to the one man who might be able to find the *Atocha* for him.

6

The Documents

Across the street from Seville's vast and gloomy thirteenth-century cathedral stands an equally grandiose but somewhat newer building. It was begun in 1582 and fashioned in the style of a Renaissance palace. During the years when Spanish galleons ruled all the oceans of the world and Seville was the center of the world's commerce, this building served as the world's principal stock exchange.

It is still a structure of tremendous dimensions and considerable beauty, but its function has changed. Now it serves as Archive of the Indies and it contains much of what remains of those glorious centuries, principally the millions upon millions of handwritten documents that once regulated the seemingly inexhaustible riches of the Indies trade.

In February 1970, the Archive was managed by a small staff, probably fewer than twenty, most of them porters who fetched bundles of documents upon request for the small group of mostly young, mostly penniless scholars who were accredited to the Archive and who worked there each day. Only one room was set aside for the scholars. The rest of the building housed the ancient maps and portraits, and the documents. The documents were tied in bundles, and the bundles were stacked from floor to ceiling in every room, in every corridor and hallway.

The scholars' room was long and narrow. It was a cold, churchlike room with marble floors and a series of vaulted cathedral ceilings. It contained two rows of heavy oak tables, twenty in all, each with a single chair to either side. The chairs had straight backs and their leather seats and backrests were rimmed by brass studs. In this imposing room the porters in their blue smocks marched up and down the aisle, enforcing silence, like proctors during an examination, though the young scholars whispered and giggled nonetheless. Along the length of one wall were great arched windows that gave onto the building's elegant courtyard. They also admitted the room's only useful light, though not much of it, and Eugene Lyon, the man Fisher was coming to see, had learned to grab a table close to the window, for the sun set early in winter in Seville. Lyon was not young, and he never giggled, but he was a scholar like the others, and happy in Seville. His life seemed on an even keel at last, and finding enough light by which to read old documents was almost the worst of his worries, until the day Fisher arrived.

Each end of the research hall was closed off by red velvet drapes that the porters pushed aside as they moved in and out carrying bundles of documents. The documents were wrapped in copious flexible folders and tied with heavy-duty ribbon, and most tied bundles were the size and weight of a case of wine.

There was such a bundle open on Lyon's table now, and he was poring over it, when a porter touched his shoulder, and whispered that an American señor awaited him in the hall. Lyon was surprised. He had been thoroughly absorbed in a time that had ceased to exist hundreds of years ago, and he was loathe to leave there, a place where he was safe. Lyon was not alarmed, though from that moment a great deal of suffering became, for him, inevitable. He went out through the glass and wrought-iron doors onto a marble landing from which a great marble staircase dropped to street level below. On this landing stood a reception desk, a guard, some porters in blue smocks who were smoking—and Mel and Deo Fisher, representatives of the world Lyon had left behind him. They were grinning at him, and now Deo kissed him, while Mel wrung his hand.

Eugene Lyon was forty, tall, skinny, and studious. He was unathletic. He had never been tempted to dive for treasure. He could see nothing without his glasses. To be correct in his dealings with every person and situation was what he always strove for. He was a faithful husband and dutiful father who took his domestic responsibilities seriously. He was a churchgoing man who, after his life caved in around him, had found solace teaching Sunday school at Christ Methodist Church in Vero Beach. Indeed, that was where he first met Mel and Dolores Fisher, who had been among his students.

At this stage of his life Lyon should have been managing some major American city—Miami, perhaps—for that was where most of his previous education and experience had been leading. After graduating from Florida with honors (B.A. in Political Science) and Denver (M.A. in Government Management), he had served five years as assistant city manager of Coral Gables, Florida. A good many American cities were turning away from the idea of an elected mayor, and instead were hiring professionals such as Lyon. His grasp of the realities of municipal government had been astonishing in a man so young, and it was clear that he was destined soon to run a city of his own.

So it was that in 1958, at the age of only twenty-nine, Eugene Lyon was hired away from Carol Gables by Vero Beach. Riding an enormous reputation, Lyon was clearly on his way to the top, and the five members of the Vero Beach city council were thrilled when, having carefully looked over their town, he had agreed to manage it for them.

He lasted three years. The experience disillusioned him and very nearly destroyed him, and he had been trying ever since to find a new life. The sudden appearance of Mel Fisher now in Seville would simplify nothing for Eugene Lyon.

Upon first arriving in Vero Beach, Lyon had considered himself astute, a man of experience. He was not a boy scout. He was no crusader. But what he found in his new town amazed him. It brought out a reforming zeal which perhaps was always in him, which perhaps he had always been afraid of, and with which now he destroyed himself politically.

The town Lyon began to manage was not the sleepy and rather beautiful tourist resort where the Dodgers baseball team trained each winter, but a place controlled by and for a very few men against whom no one dared move. These men were rich, and getting richer. A single man held a lifetime deed to three hundred and fifty feet of the city's choicest waterfront property. Another held a deed to the city's thousand-acre airport, and pocketed all it brought in. On the airport alone the city was losing hundreds of thousands of dollars in potential revenue.

Lyon's zeal focused in on this airport, and he instituted a civil suit against the man who controlled it, who, as it happened, was not only the richest man in town, but also among the most popular—it was he who had brought the Dodgers to Vero.

It was clear that Lyon would bring other suits later, if this one was successful.

The rich men who controlled Vero Beach did not feel particularly threatened by Lyon. They did not decide to have him killed, or order his arms broken.

The president of one of the major banks summoned Lyon to his office.

"We like you very much," the banker told him.

"Thank you."

"We need an honest man like you in Vero. But you're young. You don't seem to perceive how things work here."

"The law seems clear enough."

After a moment's thought, the banker noted that Lyon had a grueling job. Doubtless he would not want to keep it forever. "If you were looking around for something better, I could use an executive like you in this bank."

Lyon said nothing.

"How would you like to be an officer of this bank?"

Lyon said he would think about it, and hurried away.

The city's suit moved toward trial.

Dodgers' owner Walter O'Malley appeared at a meeting of the Vero Beach City Council, and publicly excoriated Lyon.

The worst insult came last. Pointing an accusing finger, O'Malley sputtered, "You—you're against baseball!"

Unfortunately, this also was the way many ordinary citizens of the town saw the matter.

Trial date neared. The city's case was strong, Lyon's lawyers assured him. But the city's key witness, a representative of the Federal Aviation Administration, on orders from Washington, abruptly refused to appear to testify. No reason was ever given. And the city's case failed.

The City Council met and, by a vote of three to two, fired its city manager.

Lyon, out of a job, now began to put together a cabal of his own. New elections were coming up soon. It was going to be possible to throw the rascals out and end official corruption in Vero Beach. Day after day he buttonholed friends and acquaintances, visited homes, and spoke at lunches and dinners.

A new majority was elected to the City Council. Lyon had won, and was promptly hired back as city manager.

He stayed only long enough to prove himself vindicated, then resigned and went with his wife and two small children to the Congo as business manager of a church group which planned to build free schools there. But Lyon seemed a man pursued by traumatic events. The Congo was not the religious experience he hoped for. The Congo erupted into civil war. Lyon caught malaria. His third child was born.

Lyon came back to Vero Beach. His dream of a career in city government was over, but the Third World was no solution either. He was floundering. He taught Sunday school and there met Fisher.

In fact, learning that Lyon was fluent in Spanish, Fisher had invited him home that very afternoon, and Lyon had spent the next several hours reading to the Fishers out of Spanish treasure books. That was the day Fisher's seduction of Lyon began. All afternoon, as Lyon translated aloud, the Fishers always cordial hosts, kept trying to ply him with food and drink, even though Lyon, especially now after his disillusionments, was a reserved kind of man who rarely drank liquor.

But the situation was extremely flattering to Lyon—the Vero Beach Treasure King sat at his feet—and as the hours passed Lyon had expanded visibly.

Fisher recognized this. He had an eye for vulnerability.

He did not so much entrap people as expose them to their own weaknesses, and then, if he had no immediate use for that particular person or weakness, he would file the knowledge away for possible use later.

Fisher soon learned of Lyon's political past. He soon learned the second of Lyon's somewhat guilty secrets too.

After Fisher's discoveries just offshore, gold fever had swept Vero Beach. Lyon had not been immune to this mood. True, he was no diver. But a man could pick up coins on the beach after each northeast storm, so it was said.

Lyon had gone one step further, acquiring a forty-eight-pound, World War II mine detector. He had tramped the beach with a pack strapped to his back, wearing earphones, sweeping the sand with a long crooked pole and listening for a hit. Lyon's score, after years of tramping, was a single piece of eight.

This modest passion for treasure hunting was Lyon's secret vice, and Fisher found out about it when he ran into Lyon on the beach after a northeast storm. Lyon, wearing all his gear, was combing the sand for treasure.

Fisher, having caught Lyon in the act, had flashed a knowing smile. And he had remembered.

Some years passed. Lyon began to study for a Ph. D. in Latin American history at the University of Florida. His thesis would deal with the history of the Pedro Menéndez de Aviles expedition that had conquered Florida for Spain during the years 1565–68.

Just before Lyon left for Seville to research this thesis, Fisher had arranged another meeting. If Lyon could gather any information about the *Atocha*, then Fisher would like to be guided by such information.

However desperate for new research Fisher may have been, he did not sound desperate. Nor did he offer hard money, and so Lyon, after reaching Seville, had concentrated on his own research. For five months he expended no effort at all on Fisher's behalf.

In Seville the former city manager of Vero Beach and his family lived in a small, inexpensive apartment, for Lyon had almost no money. On Sundays, Dorothy Lyon would pack a picnic lunch and they would ride a bus out into the country. This was almost the only entertainment

Lyon could afford. But he was happy. In Seville no tribal chieftain threatened them. No city council could vote him out of a job. In the Archive of the Indies no one could hurt him, and each day he found one or more nuggets of information which for him shone more brilliantly than any gold Mel Fisher had ever plucked from the bottom of the sea.

But at the beginning of February a letter had come from Fisher. Fisher expected to open up a new galleon in the Caribbean, and to close a contract for an even richer galleon off Honduras.

The letter sounded prosperous and confident. But in fact the Honduras contract would fall through, and the Caribbean galleon would prove empty. Meanwhile Fisher had continued to pour vast amounts of time and treasure into his so far fruitless search for the *Atocha.*

But his bright letter produced its desired effect. Lyon felt guilty. Fisher had been counting on him, and he had let him down. Well, his own work was ahead of schedule. He could well afford to devote a few days or weeks to his friend's problem.

And so Eugene Lyon had plunged for the first time into the search for the *Atocha.* It was no profound search. He merely glanced into a bundle of documents pertaining to the Avería Administration. Because he had studied Spanish colonial history so assiduously, Lyon knew all about the Avería, whose job it was to collect taxes on goods sailing to or from the New World. These taxes paid for defense costs, specifically the costs of the war galleons that guarded each convoy. In 1622 one such galleon was the *Atocha* so the Avería records for 1622, if Lyon could find them, ought to mention the *Atocha's* loss.

Lyon began to page through the bundle of documents labeled Contratación 3,003. He found a summary of the *Atocha's* cargo registry almost at once—the quantity of treasure aboard had been truly enormous. He sent a brief summary off to Fisher in Florida and resumed his own work.

But Fisher had arrived in Seville on the next plane, and there he stood now with Deo, grinning at the astonished Eugene Lyon.

They went down the marble staircase and out into the cold, foggy afternoon. After crossing the Avenida Queipo de Llano through Seville's late afternoon traffic, they sat down in the cafe that all the scholars frequented. Fisher immediately renewed his request for research on the *Atocha*. He made no mention of money, so Lyon, although somewhat embarrassed, hesitantly brought the subject up—he was desperately short of money himself, as short as Fisher, though on a smaller scale.

Fisher had a counterproposal. He spoke of bonuses, stock options. Lyon explained that he was trying to carry a house in Vero Beach and live here on no income, and it was hard. If he was to do the work Fisher wanted, he should get paid. With a few dollars, Lyon was thinking, he could buy a present for his wife, or a bottle of wine to drink with dinner on Sunday.

They talked all that afternoon, and the following morning, too, mostly about the *Atocha* and what Lyon might find, rarely about what Lyon might get paid. Then Fisher departed. Lyon was stuck with Fisher's last best offer, which was hardly an offer at all, but a gesture. A stupendous gesture, the kind only a man like Fisher, in these hardened times, would dare to make.

"Put me within a quarter of a mile of the *Atocha*," said Fisher grandly, "and I'll pay you $10,000."

The Archive of the Indies in winter was open from nine to one, and again from three to seven, but the reading room was so badly lit that by midafternoon, and all day when the weather was overcast, one could barely read a printed line in there, much less archaic handwritten script. Dim lamps high up in the vaults illuminated mostly the ceiling, not the tables. In addition, the stone hall was scarcely heated at all, and Lyon was a Floridian with thin Florida blood and equally thin Florida clothing. In winter in the Archive Lyon felt half blind, and he was always cold.

That afternoon, reaching the Archive early as was his habit, he sat down on the steps in front of the locked doors and contemplated his problem. Inside, beginning with some of the very first letters from Columbus, were fifty million items pertaining to the Spanish conquest of the Americas. These documents were apportioned among fourteen sections and within each section they were further divided into bundles, *legajos*, each of which would be eight to ten inches thick. A single bundle might contain five thousand handwritten documents, or even ten thousand; sometimes they were related to each other in some way, but usually there was no order within a bundle, or even within a section, at all. Most often the documents were not even in order by date. One entire section of the archive was labeled simply "Indiferente General," an accurate translation of which might be "odds and ends." Another was labeled "Escribanía de Cámara"; each legajo in this section was simply an eight-inch-thick stack of letters written by various parties engaged in the Indies trade to various other parties engaged in the Indies trade, and there was no way to learn what the thousands of letters in each bundle referred to except by reading them all.

Waiting for the great iron doors behind him to swing open, Lyon brooded. Fifty million items. Some sections had been indexed, though only vaguely. Some were not indexed at all. For instance, there was said to be a letter in there from Cortes to the Crown, describing the conquest of Mexico. Such a letter would be one of the most valuable historical documents of all time, if it could be located; people had been searching for it for hundreds of years. Documents relating to the *Atocha,* assuming they had survived at all, might be similarly misfiled.

The Archive of the Indies is set well back from the street. In front is a formal garden, and Lyon gazed out on orange and palm trees surrounded by manicured box hedges. Paths that crisscrossed the garden were formed of small stones set on their edges. In the center of the garden was a marble fountain surrounded by stone lions, each with a front paw resting on a stone globe of the world, and this symbolized Spain, master once upon a time of most of mankind. Behind Lyon's back were fifty million documents attesting to those days of glory. Fifty million.

Behind him the porters threw open the heavy doors, and Lyon, still brooding, slowly climbed the sweeping marble staircase, unaware that he was about to embark on the greatest intellectual adventure of his life.

As Lyon entered the reading hall he was conscious only of the cold and of the bad light. The light was so weak that Lyon took off his glasses and, blinking, began to clean them, as if this would help him to see.

Portraits of Columbus and other great captains stared down at him from the walls.

Fifty million items. Where did one start?

There was no mention of the *Atocha* in any modern history book Lyon had seen. One could assume that its loss had been a disaster for Spain, but that more recent disasters had submerged it completely. Perhaps records relating to it had not even been kept. Or perhaps they were there, but he would be unable to find them. Or perhaps he would find them, would devote months to the job, but would discover no specific mention of the *Atocha*'s grave site—which was all Fisher would pay the $10,000 for.

Fifty million items.

There stood the index shelf, about twenty-seven giant volumes, plus about a dozen smaller ones, and these related to many of the tens of thousands of legajos, though not to all. The partial indexing of Archive documents, Lyon saw as he opened the first handwritten ledger, had been concluded during the closing years of the eighteenth century.

He began to flip the pages of this first ledger, scarcely knowing what he was looking for. He was starting out with two clues, and two only: the ship had been named *Nuestra Señora de Atocha*, and it had sunk in 1622. He did not even know how or why it had sunk, and yet he was hoping to stumble upon a document which would tell him where.

Were there any survivors? Any eyewitnesses? That's what he ought to try to find out first.

In an index relating to the House of Trade his eye was caught by the notation "Armada Papers 1620–1630." This might prove pertinent, so he copied out a request slip for the legajo indicated: CT2987. The porter took it and disappeared through the velvet drapes.

Lyon waited.

At length the velvet drapes parted again, and the porter approached his table, carrying the legajo as casually as a box of groceries, heavy groceries, food for thought. With a thump the legajo went down on the table.

Lyon pulled the bows loose, peeled back the folders and saw thinner bundles inside. One was labeled "Papeles de Armada del Marqués de Cadereita 1622." The name meant nothing to Lyon, but the year did. Untying these ribbons too, Lyon lifted documents, looking for a single word: *Atocha.*

It was Lyon's habit always to page through legajos swiftly, rarely pausing to read more than a line or two, trying only to judge whether or not the legajo was rich enough to spend time on. This one, he saw immediately, was rich. The *Atocha* was mentioned many times. Furthermore, this man Cadereita had apparently commanded the entire fleet. So Lyon went through the thick stack again, more slowly this time, hoping to find the official report that Cadereita must have written almost immediately after the disaster. Unfortunately there was no such report, and so Lyon was obliged to go back to the beginning still again, and start the painstaking, painfully slow reading of individual documents. Whatever facts and details each contained Lyon jotted down, trying to put together a report of his own. What actually happened on September 6, 1622?

When he had waded through the entire legajo, he had a semblance of the story.

To begin with, the *Atocha* had not gone to the bottom as a result of fire, or pirates, or enemy action. Nor had it sunk alone. The Marqués de Cadereita's twenty-eight-ship fleet, scarcely twenty-four hours out of Havana harbor, had sailed directly into a hurricane. Nine ships, possibly ten, were lost. The exact number was not clear. Some were driven up onto reefs and shoals, and some capsized in the open sea. Those ships that the hurricane did not sink were devastated. Decks were stripped clean of masts, of sails, of frantic screaming seamen. One by one over the next ten days the surviving hulks straggled back toward Havana bearing their tales of horror. All were leaking, most were sinking, and the 1622 Mainland Fleet did not sail for Spain again until the spring of 1623.

More than a thousand seamen, artillerymen, officers, and passengers had been drowned; 259 went down with the *Atocha,* leaving five survivors: two cabin boys, one seaman, and two others who were presumably slaves, for their names were not given in the casualty list that Eugene Lyon now held in his fingers. The list was of course handwritten. It was many pages in length and, although the ink was faint, the words seemed stark to Lyon, for in them he saw the loss of the *Atocha* in human terms. There had been forty-eight passengers aboard. All were wealthy. The name of the Augustinian friar Pedro de la Madriz led the list. He had just completed a missionary visit to Peru and was on his way home, and he had shared a tiny cabin with three Franciscan friars. All four priests had drowned. Lorenzo de Arriola and Miguel de Munibe, two of the most important of Spain's merchant shippers, drowned. An entire family—father, mother, two young children, two servants—drowned. Don Diego de Guzmán, an important civic official from Cuzco, drowned. Vice Admiral Pedro Pasquier de Esparza, commanding, drowned. Captain Bartolomé Garcia de Nodal, a noted discoverer and conquistador, drowned. Martin Jimenez, a famous pilot, drowned. Jacove de Vreder, who had grown wealthy while serving as silver master aboard Indies galleons, and who had shipped cargo on several vessels in the fleet this year, drowned. There had been seventy-nine soldiers and two drummers aboard the *Atocha*. All drowned. There had been forty able seamen, and forty-one *grumetes* (apprentice seamen). All but one drowned.

Lyon's eyes ran down the lists of names. It was like reading the report of an airline crash. There had been a company of soldiers aboard. There had been barrel makers, carpenters, and other such workmen. There had been fifteen cabin boys, the youngest, Lyon saw, only twelve years old. Most had been thirteen—one was eighteen and probably about to be promoted to grumete. But his promotion would never come through; most grumetes had been in their late teens, and the able seamen were all in their early twenties except for one or two middle-aged men.

Lyon read the details; each victim's age, hometown, and station aboard ship were given, and in some cases so were distinguishing marks: Juan Felipe Romero, a twenty-year-old soldier from Seville had been *herido en frente*. Lyon's eyes closed involuntarily and he pictured the scarred forehead of the twenty-year-old boy from Seville.

The majority of the sailors and grumetes, Lyon saw, had hailed from the coastal village of Sanlúcar de Barrameda. There must have been a hundred of them from Sanlúcar. The sinking of a single galleon had virtually wiped out the youth of the town. Lyon imagined the grief when news of the loss got back there.

There was a similar casualty list for the galleon *Santa Margarita*. It was shorter, for sixty-six people aboard the *Margarita*, had been rescued. Lyon felt twinges of grief when fingering this document too. The whole thing was becoming entirely too personal.

After a while he put the casualty lists aside. However moving they might be, they would not help Mel Fisher find the remains of the *Atocha*.

Lyon studied other documents in this legajo, and also in the one following it. The *Margarita* and the *Atocha* had gone down within sight of each other, and a third treasure galleon, *Nuestra Señora de Rosario*, had also been sunk. The other six or seven wrecked vessels had been *pataches*, which were small armed warships, or else merchantmen, none of which had carried treasure. Their loss would have been of little concern to the Crown, but the three treasure galleons were another matter. Urgent measures would have been taken to salvage the treasure and cannons. Lyon paged quickly through documents, hoping to find further news. Had the *Atocha* been salvaged in 1622? Was Fisher in fact wasting his time? Lyon found correspondence between the Marqués de Cadereita in Havana and salvors he must have sent to the wrck sites, but these letters told little, and he put them aside, continuing his search for what would be even more telling, Cadereita's progress reports to the king. Cadereita must have written many such reports, and surely one or more still existed. But Lyon soon saw to his disappointment that nothing of the kind was included here. Perhaps he would find one somewhere else later, misfiled. Perhaps not. Paging back as far as the casualty lists, he slowly came forward again, carefully deciphering each line of each document that mentioned any of the three lost galleons.

Information came slowly. Lyon learned that on September 15, 1622, ten days after the hurricane struck and nine days after the three galleons sank, Cadereita had called a meeting in Havana which was attended by the civil governor of Cuba and by all the captains and pilots of the armada who had survived, and these men discussed the possible recovery of the treasure, artillery, and other valuables that the *Atocha* and the *Margarita* had carried. At this point the fate of the *Rosario* was still unknown. Cadereita's agents had already interrogated the five *Atocha* survivors, and the sixty-six *Margarita* survivors, and these people, it was clear, had given Cadereita a rough idea of where the two galleons had gone down.

But however carefully Lyon read and reread them, the documents gave no clue as to where this location might be.

At this meeting Cadereita appointed Captain Gaspar de Vargas to search for the two galleons whose approximate location was known, and for the *Rosario* too. The following morning Vargas sailed out of Havana with three pataches and two smaller boats plus all the divers, instruments, and gear that were to be found in Cuba.

Vargas was lucky. Apparently he sailed directly to the spot where the *Atocha* lay. Half of its mizzenmast still jutted above the water, so he anchored close alongside, climbed down into a small boat and himself sounded the depth of water there: ten arms. Lyon translated this figure: fifty-four feet. Vargas then put divers down to try to enter the silver storage rooms, but to naked Indians these proved impregnable. All of the *Atocha's* hatches and gunports were still securely battened down as if, on the bottom and filled with dead men, it was still trying to ride out the hurricane.

Lyon, reading this, imagined two all too vivid pictures. One was of hatches opening and the corpses floating out. The divers, had they swum down into the storage rooms, would have had to push the bodies aside. The other vision was of the *Atocha,* locked up tight, sinking. As the water rose up inside, all those doomed people were unable, whatever their strength, to batter their way out.

Vargas had decided that nothing could be salvaged from inside the *Atocha* now. He would have to come back with explosives and other instruments. Vargas did salvage two pieces of artillery—Lyon speculated that these must have been stern chasers mounted on top of the sterncastle. Possibly the sterncastle was only ten feet or so under water.

Before sailing away, Vargas had tied a buoy to the *Atocha,* for should the galleon roll onto its side on the bottom, the stump of mizzenmast would no longer be visible above the waves. The buoy was Vargas's insurance policy. It was a spare yardarm, and bobbing amid the waves, it must have looked not unlike one of Fisher's buoys at the same spot three and a half centuries later.

Vargas then moved off some distance and began searching for the *Margarita*.

The infantry captain, Don Bernardino de Lugo, had been among the survivors of the *Margarita*, and his had been the most complete narrative of the sinking of both galleons. According to the official interrogation, he had stood on the pitching deck of the *Margarita* at seven in the morning on September 6. Despite the spray and surging waves, so he testified, he had perceived the foundering *Atocha* one league to the east; it was already stripped of all its masts except the mizzen, and was carrying no sail. Even as he watched, it struck a rise and then sank very quickly.

The *Margarita*, according to de Lugo, had grounded on a sandbank, where it clung for three hours while the mighty seas battered it to death. At last it was washed off the sandbank, and then it too sank, and the greater part of its crew and passengers drowned. A single heavy wave had washed de Lugo overboard, and he had clung to a plank in the open sea for seven hours. Finally the weather moderated, and he was picked up by a small boat from a ship en route to Jamaica. Before leaving the site, he had managed to tie a floating yardarm to one of the *Margarita*'s cannons, he claimed.

That meant that the top of the *Margarita*'s sterncastle must have been barely underwater, Lyon speculated.

Turning away from the *Atocha*, Vargas now spent two days searching for de Lugo's buoys, or for any sign at all of the *Margarita*. He found nothing.

A storm arose. Vargas ran before it in the direction of the Tortugas, and once again his luck was astonishing: aground on the last key of the Tortugas he found the missing *Rosario*, and on the low-lying island, stranded, were all its people. On another tiny island nearby Vargas found one of the fleet's missing pataches; he was able to save all of those people, too.

Vargas's several small vessels must have been jammed

with survivors by now. Lyon found himself wondering how the groceries held out so long, because Vargas did not sail back to Havana. Instead, he studied the sunken *Rosario* carefully and decided that nothing could be salvaged from it until the main deck and all of the fore and stern decks above that had been put to the torch. He put this plan into execution at once. For hours the *Rosario* blazed. When nothing but charred edges showed amid the swells, Vargas sent his divers down into the hull.

Vargas remained at the scene until October 17, an entire month, and during this period his divers salvaged all of the *Rosario's* silver and all of her twenty pieces of artillery; he also recovered four pieces of artillery from the nearby sunken patache.

Midway through the work a second hurricane struck. Lyon, reading, judged that this was perhaps worse than the first one, for the key on which Vargas had grouped his survivors and stacked his silver bars, though a mile and a half long, was totally submerged except for a single rise of land. There the battered survivors clung to mangrove roots and to each other while the winds and waves terrorized them a second time. When the hurricane ended, Vargas got on with the salvage.

In Havana the second hurricane evidently made Cadereita frantic. Another search expedition, this one consisting of three more pataches, two smaller vessels, some canoes, and many drags, grapnels, and other instruments was put under the command of Don Pedro de Ursua. It set sail at once.

Six weeks passed before Ursua returned to Havana. By then all his ships were in disrepair from storms. He had found no sign of the *Atocha's* upthrust mizzenmast, of de Lugo's yardarm buoy over the *Margarita*, of the *Rosario*, or of Vargas. At length, having concluded that the second hurricane, and all of the great storms that had followed it, had broken up the sunken galleons, Ursua had gone searching for pieces from key to key, and on one, which had no name in 1622, he had found a portion of the *Atocha's* bow—apparently the front twenty or thirty feet of the ship. Ursua judged that the *Atocha* had broken in half and had also separated along the line of the gunports, which had acted like serrations in paper. The bow was empty. Most of whatever valuables it had carried had no doubt dribbled out as it floated toward shore. The Indians had grabbed any colorful items that remained; Ursua now traded these, regaining approximately two chests of pieces of eight.

It was Ursua's theory that the keel and floor timbers of the *Atocha*, plus the silver, artillery, and other weighty things, still sat on the bottom where the ship had sunk—wherever that spot might be.

The personalities involved were becoming vivid to Lyon, especially Cadereita. Lyon had never heard of him before, and the man was virtually unknown to historians, but clearly he had been one of the giants of his age. Born Lope Díaz de Armendariz in 1575 in Quito, in the vice-royalty of Peru, he had sailed the Carrera de Indias from 1606 until 1635, when he was appointed viceroy and governor of New Spain (Mexico), a post he held for the next five years. Many of his ships were lost to enemy action, and to storms, over those decades, but in 1633 he had won a famous naval victory over the Dutch off San Martin Island. Personal details about Cadereita's life remained obscure. No historian that Lyon was ever to read chose even to mention Cadereita's date of death. But there was a portrait, painted when Cadereita was about sixty-five years old, that showed a thin-faced, ascetic man dressed all in black. The wide brim of his hat was worn high on one side and low on the other. His white mustache swept up at both ends, finishing in the middle of his cheeks, and his white goatee was trimmed in an inverted V. He was not smiling. His garments were adorned with no decoration of any kind—no jewelry, no medals—so perhaps he was a simple, plain kind of man, a seafaring man, despite his great rank.

He must certainly have been a brilliant seaman; just to survive thirty years at sea in Spanish war galleons proved that.

Lyon was allowing himself to be distracted by the personality of Cadereita, because he did not know where else to look for the information Fisher wanted.

In the folder in his hands Lyon found a great many letters that Cadereita had dictated and signed between September 15 and 17. Even as salvage attempts began,

Cadereita was setting up a new chain of command. One by one, he apportioned the jobs, personally assigning even the least of them. One letter, dated September 17, 1622, went to a soldier named Pedro de Arenas, promoting him to the rank of sergeant of company, and putting him in command of the security troops at sea. Cadereita wrote that Vargas and the main salvage force had gone out the day before and Arenas and his troops would go out that day aboard a frigate. Cadereita even remembered to mention that one copy of this letter would go to the king, who could be expected to confirm Arenas's new rank, and that a second copy would go into Arenas's service record.

By now Lyon was extremely impressed with both the modesty and the competence of Cadereita, and this would prove important. Eventually those very qualities would provide Lyon with the key to the riddle Mel Fisher had been trying to solve for five years, the location of the *Atocha*.

Continuing to read, Lyon found that Cadereita had ordered his chief pilot, one Lorenzo Bernal, arrested and imprisoned—presumably for the crime of leading the 1622 Mainland Fleet into the hurricane. Obviously Cadereita had been no saint. Even though the ultimate responsibility had been, of course, his own, he needed a scapegoat, and Bernal would do. Just as obviously, Cadereita's prestige was so enormous that even the loss of ten ships in a single day could not dent it.

In the documents, Cadereita made mulitple decisions on his own authority, and this was in itself impressive. It was rare to find someone in the Empire doing anything on his own. The Crown did not make an effort to encourage free thinking in 1622. Yet Cadereita, it seemed, had been a man of enormous initiative.

A great many documents concerned Vargas, and Lyon began to form a picture of him, too. After salvaging the *Rosario*, Vargas had immediately been sent out again, and for the next nine months he apparently searched for the *Atocha* and the *Margarita* almost uninterruptedly.

Was he going to find them or not? Lyon, reading on, saw Vargas alternate regularly between hope and despair. Although he had already served as vice admiral of one of the Pacific fleets, he was apparently considerably younger than Cadereita, for there was a slightly patronizing tone to certain of Cadereita's letters to him. In one of them, dated April 16, 1623, Cadereita in alternating paragraphs had patted Vargas on the back with one hand and urged him forward with the other. Cadereita wrote that he realized how difficult it was out there when the sea was high; nonetheless he urged haste. Every fifteen days from then on, Vargas would come into port. Cadereita was pleased that Vargas had found some military stores; the royal treasurer of artillery was pleased also. And Vargas had indeed done very good work on the *Rosario* previously. Vargas should just keep doing his job, but he should hurry. Cadereita's four-page letter closed with the usual flowery words, but his signature wasn't there. The signed copy must have gone to Vargas, Lyon speculated, and perhaps Vargas had kept it and it was to be found today in some other legajo. Or perhaps he crumpled it up in disgust and threw it overboard, because in effect it sentenced him to still more months out in the open sea looking for wrecks that he could not find.

Cadereita himself had sailed out to the site on February 26, 1623, and had remained there until March 26, according to an April 3 letter he wrote to one of his admirals. Cadereita must have set sail on the usual two-month voyage to Spain immediately thereafter, because the next letter that Lyon found was dated June 4, 1623, and was written to the king from the vicinity of Sanlúcar de Barrameda. "For four months Vargas and I worked. There were not fifteen good days. We got two silver bars, a chest of reales, and some silverware." Lyon could imagine Cadereita standing at the rail of his galleon as the coast of Spain at last hove into sight. Cadereita had excuses to make to the king in advance, and he had gone down to his cabin to make them.

The letters Lyon found next seemed encouraging at first. Captain Nicholas de Cardona had come to join Vargas bringing fourteen black divers from Acapulco. Surely they would soon find the hulks and the treasure. But gradually the enthusiasm in these documents tapered off: "Vargas is working with twenty-four divers, hopes to find it. . . ." "Gaspar de Vargas hasn't found the two ships where they were lost . . ." "Vargas has written saying he has lost hope of finding the silver of the lost galleons." Late in 1623 both Vargas and Cardona withdrew from the search.

Lyon discovered that for the next two years the officials of Havana, at royal order, had kept buoys renewed over the presumed wreck site, and in 1625 one ship sent to do this, commanded by Francisco de la Luz, had simply disappeared in a storm. It was never heard from again, nor any of its thirty or forty men.

At last Lyon came to the end of the fleet papers. Although he was fascinated by what he had found so far, Fisher would not be. Fisher wanted to know only one thing, where the *Atocha* had gone down, and Lyon couldn't tell him. All Lyon knew so far was that the *Atocha*, for unknown reasons, had resisted all salvage attempts up to at least 1625. Lyon not only didn't know where the *Atocha* had gone down, he didn't even know where to look next for this information.

So he decided to find, if he could, the *Atocha's* cargo registry. This registry, since it predated the shipwreck, would of course contain no location information. Still, Fisher would be glad to have it. He could wave it at all the other treasure hunters.

So Lyon searched for most of a week in all likely legajos. He found many other registries from the 1622 fleet, and from other fleets, but not the *Atocha's*.

His failure filled him with despair. If he could not even locate this single most central document, how was he supposed to find out where the galleon had gone down?

Where to look next?

Faced once again by fifty million documents, Lyon began to leaf through index ledgers relating to other sections of the Archive.

One, called *Contaduría* and devoted totally to audits by royal accountants, gave him pause. He knew that a great deal of previous research had been done on behalf of treasure hunters. But had anybody ever searched among these financial audits? Lyon doubted it. Not only was the accountants' official script particularly difficult to decipher, but audits, then as now, were boring.

The "Inventario Analítico de Todos Los Papeles qui Vinieron de la Contaduría General del Consejo de Indias" ledger was heavy. It measured ten by fourteen inches. It was about an inch and a half thick. It had been completed, Lyon saw, on December 17, 1792. There were a number of similar index ledgers. Lyon picked up one marked "Cuba" and began to turn pages. He turned and scanned 389 pages without finding a single entry that looked interesting, and then on the next page one virtually leaped off the desk at him, and his heart began to beat fast. He read: "Accounts of Francisco Nuñez Melián, Treasurer General of the Crusades of the Island of Cuba, and Governor of the Province of Venezuela, of the Salvage of the Galleon Margarita, One of Those of the Fleet of the Marqués de Cadereita which Shipwrecked in the Matacumbe Keys in the year 1622."

Lyon carefully wrote out a slip requesting legajo Contaduría 1112 and gave it to the *portero*. Then he sat motionless, waiting.

The legajo that the portero set down before him was a relatively slight one, only two inches thick—about eight hundred pages. Having untied the ribbons, Lyon folded back the covers. His first glimpse of these documents, the most important he would ever find, was not encouraging, for this was the most worm-eaten sheaf he had yet seen. At some point over the past three hundred and fifty years tiny *pollila* worms had gotten into it. They had had a banquet. One entire corner was eaten away. They had burrowed straight down into the heart of the documents too, so that page one, when Lyon lifted it, was a mass of perforations; scarcely a word was legible. Carefully Lyon began lifting away documents. There were so many wormholes that not a single sentence could be read on any page. Lyon turned the entire sheaf over. The back was the same. The worms had feasted from that side too. However, when he had paged carefully through the entire sheaf from beginning to end he saw that the wormholes ended after about sixty pages in both directions. It was going to be possible to read the middle section of the accounts after all.

And so Lyon began to plod slowly and painstakingly through what was neither more nor less than an eight-hundred-page expense account written in 1630 script. Lyon had never slogged through duller stuff in his life.

Salvors in those days kept one-third of what they found, and they were allowed to write off a second third against expenses, if these could be justified. The final third went to the king. So the salvor was obviously going to pad his expenses as much as he could, and Melián, Lyon saw, had done just that. Every bag of nails was counted, every jug of wine—for page after page.

Melián had not been a professional salvor. He was not even a seaman. By trade he was a salesman, and thanks to political connections, he had obtained the lucrative papal bull concession for Havana; Melian had lived on commissions from selling indulgences on behalf of the Crown.

Melián must have been a man much like Mel Fisher, Lyon thought, a man with oversize dreams. A gambler. He must have had a tremendous ego. Admiral Gaspar de Vargas had looked for the two galleons for the best part of a year without success, and Vargas was one of the greatest captains of Spain, with the entire might of the Spanish navy behind him. It was incredible that Melián could imagine himself succeeding where Vargas had failed, but he did, and he had bid for a royal contract to find and salvage the two galleons; this was awarded to him in 1624.

Melián had spent the next year and a half raising the money with which to hire the ships, sailors, divers, and security troops such an expedition required. It was an operation exactly in the Fisher style—grandiose: two frigates, two smaller ships, numerous boats, and two teams totaling twenty divers in all.

Vargas had searched for the two wrecks using the standard salvage technique of the time: a cable was hung between long boats and weighted in about six places by cannon balls and grappling hooks; then, with a dozen or so men hauling at the oars, the long boats proceeded along parallel lines, the grappling hooks sweeping all the ocean bottom in between. Every time a hook snagged on something, a diver was sent down to investigate.

The wreck site, in 1626, was supposed to be still littered with Vargas's buoys, but Melián found no buoys there at all, not one, though he looked hard for a month. This did not faze him though, for it was his own secret weapon he was counting on, not buoys. Mel Fisher would

have been proud of Melián. The Spaniard had invented a
bronze diving bell equipped with windows. It was an inverted cone open at the bottom that could be dragged behind ships. A kind of platform hung from the open end by
chains, and on this a diver stood in water up to his waist
and he peered out at the depths rushing by, breathing the
air trapped in the top part of the bell until such time as he
passed out. Melián's diving bell used up a good many divers, but it was to treasure hunting in 1626 what Fisher's
mailbox seemed to be in 1964—it changed the rules of the
entire game. Melián later sent a letter to the king explain-
ing his *filosofía* and demanding an exclusive world-wide
patent on it.

Well, Fisher had filed for a world-wide patent on his
mailbox, too, though there was no way he could control
the installation of homemade versions. Lyon could find no
record that Melián had cashed in on his diving bell patent
either.

But the bell did work. Through its window in June of
1626, four years after the shipwreck, a slave named Juan
Bañon descried all that was left on the bottom of the sea
of what had once been the galleon *Margarita*.

Three of Melián's divers, Lyon noted, must have been
Spaniards imported from Europe, for they were highly
paid. The accounting ledger showed their salaries to be a
hundred pesos a month. The salary of the governor of Florida, Lyon knew, was only twice that sum in 1626.

The rest were slaves, either blacks or Indians, and if one
of them suffocated, or drowned, or died of an embolism,
or got eaten by sharks, this was a simply nuisance—his
monetary value had to be deducted from accumulated
profit. The slave's death was not otherwise remarkable.
On the other hand, Melián had promised freedom if one
of them should find the *Margarita* or the *Atocha*. Like
Mel Fisher hundreds of years later, Melián was a man
who lived on hope and paid his bills in promises whenever
possible. As a result of finding the *Margarita* Melián became rich, Bañon went free, and Melián (the accounting
ledger showed) laid the cost of a replacement slave on the
king.

Lyon allowed himself to be captivated by the vivid details that glittered amidst these dry columns of sums. He

visualized Juan Bañon, naked and dripping on the deck of Melián's salvage vessel, holding in his arms the first bar of *Margarita* silver, and begging Melián for his promised bonus—freedom. Melián would have been ebullient. His great gamble had paid off. Probably he saw already how he could parlay this success into the governorship of, say, Venezuela, at the time a province of about forty thousand Spaniards; he would return so much treasure to Spain that the king would accord him any boon. Perhaps Melián embraced his dripping slave or pounded him on the back. He would have granted the slave's freedom with the same giddy largess that Fisher showed passing out gold doubloons to his divers after his big strikes off Vero Beach.

There was much other detail within the account papers. They had ceased to be dull, and Lyon read on with mounting excitement.

Melián's salvage of the *Margarita* had lasted for most of four years, and it was interrupted as often by Dutch warships as by storms. Everyone in those waters was hostile to the Spaniards. Representatives of the greatest nation on earth did not have to be nice to people, and the Spaniards never tried to be, but there was a price, and the Spaniards were paying it now. Indians on the nearest keys and atolls harassed them. So did the Dutch.

In the summer of 1627 the governor of Cuba sent a longboat out to the wreck site to renew the buoys. The boat and its crew of rowers, under the command of a navy corporal named Bernave de Salvatierra, were captured by a Dutch warship. Corporals, to the Spaniards, had little more status than slaves; this corporal must have been terrified. But the Dutch declined to kill Salvatierra. Instead, with macabre humor, they marooned him and his men on a key inhabited by Indians. The Spaniards were still alive when Melián found them there. He paid their ransom: six bundles of knives costing 84 reales, twelve hatchets costing 240 reales, and six jugs of melado at 14 reales the jug. Lyon read these sums in Melián's expense account, together with an explanatory paragraph justifying them.

Lyon continued to turn pages. Most provided no useful information at all. He slogged through the legajo anyway, reading, or attempting to read, all eight hundred pages, searching through endless columns of stores for clues to the location of the wreck site. He found a few clues, or so he thought, but they were faint and he could not decide what they meant.

After Bañon's find, the *Margarita's* treasure rose to the surface, bar by bar. By the end of the first diving season Melián had salvaged 350 silver ingots, 64,750 pieces of eight, 109 copper plates, 10 pieces of worked silver, 4 silver lamps, 3 silver vases, 11 bronze cannons weighing between 2,600 and 4,900 pounds each, 2 mortars weighing 1,600 pounds each, plus numerous guns, muskets, swords, arquebuses, spoons, plates, and bowls. No gold at all was noted, but each silver bar was identified by serial number, weight, fineness, and current (1622) value. Lyon copied these figures down and later on a calculator worked out the 1970 bullion value of the silver that Melián had brought up in one summer—it came to $652,832, and Lyon sent the record of this sum to Fisher, knowing that it would inflame him.

What percentage of the *Margarita's* total treasure this haul represented, Lyon did not know. Not all, certainly, for the Spaniards were back the next year, and the next, and the next—though the last expedition was commanded by Juan de Anuez, Melián's deputy. By then Melián's coveted appointment as governor of Venezuela had come through, and he was already on the job there, a rich and famous man and, henceforth, everywhere he went, a fabulous catch for hostesses of dinner parties. Anuez got very little out of the wreckage that last year; in fact the loot became slimmer season by season, and so in 1630, as Eugene Lyon saw by the date on the final page, these accounts had been signed, sealed, and sent to the Crown.

How much bullion remained inside the hulk of the *Margarita* today? Lyon asked himself. Assuming that none had been brought up at a later date, the answer was plenty. The last two fully equipped and enormously expensive expeditions had not been sent out there merely to retrieve five silver bars and seven hundred pieces of eight, which was all they had found. Lyon guessed that a third of the *Margarita's* wealth, or close to it, must still have been down there when the Spaniards called off the search because of the diminishing returns. And was still down there today. Within sight of where the *Atocha* lay.

This gave Fisher two potential targets in the same general area. But where was that area? Lyon sat in the Archive of the Indies, in the wooden chair with the studded leather backrest, and brooded. In documents studied so far he had noted repeated mention of the Matecumbe Keys. But there had also been repeated mention of the Tortugas, of the Caveza de los Mártires, of the Cayo del Marques, and of the Cayo de Cuchiaga.

The more he brooded the more Lyon realized that the Spaniards had used most of these place-names almost interchangeably. His next job, then, was to work out the origins of each of them, and then attempt to relate them to modern place names and to specific Florida keys. Lyon had a number of advantages over all previous reserachers into salvage material, but one of the best of them was this: as a boy growing up near Miami he had sailed to or around most of the keys in pleasure boats. He did not now have to look up their names and locations. He already had that information in his head.

He began studying old books. One, written in 1574 by Lopes de Velasco, described an Indian tribe indigenous to the Florida keys. Its chief was named Matecumbe. Obviously this was the origin of Matecumbe as a place name. But Lope's description of Chief Matecumbe's island matched neither of the present Matecumbe Keys. Rather, it fitted the island known today as Key Largo. It was clear the tribe had inhabited a number of more southerly keys as well. All of which, Lyon reasoned, would have become known as the Matecumbe Keys to the Spaniards.

Thus for a modern salvor to look for the *Atocha* only off the modern Matecumbes was absurd.

But now Lyon's problem was even greater. Fisher wanted to be put within a quarter of a mile of *Atocha,* and Lyon had just enlarged the search area from two small islands to almost two hundred miles of reef line.

Next, Lyon considered the multiple references to the Tortugas. There is still a Tortugas group today. It lies 140 miles west of Upper and Lower Matecumbe Keys, seventy miles west of Key West, and its name originated with Ponce de León, discoverer of Florida in 1513, who had slapped "Tortuga Keys" on the last group in the archipelago because of all the turtles he found there. Lyon traced the name all the way back. Same place then as now.

The *Rosario* it was specifically noted had struck "the last key of the Tortugas," and had been completely salvaged. Since it had been the flagship of the Tierra Firme merchantmen, it would have led the column—with the *Atocha* bringing up the rear. The ships would have been compact when the storm struck and, driven by the same winds, surely they could not have fetched up on shoals or reefs 140 miles apart. This seemed to put the *Atocha* at the Tortuga end of the Florida Keys archipelago, not the Matecumbe end. In the chart he began to sketch in his mind, Lyon penciled it in there, with a question mark beside it.

Lyon now spent days searching for sixteenth- and seventeeth-century maps that would pinpoint a few of the other place names that puzzled him, but he found none. He went back and reread the textual references in the documents studied so far and he kept stumbling across the words "Cayo del Marques."

Melián's salvage camp had been on the Cayo del Marques. In the accounting papers there were numerous references to the *Margarita's* salvage having taken place in the sea and keys "del Marques" which must mean that the Cayo del Marques was the closest land to where the *Margarita* and the *Atocha* had gone down. But which island today was the Cayo del Marques of the Spaniards? Why had none of the other researchers been struck by references to this Cayo del Marques? Could this island have been today's Marquesas Atoll ? What were the origins of the names Cayo del Marques and Marquesas? Did they refer to the same island?

Instinctively Lyon concluded that of course the Cayo del Marques and today's Marquesas were one and the same. And then he went back and sought to buttress his guess.

Question: Why had no other researcher thought references to the Cayo del Marques important? Answer: Because not one had ever found any such reference. Not one treasure hunter, with the possible exception of Robert Marx, had ever been able to read the documents himself.

All had hired Spaniards and in most cases it had been the same Spaniard—Señora Flores Rodriguez. She had looked only amid documents dated 1622 or 1623. She had found references to the "last key of the Matecumbes," and had stopped. All other researchers had done exactly the same.

Question: Why had there been no mention of the Cayo del Marques in those contemporary documents? Answer: Because the Cayo del Marques by that name did not yet exist. The Cayo del Marques, at the time the *Atocha* sank, had had no name at all.

It had been named, Lyon was convinced, for the Marqués de Cadereita. Being a hard-working, competent executive, Cadereita had lived and worked as close as possible to the site of Vargas's salvage attempts in the winter of 1623. Being a modest man, Cadereita had never called the island by its new name in his own dispatches. Cayo del Marques had become current only in the documents of others beginning about 1626. And only Lyon so far had thought to look into documents dated that late.

Working all this out, Lyon became more and more excited. How far off the Marquesas would the two wrecks lie? There was as yet no way of telling exactly, but with a chart of the area one could make some good guesses. The Marquesas were thirty miles west of Key West, and the Tortugas were about forty miles west of that. One could draw a vertical line halfway between the two groups. The wreck would lie on the Marquesas side of this line; otherwise the salvage camp would have been in the Tortugas. The wrecks had to be north of the reef line. South was the Gulf Stream, where the water became almost bottomless.

The *Atocha* would lie in fifty-five feet of water—assuming that the water depths had remained constant for three and a half centuries—so all areas very much deeper or very much shallower could be ruled out. There would need to be a point of reef close by which the *Atocha* would have struck.

Lyon sent this hypothesis to Fisher, who quickly sent back a copy of Coast Guard chart number 1252. On this chart, working from the official Coast Guard notations of water depth, Lyon blocked out what seemed to him the most likely area in which to find *Atocha's* bones.

Then he found a second promising area near the first, and he inked that in too.

After sending the chart back to Fisher, Lyon resumed work on his doctoral thesis and began to wait.

It was now April, 1970. As the weeks passed and no word came from Florida, Lyon repeatedly sought to convince himself that his guess was valid. The former city manager of Vero Beach had moved Fisher's entire search operation more than one hundred miles due west of where it had been, or so he assumed, and this was a burden on his conscience.

The weeks became months, but no word reached Lyon from Florida. He waited and worried.

7

A New Start

Lyon had made most of his computations in his head, and all his decisions had been intellectual ones. Intellectually, he had been to El Dorado and back. But Fisher had not yet left the harbor. Lyon had found the *Atocha*. Fisher had not. Though the stakes were huge for both, it was Fisher who had to convert Lyon's theories into boats and gear, into divers, into an expedition, into sweat, groceries, and toilet paper. Lyon had faced documents. It was Fisher who would have to face the sea.

According to Lyon's hypotheses, the galleons were lost in a "relatively small area." And so it was small on a chart. It measured nowhere more than six inches in length and four in width. On a chart Lyon's segment of the ocean seemed entirely comprehensible. But from the pitching deck of a boat one couldn't even see all of it at once, much less see what was under it. And one could never understand its moods at all.

Six inches by four translated to about twenty square miles, an area five times the size of Key West island. It was as big as Manhattan, as big as all of greater Miami.

Fisher would have to find the *Atocha* in a city-sized

place where no streets had ever been laid out, and where, therefore, a man could never be sure where he was. There were no houses or stores to use as reference points, and the skyline was wave tops. Down on the bottom, features were no more recognizable than on the surface. Here and there rose some dunes. Elsewhere waved a patch of turtle grass. Otherwise nothing. A diver could not see much anyway. Visibility fifty feet down was the equivalent of night all the time, and divers would be nearly blind.

While the seas above tossed his boats about, Fisher and his divers would have to find a target that, afloat, had been no greater in length than four or five cars parked bumper to bumper, a target that time had most likely had made unrecognizable and, worse, that time had most likely buried under the sand.

Close inshore off Upper or Lower Matecumbe Key, the *Atocha* had seemed reasonably attainable. The shoreline was always there to give confidence. In sight during most of each day's search was the saloon where a treasure hunter would drink his rum when evening came. One never felt totally disoriented, totally lost. But out in the open sea it was going to be quite another thing. To dive, to work, to live out of sight of land was going to be a terrific drain on the human spirit.

Lyon was asking a lot of Mel Fisher.

Fisher had paid the state of Florida good money for his leases off Upper and Lower Matecumbe Keys. He would have to kiss this money good-bye. After five years he must feel married to the waters there. He would have to leave them. He would not want to abandon a place in which he felt secure, but must.

Lyon was asking even more. Fisher should admit not only that he had been searching in the wrong place, but that he had persisted in this mistake for five years. Fisher should grin at everyone, give a cheerful wave, and head for the empty ocean a hundred miles away.

For a man of little faith, what Lyon was asking would have been impossible. But Fisher was not a man of little faith. Faith, to Fisher, was as easy to fire up as a fresh cigaret. He could ignite a new faith off whatever burned-down faith was already in his mouth. One puff and the new one was blazing. Receiving Lyon's hypothesis, he turned his back on Upper and Lower Matecumbe Keys. His expensive leases he abandoned without a qualm—other treasure hunters snapped them up joyfully behind him. And he pointed all his ships, boats, gear, and divers toward the empty ocean fifty miles from Key West, twenty miles west of the uninhabited Marquesas. He had applied to Florida for a variance out there measuring three miles by six, but even before it was accorded he was on the scene. Most of the primary search area outlined in Spain by Lyon fit within this variance, but not all. Fisher would search what overlapped anyway. Who could stop him? Was Florida going to send agents out into the open sea to spy on him?

Virtually all of the water within his variance measured fifty-five feet deep more or less on the Coast Guard chart. At that time Fisher took Coast Guard charts on faith, also. Later he would learn that these charts, though indubitably official, were no more accurate than other official documents. That is, Fisher, as he started this new search for the *Atocha*, was taking into account no variables at all. He approached the job with the absolute guilelessness of a child. It was amazing that a man his age could believe so deeply. He was extremely cheerful and tolerant. He didn't mind if others doubted. But he himself believed—in the Coast Guard, in Lyon, in his instruments, in his own lucky star.

Said one man: "Start him in a direction, and nothing will stand in his way. He will attain that goal." Said another: "He maintains this cheerful attitude. He's so confident of success. He knows the pot of gold is there. Tomorrow's the day. Or maybe today is the day." Said a third: "He's not held back by things that would hold back others. He never says to himself, this won't work, or I don't have the money. He sets his mind to accomplish what he wants one way or the other. He goes from point A to point B and there's no deviation from it. If it's a jury-rig that is deemed totally unsafe by all experts and it's going to blow up any second, that doesn't make any difference to Mel. If it will accomplish his aim, he'll go ahead and use it anyway."

Fisher seemed happier than ever before. He believed he was going to find the *Atocha* at once, within ninety days certainly. "This is fact, not fairy tale," he chortled. "This time we have the research."

He would find it with his trusty magnetometer. To this instrument he attributed almost magical properties, though there was nothing magical about it. One could not just wave it over the sea. To register a hit it had to be brought within sixty feet of iron or steel, closer if possible. In an area as vast as Lyon had outlined, this meant that it would have to be dragged back and forth on a rigidly prescribed grid pattern. Each line had to be absolutely straight and absolutely equidistant from the ones to either side of it. Otherwise some areas would get searched multiple times and others not at all. In addition because the water was so deep—deeper than any Fisher had ever worked in before—the grid lines would have to be no more than twenty or so feet apart. Control must be perfect.

Which brought up the first of his enormous problems: how was he to control his search pattern in the open sea, to draw straight lines across waves? How was he to remember which waves he had already magged, and which came next? None of the methods that had served him in the past was going to serve him here.

In the north, off Upper and Lower Matecumbe Keys, Fisher had each day marked off on his chart the next rectangle to be searched. One side of each rectangle was land. The opposite side was the Gulf Stream; anything lost in the very deep water from the Gulf Stream on out was lost forever. The Gulf Stream was easily discernible, for in color it was a darker blue than water trapped between it and shore, and to run courses parallel to the Gulf Stream was a simple matter. One dropped buoys at the end of each run and, because the water was fairly shallow, started the next one as much as fifty feet closer to shore.

But it would be impossible to use that technique now because one side of the rectangle was missing. There was no land in sight anywhere.

In the north it had been equally simple to mag on courses perpendicular to shore. One drove pairs of stakes into the beach every fifty feet or so, the forward stake three feet high, the one behind it six feet high. The two stakes were painted in contrasting Day-Glo colors. The mag boat captain would then run courses in toward the beach, and out toward the Gulf Stream again, and by keeping each pair of vivid stakes in turn exactly in line one with the other, an exact search grid could be maintained indefinitely. The only worry was that sometimes stakes got knocked down by dune buggies.

But the nearest beach to the new search area was beyond the curvature of the earth.

Still a third technique had been available in the north. A mag boat could also be controlled by an instrument called a theodolite, a kind of surveyor's transit attached to a compass—one set the theodolite up on a tripod on a rooftop or a fire tower. If a man stood with his eye glued to the eyepiece for hours and shouted corrections into a radio, he could send a mag boat out on an exact bearing, and then, by shifting his instrument a fraction of a degree, bring the boat back on an exact adjacent bearing.

However, there were no rooftops or fire towers available in this new part of the ocean, only waves, and one could not stand a theodolite on waves.

Or could one? Of course one could, thought Fisher.

In water fifty or more feet deep? Of course, thought Fisher, after staring carefully at his chart, and he announced that he would build a tower up out of the water, and mount a platform and a theodolite tripod on top of that.

But a tower that came up from so deep would lack stability. In heavy seas it would sway like a treetop. One might just as well mount the theodolite on a boat. Accurate readings would be impossible.

Not necessarily, said Fisher, his finger caressing the spot, plainly marked on his chart, where the shipwrecked *Barbinero* lay—that freighter laden with bad women and bad wine that had been turned away from Havana in 1929 only to capsize here in a hurricane. The *Barbinero*—the same upside-down hull that Fisher and Deo had dived on during their honeymoon.

It lay close to the area Lyon had chosen; it would help him find the *Atocha*. Fisher was a sentimental man. If he had accepted Lyon's hypothesis so easily, this was partly because he knew those waters already. They meant a good deal to him, and he wanted to go back there.

So he loaded his dive boat with all the used angle iron and other such rusty junk that he could find, and sailed on out there, intending to make his tower sprout up out of the *Barbinero*'s hull, a job that none of his divers thought could be done, given the total absence of sophisticated tools aboard. How did you mount a tower on the smoothness of that hull? Did Fisher plan to use magnets, or what? "You'll see," said Fisher confidently.

But when his boat was still ten miles distant from the *Barbinero*, Fisher suddenly changed his mind. They would not go to the *Barbinero* yet. They would stop here first. The "Fisher Factor" was sending signals, and he was listening to them. He ordered the anchors thrown down, and divers over the side.

All day, as his boat had chugged toward the freighter, Fisher had stared hard at his charts. At times he had seemed to go into a trance, in which he saw himself as captain of the doomed *Atocha*. Mountainous waves crashed down on him. He heard his sails split, saw his masts toppling, until only splintered stubs were left, the mass of each hanging over the side.

Trances were a talent Fisher had—whether due to mysticism or self-delusion it was impossible to say. But the scene aboard the *Atocha* was as clear to him as if he had been there. He watched every line on board being fastened to the *Atocha*'s enormous anchors: each anchor was twenty feet long, nearly a quarter the length of the galleon. They were sent to the bottom. In thunderous seas, the *Atocha* swung on them. With seven or eight hawsers attached to each anchor, the inevitable happened—the shortest line on each anchor snapped with a report as mortal as a gunshot, and then the others, one by one, and Captain Fisher and his doomed *Atocha* were swept toward perdition.

When the trance passed, Fisher had searched his charts for a reef with deep water just behind it, a reef that might have sunk the *Atocha*. He found no such reef close to the area Eugene Lyon had selected, and none within the variance he had requested from the state, though there were a number of promising ones on his chart. The most likely, Fisher sensed, hovered here, ten miles east of the *Barbinero*, seventeen feet below the wave tops. Seventeen feet was about what the *Atocha* would have drawn.

It was what is called a patch reef. It was only half a mile long, and the water behind it, according to the chart, was forty feet deep, no more. This reef had not impressed Lyon, because the great Gaspar de Vargas himself had measured the *Atocha*'s depth, and to Lyon fifty-five feet meant fifty-five feet.

However, the more Fisher stared at his chart, the more he believed that this was the reef that the *Atocha* had tumbled across, and it lay directly in his way as he sailed from Key West toward the *Barbinero*. As soon as Fisher had delineated the reef, he sent two divers over the side, ordering them simply to swim around down there and look for a point of impact. The galleon had weighed more than six hundred tons, and probably would have scarred the reef. This scar might still be visible today. The two divers should also study the bottom to either side for ballast stones.

Fisher, in common with Lyon, in common with everyone, had no idea what happened to the bottom of the sea over the course of three and a half centuries. Leaning over the rail, not in any trance now, he watched the trails of bubbles of his divers and waited for news. The reef they were searching no doubt already existed in 1622, but a reef was like a tree, it lived and grew; a ship slamming into it, or even a series of storms, could break branches off. In other words, the reef beneath his feet could have been higher or lower in 1622. The same was true of the ocean floor all around this reef. The fact that Gaspar de Vargas had found ten arms of water over the *Atocha* in 1622 did not impress Fisher at all, for sandbanks moved, so that same water might be only thirty feet deep today. Or seventy-five feet deep. Besides, Fisher was not convinced that an arm was 5.4 feet, as Lyon maintained. Fisher knew a treasure hunter in Bermuda who claimed that an arm was less. Fisher's faith was, at times, curiously tainted by skepticism. Lyon would later waste weeks tracing the origin of the word *braza* all the way back to the thirteenth century in an effort to prove that to Spaniards a braza in 1622 was what it always had been, 5.4 feet, exactly as he had said. The Bermuda treasure hunter was therefore dead wrong. But Fisher would remain unconvinced.

The first of Fisher's two divers, having used up all his air, climbed on board.

"Anything?" Fisher asked.

"Nothing."

"Not even a ballast stone?"

"No."

The second diver surfaced. "Anything?"

"No."

Fisher started up his engines. From time to time, as he steamed away, he would gaze back toward the unseen reef that his divers had just searched. It kept nagging at him. The "Fisher Factor" had sent him signals before, though seldom this strong. How could it be so wrong, he asked himself. But soon the reef was ten miles away.

Another year and a half would pass before the search returned to this reef, at which point Fisher would learn that the Coast Guard chart was wrong, that the water alongside it was in places fifty-five feet deep, precisely.

In the vicinity of the *Barbinero*, Fisher trailed his magnetometer in the water until it registered a hit on the freighter's hull. He then anchored. The "final" search for the *Atocha* was about to begin.

8

The Night-and-Day Search

As Fisher swam down, the
Barbinero seemed to swim up to meet him, and he saw
that the passage of seventeen years had changed nothing.
Its colors were as brilliant and exotic as he remembered.
Bubbles rising above his head, swim fins kicking lazily, he
glided completely around the sunken vessel, and there
were moments when Deo as a very young bride seemed to
be swimming beside him. The hull was pink and mauve
and rust red. It was a hundred shades of green from the
waving rooted sea grasses, and purple and tan from the
barnacles, sea snails, and other encrustations. It swelled
up out of the breast of the seabed like some enormous
steel mollusk, a gigantic tumor whose too vividly colored
cells indicated its abnormality.

Choosing the highest part of the hull, Fisher swung his
hammer and banged the clotted steel. The fishes that had
buzzed like insects around him took flight, and a cloud of
rust arose that, for a moment, obscured both Fisher and
the world. One leg of his tower should be bolted to the
hull just here, Fisher determined, and in slow motion he
swung, heavy armed, against the water, striking the hull

again and again, banging until he had exposed the steel plate itself. Then he measured out the three other points to which the tower's legs would be anchored, and did the same.

The hull was half an inch thick at least, not very much of which had rusted away, and Fisher's divers, some of whom swam beside him, wondered how he proposed to bore through that much steel. Some kind of heavy-duty underwater drill would be necessary, but there was none on board the dive boat. Or else they could use an acetylene torch that would burn underwater, but no such torch was on board either.

Fisher couldn't afford such exotic toys and would have to make do without them. Very likely, he was happier that way. To Fisher making do was a need, making do was his art form. Vital tools got in the way of his pleasure, got in the way of that image of himself he was most proud of.

Swimming to the surface, he climbed dripping from the sea and set to work.

Fisher had brought along a number of lengths of half-inch conduit. The pipes were stuffed full of iron wire wrapped tightly around a slim strand of magnesium.

Grasping a length of conduit, Fisher attached a oxygen hose to one end, and turned on the gas. To the other end of the conduit, which was now gushing pure oxygen, he held a blow torch. The combination of blazing torch and gushing oxygen at last caused the magnesium strand to catch fire, and magnesium burns with such incredible heat that all the iron wire around it caught fire, too; finally the whole conduit caught fire. The thing was like an enormous Roman candle. Still wearing air tank and flippers, Fisher now pulled his mask into place and, carrying his blazing Roman candle, plunged into the sea again. Twenty feet down he touched his Roman candle to the thick steel hull of the *Barbinero*, and it began to melt a hole through the hull. What Fisher was doing was burning steel.

Under water the Roman candle made a slightly smaller but still enormous ball of fire; the water around it was boiling, and the oxygen was escaping in thousands of great bubbles. It attracted dozens and then hundreds of fish. They came toward Fisher from all over the ocean. In a moment barracudas were swimming all around him in a frenzy. Vastly amused, Fisher thrust his Roman candle into the face of the nearest one, and when it bolted, he lunged at another. Behind his mask he was laughing. As he turned back to his task he was totally confident, totally happy.

When the first conduit had burned itself out, he swam to the surface and ignited another.

In this way Fisher burned the necessary holes through the steel plates of the *Barbinero,* and then he sent divers down inside the hull with handfuls of bolts. It was like swimming in a vast steel cave illuminated by slim spears of light coming through the bolt holes. At each of these, the divers pushed bolts through and then held each in place while someone on the other side bolted the correct piece of angle iron to the hull.

And so Fisher's miniature Eiffel Tower began to rise up out of the sea beside his pitching dive boat. Strip by strip, bolt by bolt, day by day, lengths of rusted angle iron were fastened together, until after a month's work the tower stood twenty feet above the waves that crashed into it. This, Fisher judged, was high enough, and he attached a platform into place on top. His theodolite tower was ready. Never mind that this tower was also a permanent navigation hazard. Fisher had needed it and so he had built it. Navigation hazards never bothered Fisher. When he was through with this one he would sail away and leave it there.

The tower had come out rather crooked. It leaned precipitously to one side, and so, although Fisher proudly called it his Eiffel Tower, his divers began to call it the Leaning Tower of Pisa.

It was not really stable, either. The currents and the winds were moving it slightly. Unfortunately, if the theodolite tower moved even an eighth of an inch, the mag boat would be half a mile off course as it reached the outer horizon. Divers and torches had to attack the *Barbinero*'s hull once again, and anchor the tower into position with taut cables. The navigation hazard had become even more formidable. But now at last a course could be fixed that would be accurate to within a foot and a half at a distance of twelve miles, and a skillful mag boat driver, obeying each correction as it was called to him, would deviate hardly at all from that line.

The theodolite tower was the hub of a wheel, which Fisher had divided into segments to be searched. The first segment, about a quarter of the wheel, measured roughly twelve miles on all three sides. It encompassed all of Lyon's area and a good bit more.

Twelve miles is farther than a man can see from a tower only twenty feet above the waves, and in addition Fisher had decided to mag around the clock, using three different crews, for he intended to find the *Atocha* inside of two months. He was that confident. But how does a theodolite operator track a boat once it disappears over the horizon; and how, at night, does he track it at all?

Fisher had solutions. Fisher had solutions for everything. They were never elegant. They always worked, at least for a time.

His solution now was to mount a seventy-foot mast on his boat. By day this mast floated a plastic garbage bag. By night the mast blazed with an airliner's strobe light.

And so the magnetometer was dropped over the dive boat's transom, and the first run was made from the theodolite tower out to the horizon and beyond. At the reef line Fisher turned around and came back on a course virtually parallel to the first one and only about twenty feet away. Then came the third course, the fourth, the tenth, the hundredth, the thousandth.

From time to time there were hits. Buoys were pushed over the side to be checked out by divers, each of whom expected each time to be the first man to sight the *Atocha*. But often the divers spotted nothing at all. Whatever had rung the magnetometer was buried in sand. That meant dropping the mailboxes and digging until it appeared. In this way divers found a great deal of iron junk thrown overboard by passing ships one year ago, or fifty: fifty-five-gallon oil drums, metal fish traps. But they did not find the *Atocha*.

The weeks passed. The search was rapidly using up the city-sized area Eugene Lyon had marked on the chart.

Fisher and his crews magged all night every night, and they magged or dove all day every day. They scrutinized

vast areas of ocean bottom electronically and also personally, swimming their noses down close to it. It was the
most intensive search Fisher had ever organized. The divers were no longer the original Treasure Salvors, of whom
all but Fisher and Demostines Molinar had returned to
more prosaic jobs. The new divers were not really professionals at all, but youths with tanks on their backs whom
Fisher recruited as he needed them. But they were disciplined, extremely enthusiastic, and they worked to the point
of exhaustion. So did Fisher, who did much of the diving
himself, even though he was almost fifty years old.

The currents were powerful, and every six hours they
changed. When Fisher dove they were forever pushing
him in directions he did not want to go. He was using up
all his strength just to stay stationary. When he rose to the
surface and looked around he noted each time that there
was nothing in sight except his dive boat. No land. No
other ship. He could not even see the tower most times.
What a big, big ocean it was, he thought over and over
again.

And so Fisher searched all of the area included in the
variance accorded by the state of Florida, and very soon
thereafter completed all the area selected by Eugene
Lyon. If the *Atocha* was in there, Fisher hadn't found it.

Though immune to silver, gold, and other nonferrous
metals, the magnetometer was infallible on iron, or so
Fisher believed. If the *Atocha* was in there, then the mag
should have recorded multiple hits on it. Every galleon
Fisher had ever dived on had carried slews of iron cannons, and the mag should have rung up each one of the
Atocha's. It should have signaled the accompanying mass
of iron cannonballs as well, plus much else. Galleons, in
Fisher's experience, carried blacksmith's anvils and great
iron galley stoves, and they had been hammered together
with about seven thousand pounds of iron nails.

What Fisher did not know was that the *Atocha* was no
mass of iron at all. It was nearly a hundred years older than
other galleons he had found, belonging to an earlier and
more gracious age, when cannons were bronze with richly
decorated escutcheons, and cannon balls were often hand-
carved stone; when galley stoves consisted principally of

decorated ceramic fire tile; when dowels were used, not nails.

Innocent of these facts, Fisher recognized only that the *Atocha* had not been found in Lyon's segment; therefore he would search elsewhere. He saw also that, after two months of round-the-clock search, his divers were exhausted; henceforth he would be reduced to working only one shift a day. This meant that probably he would not find the *Atocha* for another several months.

He was in no way discouraged. One city-sized area had been searched; he would now move on to a second, and he was ready to search a third, a fourth, a fifth—however many were necessary. He was still supremely confident, still tasting in advance the joy of bringing the *Atocha*'s treasure, piece by piece, to the surface. He was still expecting any day do score mag hits on iron that had never existed.

From his Eiffel Tower, Fisher selected a second segment of the wheel to be scanned, this one heading dead west toward Rebecca Shoals, a segment only half the size of the first one, for the sea out here was tremendously rough. Even Fisher felt constrained to think in smaller terms than was his habit. But he did not find the *Atocha* in this segment either.

Next he searched an even smaller section, a kind of corridor extending northeast from the tower, most of it lying across Halfmoon Shoal. Fisher knew that shoal. There were lots of points sharp enough to disembowel a galleon. But again he did not find the *Atocha*.

As failure followed failure members of his crew became despondent, but this emotion apparently was unknown to Fisher, who, on the surface at least, remained as optimistic as ever.

Deciding that the *Atocha* wasn't in the vicinity of his Eiffel Tower at all, Fisher studied his charts once again and decided that the *Atocha* might have disemboweled itself on Cosgrove Shoal some fifteen miles to the southeast. On Cosgrove Shoal stood a Coast Guard lighthouse, and there, sixty feet above the waves, Fisher—without permission—set up his theodolite, and this lighthouse served for a time as tower number two.

Cosgrove Shoal was part of the reef line. Behind it was the Gulf Stream; the bottom dropped precipitously. In front of it the water was nowhere more than sixty feet deep, and often it was very much shallower than that, according to the Coast Guard chart.

From Cosgrove Shoal, Fisher cast back the way he had come. One side of his new search pattern abutted, as a disciplined search demanded, the area on which Lyon had bet $10,000 and lost. The second side almost touched the patch reef that Fisher had stopped at on his way out to the *Barbinero*. But again he turned away from this reef.

Cosgrove Lighthouse was an exquisite theodolite tower, a perfect one, but as soon as the Coast Guard discovered that Fisher had a man and instruments up there, it kicked him off and padlocked the place behind him. So he moved to a bird-watcher's tower on the Marquesas atoll, where he also had no right to be, and that became theodolite station number three. This tower was a wood scaffold four stories high on the beach at the edge of a bird sanctuary. The entire, vast Marquesas atoll was deserted, exactly as it must have been in 1623, when the Marqés de Cadereita had camped there, if, in fact, he had camped there, as Lyon had thorized.

From this tower Fisher magged another huge area southwards toward the reef line, a triangle measuring about ten by seven miles. But he did not find the *Atocha* in it.

Next Fisher swung his theodolite to the southeast, intending to mag that segment of sea adjacent to the last one, but trees on one of the other islets forming the atoll interfered with his sightline. Without hesitation Fisher sent men onto this islet with axes, and they cut the offending trees down. After that the area was magged without incident. Fisher was hopeful every day and often instilled this same hope, against their better judgment, in everybody. But the mag did not find the *Atocha*.

Fisher was perplexed. He had now magged all of the best and most likely spots, but he had found nothing and he could not figure out why.

At this juncture a document arrived from Spain from Angeles Flores Rodriguez who, despite everything, was still on Fisher's payroll. Fisher could never bring himself to fire anybody and he would not fire Señora Flores Rodriguez even after the results of this present document were known. In fact, she would still be working for him years later.

The document that arrived purported to be Cadereita's official report to the king. Señora Flores Rodriguez had found it at last, by dint of herculean searches, she said, in the legajo marked Santo Domingo 132. Her transcription of this report she now sent on for Fisher's perusal. Señora Flores Rodriguez, whose English was poor, worked in this way with all her clients. She had, with painstaking care, deciphered the scribblings of Cadereita's 1623 scribe—the report had been dated Jan. 10, 1623—and had typed the report out clearly and plainly in modern Spanish so that anyone could read it who understood the Christian tongue.

Fisher was elated. Now at last he would find solid information as to where the *Atocha* had gone down. Cadereita must have mentioned where. Of course, Fisher couldn't read the document in his hands. He could only scan it, finger it lovingly.

In great excitement Fisher sent the single-spaced seven-page typescript to Lyon, but then couldn't wait for Lyon's translation to come back. He was on the phone with Lyon almost at once, and Lyon read to him the single most important paragraph yet discovered, so it seemed, an eyewitness account of the sinkings of the *Margarita* and the *Atocha* both: "Dragging her cables," Lyon read, "the *Margarita* was lost upon a bank of sand which is to the east of the last key of Matecumbe." After a moment, during which both men digested this electrifying news, Lyon read on, but Fisher stopped him.

"Read that part to me again," said Fisher.

"She was lost to the east of the last key of Matecumbe."

"The last key of Matecumbe, as we've already decided, is the Marquesas," said Fisher.

"Yes."

"To the east of it."

"Yes."

And all these recent months Fisher had been searching west.

"To the east," Fisher said. "Between the Marquesas and Key West."

"That's what it seems to indicate."

All that frantic magging west, when he should have been looking east! If Señora Flores Rodriguez had been present, Fisher would have kissed her.

A new article of faith had just become part of Fisher's creed. He was always able to discard any one of these without disturbing the others. His faith remained solid, but the articles changed constantly. For instance, he still believed absolutely that the "last key of Matecumbe" was the Marquesas, because Lyon had told him so; but his faith in Lyon's first search area, which had once been equally absolute, he had abjured as soon as he had magged it.

His faith in Señora Flores Rodriguez had made him mag off Upper and Lower Matecumbe Keys for five years, and he had abjured her for Lyon. Now here he was listening to another of her sermons and allowing himself to be converted once again. It meant renouncing his belief in the fifty-five-foot depth Gaspar de Vargas had sounded— for there were no such depths east of the Marquesas—but then his faith in this depth had never been strong anyway.

Putting to sea again, Fisher landed with his divers on Boca Grande Key, the next island east of the Marquesas, a place of beaches and mangrove trees, and there he began to construct out of wood he brought with him the new tower he needed for his theodolite. Boca Grande was uninhabited. Fisher and his divers had as much right there as anybody, and no one heard their fierce hammering except the birds.

His entire crew seemed infected with Fisher's own eagerness and enthusiasm. They seemed sure to find the *Atocha* now, and as soon as tower number four, the Boca Grande tower, was ready, they began to mag again and to dive on every buoy tossed over the side. And each of them firmly believed that the next buoy, or the one after that, would lead straight to the *Atocha*'s strongroom.

9

Swimming the Minefield

To do the magging Fisher
had by now hired Bob Holloway, called Holly, fifty-one years
old that year, a former building contractor from South
Bend, Indiana. Holloway was a tall, gray-haired man who
looked, at first glance, like a pirate, with his bare feet and
chest, his beautiful tan, his single gold earring. But he was
no pirate. His job was a meticulous one, and it was done
by a meticulous man. Someone once described Holloway
as incredibly neat: "He can paint anything, and not get a
drop on him." He also could drive a mag boat all day
without ever deviating from his line.

Holloway drove his own thirty-five-foot Chris-Craft,
Holly's Folly, and he drove it fast, at a steady 900 revs,
timing each run so that in length they were identical.

He drove fast partly because of the size of the sea—each
individual sector meant thousands and thousands of miles
to cover—and partly in order to keep the cone-shaped mag
head—which trailed in the water fifty to a hundred feet behind his boat—from sinking to the bottom. If it sank, it
would give distorted readings at best. At worst, it would

THE SEARCH SITES

0   2   4   6   8   10
NAUTICAL MILES

82°30′   82°20′

24°40′

TOWER 7   NEW GROUND

13th AREA

1a AREA
REBECCA SHOAL

ISAAC SHOAL

TOWER 1
(THE BARBINERO)

HALF MOON
SHOAL

THE QUICKSANDS

TOWER 8   TOWER 6
(THE FINAL TOWER) (THE BON VENTE)

14th
AREA

STRIKE
AREA

12th
AREA

10th
AREA

REEF

9th   11th   AREA
AREA

1st AREA

24°30′

10½ MILES

GENE'S GUESS

2nd AREA

7th AREA

10½ MILES

DEEP WATER

REEF LINE

GULF

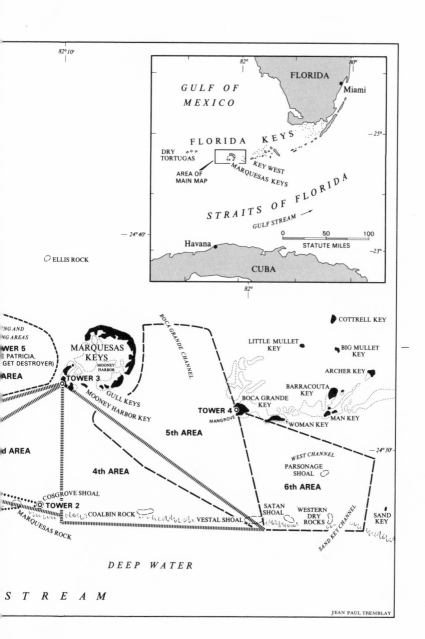

82° 10'

GULF OF MEXICO

FLORIDA

Miami

FLORIDA KEYS

—25°

DRY TORTUGAS

AREA OF MAIN MAP

KEY WEST

MARQUESAS KEYS

STRAITS OF FLORIDA

GULF STREAM

—24° 40'

Havana

0   50   100
STATUTE MILES

—23°

CUBA

82°

82°

○ ELLIS ROCK

'NG AND NG AREAS

WER 5 E PATRICIA, GET DESTROYER)

AREA

BOCA GRANDE CHANNEL

COTTRELL KEY

LITTLE MULLET KEY

BIG MULLET KEY

MARQUESAS KEYS

ARCHER KEY

MOONEY HARBOR

TOWER 3

BARRACOUTA KEY

BOCA GRANDE KEY

GULL KEYS

MOONEY HARBOR KEY

TOWER 4

MANGROVE

MAN KEY

WOMAN KEY

5th AREA

d AREA

4th AREA

—24° 30'

WEST CHANNEL

PARSONAGE SHOAL

6th AREA

COSGROVE SHOAL

TOWER 2

COALBIN ROCK

VESTAL SHOAL

SATAN SHOAL

WESTERN DRY ROCKS

SAND KEY

MARQUESAS ROCK

SAND KEY CHANNEL

DEEP WATER

STREAM

JEAN PAUL TREMBLAY

dash out all or part of its brains. Water depth varied constantly, and this was a very delicate affair.

Holloway's crew most days consisted of his recently widowed sister, Marjory Hargreaves, called Tee, and his girl friend Kay Finley. Holly would run the boat, making each minute correction as it was called to him from the theodolite tower, while one of the women scrutinized the markings on the magnetometer's slowly unreeling graph paper, and the other stood ready to drop a buoy.

Some days there were no drops. On others a dozen buoys went over the side, so many that one of the women would number each so that they could be correlated later with the markings on the graph paper. Some of the buoys were plastic milk containers, some were styrofoam balls, and some were green, plastic bottles that had once contained Janitor in a Drum, Key West's most popular bilge cleaner. On hot dull days Holly might stop to let them all plunge over the side for a swim. But other days were so busy that they ran out of buoys and would have to circle around and pull up old ones in order to continue their remorseless searching of that day's sector.

There were accidents. In a rough sea Holly injured his back. A propeller pin broke, Kay went over the side to fix it and in the surging sea got caught under there and, with the boat bouncing up and down on top of her, nearly drowned. Another day Kay's poodle fell overboard. They found it after ten minutes, head still high amid the wave tops. That surprised everyone, especially Kay, who was in tears.

It was Holly's pattern to spend five days a week at sea, then come into Key West for the weekend. Each weekday night he would anchor in the lee of the Marquesas, and after dinner he and the two women would lie out on deck, watching the stars and listening to music from Miami on the radio.

Every four months Holly would head for the shipyard in Key West to refit and repaint. He later estimated that he had magged 120,000 nautical miles of sea bottom. His engines were overhauled so many times that the bolts wore out. Twice the engines themselves wore out. Holloway had them replaced. And he went on magging.

Very often the theodolite operator was Tee Hargreaves'

young son Dave, whose ambition was to become a diver, and who first took on the theodolite job when he was eighteen. Even operating the theodolite was dangerous work. Although tower number two was the Cosgrove Lighthouse and towers three and four were wooden structures set up on land, the other towers, five in all, were iron or steel structures jutting straight up out of the waves. They were the highest points for miles around, and in electrical storms the theodolite operators were, in effect, sitting on top of lightning rods. At sea electrical storms appeared swiftly, almost without warning. The instant the first streak split open the sky, the object of the game changed, and whichever was the fastest of Fisher's boats sprinted for the tower to take the operator and the instruments off, hoping to get there before the lightning did.

In good weather the theodolite operator had only the sun, the waves, and the birds for company. The divers spoke of the operators as "The Fry Boys." A number held the job that year and later. They were boys who could stand for hours with one eye pressed to the eyepiece— though not too close or hard. They had to be careful never to jar the eyepiece; if it moved even a fraction, it had to be reset, which was time consuming, and several of the mag boat's runs would inevitably get duplicated—or else an entire sector might be missed altogether.

Each morning the operator would be deposited on the tower. Usually he had nothing with him but the instruments, a plastic milk bottle filled with water, his lunch, and some toilet paper. He would stand there all day. On those nights when the sea was exceptionally calm the magging would sometimes continue until midnight. At some point the theodolite operator would be changed, or brought supper, and then he would put his eye back to the eyepiece again, and hold in the cross hairs whatever light the mag boat was showing until Holly tired, or Fisher did, and the search shut down for the night.

The operators taught each other the job: how to level the tripod, how to set the instrument up on a zero-zero course, and how to correct the mag boat captain's errors. Although two-way radio communication between mag boat and tower did exist, the mag boat captain in

practice never spoke at all, for radio transmissions interfered with the mag. The captain merely listened to corrections, and he made them. Being a theodolite operator was
a lonely job. Some of the "Fry Boys" went all day every
day without eating, their appetites cut by the condition of
the tower itself. Within two weeks of being built, each
tower's platform was caked in birdshit. This had been
rained on, walked on. It had the consistency of soft clay,
and could not be broomed off, though some boys came
armed with brooms and tried. It was an inch and a half
thick. One could do nothing about it, only stand there and
attempt to ignore it.

From time to time, the mag boat, having ceased to run
its courses, would hover at a certain spot. To the theodolite operater that meant the boat had scored a hit of some
kind. He would watch through his telescope. These were
the most exciting moments of the day. Would the mag
boat captain dive on the hit or merely throw over a buoy?

After a while the call would come: "Put me back on
course, Tower."

To keep up their interest, Fisher had ordained that
when the workday ended, the Fry Boys should always be
allowed to dive on any significant hits. If it was already
dark, they could dive the next morning before the mag
search resumed. In this way the theodolite operators remained close members of the team. They were almost like
divers themselves.

Fisher always knew how to reward people.

To dive! For a chance to dive, the boys Fisher employed would clean bilges, peer through a theodolite all
day, and later on, diaper the pirate galleon. Many over the
years offered to work for Fisher for nothing, and although
he never permitted this, still, he knew exactly how strong
his hold on young divers was. As with Eugene Lyon,
Fisher understood the vulnerability of others. He also
knew how to use that vulnerability to advance his own
dreams.

Under perfect conditions the mag would give readings
on iron and steel anywhere within a sixty-foot radius, even
if buried under sixty feet of sand. But at sea there were no
perfect conditions. The sea out there was almost always
rough, and although Holly was an artist at keeping his

boat on course, still it was continually tossed about too, and the mag head often moved through the water in a series of spasmodic jerks. Under perfect conditions, with no ferrous metal present, the graph needle would have marked an absolutely straight black line down the center of the slowly unreeling graph paper. But in practice the line wiggled, as if mimicking on a minute scale each lunge of Holly's sea-tossed boat. It was therefore impossible to determine whether any particular wiggle was something or nothing. Though the instrument was designed to react to a single 1622 musket, to a single iron cannonball—even to a bag of nails—in actual practice one needed a much greater mass than that. One couldn't dive on every wiggle. There were an infinite number of wiggles.

And so Holly and Fisher learned to wait for what they called peg readings—hits that sent the needle zigzagging from one side of the graph to the other. The trouble was, there proved to be an almost infinite number of peg readings, too.

Most proved to be, to a greater or lesser degree, modern. Most objects lay exposed, or partially exposed, on the bottom. They could be checked out quickly. But if nothing showed then the *Virgalona*, Fisher's favorite dive boat, would have to be brought over the hit and anchored there to the four points of the compass, like a man spread-eagled upon the floor. The mailboxes, one over each prop, would then be dropped, and divers would descend to hover in the blast until the object, whatever it was, came to light. Depending upon how obstreperous the sea was that day, the checking out of a single hit could take one hour or many.

None of these hits was the *Atocha;* instead everyone by now had dived on and marveled at some really bizarre junk.

One peg reading proved to be a baby carriage. In the middle of the open sea. Another was a wrecked World War II airplane. Fisher paused to search for the pilot, but found nothing. Some fifty-five-gallon oil drums, when found, were still sealed tight. This indicated to Fisher that they contained toxic chemicals, and he moved his divers away fast.

A series of hits turned out to be torpedoes, presumably

live ones, and Fisher attempted to sell them back to the
navy, for he needed the money, but the navy wouldn't
buy. A civil war schooner was found, and a former
paddle-wheel steamer. A single enormous hit proved to be
a freighter loaded with what Fisher judged to be $2 mil-
lion worth of angle iron. He marked it on his chart and
moved on. Later he said proudly, "A businessman would
have seen dollar signs flashing. I never messed with it."

Nothing any longer surprised Fisher east of the Marquesas, where Señora Flores Rodriquez had sent him. He
had used up months, without discovering a single trace of
the galleon she said was there.

Worse was to come. At some point in prehistory that spot
had been bombarded by meteorites. Each meteorite was a
splendid interference in the earth's magnetic field, which
was all the magnetometer knew how to record. The first such
reading made Fisher ecstatic. He dove down, but the bottom
was smooth. Whatever had caused the hit was buried deep,
exactly as a 1622 galleon should be. Fisher was certain he
had the *Atocha* now; what else could such a big hit be but
all the iron cannons, cannonballs, anvils, stoves, and nails
that a galleon carcass would contain?

The mailboxes went down. The crater got deeper and
deeper, wider and wider. Tons of sand were blown away.
There was nothing there. But the magnetometer still gave
the same reading. Fisher went in search of a scientific explanation, and at last found it: meteorites.

From there he went on to other meteorites. What else
could he do? The readings were too perfect to ignore, and
the next one might the the *Atocha*.

Months went by. At last even Fisher got restless. Again
and again he read the document that Angeles Flores Ro-
drigues had transcribed and which had put him where he
was, digging up meteorites. Presently he phoned Lyon:
could Lyon check Angeles's transcription against the original document? Lyon sent to the Archive of the Indies for a
microfilm of Cadereita's report to the king from Santo
Domingo 132. When it came he took it down to the Vero
Beach public library, and threaded it through the reader.
He saw at once that a mistake in transcription was possi-

ble. The document was faded, and the scribe's script was virtually impenetrable. A good scribe in 1623 must have been a man who could write with blinding speed; never mind if the document was legible afterward. Often scribes made copies of original reports—copies that were destined for a filing cabinet somewhere from the moment the scribe scratched them out. Apparently that's what this document had been. The scribe had taken no care. Words were run together; sentences were full of the scribe's personal shorthand.

Lyon began to concentrate on the crucial line: "East of the last key of Matecumbe." In seventeenth-century Spanish, the word east was written *leste,* and west was written *veste* or *ueste.* According to the line that Lyon studied, the *Margarita* had gone to the bottom "*a la banda del . . .*"

The next word was either leste or veste, but the letter that began this word was both so faded and so crabbed that it was not obviously any letter at all. Lyon got the biggest magnifying glass he could find and stared through it at a single letter. Presently he concluded that this letter was either a *u* or a *v.* It definitely was not an *l.*

Well, then: "A la banda del *veste* . . ."

Lyon phoned Fisher. "Angeles goofed. You should be west, not east."

Fisher, without recriminations and bearing no ill will toward anyone, abandoned the wooden tower on Boca Grande Key, tower number four, moved back west—where there were several areas he had not yet explored—and from rusted angle iron constructed tower number five on the twisted carcass of a navy target ship named the *Patricia.* The former destroyer had been struck by uncounted bombs, shells, and torpedoes over the years, though a good deal of hardware had fallen long or short too—as Fisher was about to find out painfully. For here again when the divers dove on hits nothing showed on the bottom, and it was necessary to dig out each reading. But because these readings were due to bomb and shell fragments, nothing was there to find. The original fragments had sifted down to the bottom and rusted there to the consistency of coffee stains. Philosophically they no longer had being. They did not exist. They could plague only one man in the world, but they and he had found each other.

There were so many such readings that it became impractical to dive on each of them. Fisher began to study his mag tapes, looking for a pattern, and he asked Fay Feild, who had invented the instrument, to help him. Feild, having returned to the industrial world, was busy inventing other more valuable gadgets now. But he still held all his Treasure Salvor stock. Spiritually, he was still a treasure hunter. Now he looked over Fisher's shoulder at mag tapes that showed an irregular progression of hits. "That looks to me like a row of iron cannons," he said.

"That's what it looks like to me, too," said Fisher.

"How many iron cannons did the *Atocha* carry?"

"I don't know yet. Lyon's trying to find out."

Both men studied the mag tape in silence. The dive boat was anchored over the hits. They were ready to dive.

"Cannons," guessed Fisher.

"Cannons," agreed Feild. "A straight line of them. Maybe they were pushed overboard in the hurricane. Maybe she dumped them as she foundered."

Feild plunged over the side, free dove to the bottom, and searched for the corroded, iron cannon barrels he was convinced were there.

For once Fisher was both slower and more practical. He went down wearing a tank, and carrying a small sledge hammer and a stake attached to a length of rope. Pounding the stake into the ocean floor, he swam out to the end of the rope, and began circling. When the rope snagged Fisher hauled himself into the snag point. And there it was, he thought. Iron. The object of his dreams. He touched it. Iron. No doubt about it. Nearly completely buried. Only a brief curve of it showed. Fisher was so sure this was a cannon that he raised his sledge hammer to crack off the encrustations. His peril at that instant was greater than ever before in his life, though he did not know it. His hammer head even began to descend through the water before Fisher jerked it back, having realized only at the last instant what he was about to strike. It was a World War II mine, a great iron ball measuring about four feet in diameter.

He was swimming in the middle of an entire minefield. In all, the mag recorded three to four hundred still-armed mines, but never set one off. Nearly all of them were dived on. No trace of the *Atocha* was noted near them, although the same chilling thought had by now occurred to everyone. Suppose the *Atocha* lay underneath something whose signals were stronger than its own? Suppose it lay under these mines or under any of the earlier discoveries: the torpedoes, the wrecked airplane, or the nineteenth-century ships? Suppose it lay inside the bombing range, its signals totally obfuscated by the remains of millions of steel fragments?

A year had passed. They had searched all fall and winter, and now it was spring again. Money was going out, but none was coming in. Fisher sometimes spent up to $1,000 a day and he had nothing to show for it, not even any clues.

It was entirely possible that they had already passed over the *Atocha*'s remains once or many times. The mag head might have gone dead for an hour or a day because a terminal got jarred loose. And nobody noticed. Suppose one day the theodolite operator had failed to set the instrument up properly? The Fry Boys were only kids, and no one was checking them out there alone on that tower. Many, many faulty courses might have been run, and the *Atocha* might be lying in a gap in the pattern.

In the atmosphere of defeat only Fisher remained cheerful. Failure with Fisher was expressed differently. It made him erratic. So that now, instead of continuing the systematic search he had charted at the beginning, he began to cast wildly about, obeying each day's hunches.

Receiving a report that fishermen had sighted cannons on the bottom of Boca Grande channel, where all the meteorites were, Fisher hurried back there and searched the spot thoroughly. Nothing. Some lobstermen told him they had sighted bronze cannons near the *Patricia* one day when the sea was clear. Although Fisher had given this bomb-ridden area up completely—it was also much too shallow to coincide with the depths reported by Vargas— still he went back there and searched for possible bronze cannons. Again, nothing.

On no evidence whatsoever Fisher decided that the

Atocha might have smacked into New Ground Shoal back close to the *Barbinero*. He formed an entirely new subsidiary company (called the New Ground Corporation) and prepared to begin a new search twenty miles northwest of the one preceding it, ignoring all the area of sea in between.

First he needed a new tower. The world did not need a new navigation hazard, but that's what it got. Another Eiffel Tower rose up from the shallowest portion of New Ground Shoal in water only four feet deep, where it began—at first with almost infinite slowness, but later with considerable speed—to sink into the bottom. Well, only pleasure boats could slam into it in such shallow water.

And so this new search began. Holly magged and magged. Fisher and his divers dove on hit after hit. But they did not find the *Atocha*.

Again deciding to change area, Fisher leapfrogged across ten miles of unsearched sea to a place marked on Coast Guard charts as The Quick Sands. It was called this not because it swallowed up people and ships, but because the underwater dunes, which were composed of crushed shells, moved so quickly that divers could actually watch them form.

Still another tower was needed here, of course, and Fisher presently settled on a bizarre one. It would be his most formidable navigation hazard yet.

He had been having lunch at the Pier House, Key West's best hotel, when across the harbor an abandoned tug boat had caught his eye. It was called the *Bon Vente*. He knew it had no engines. He saw that it was roughly 125 feet long and four stories high, and he said to himself that it would make a damn good tower.

So he raised $2,500, bought the tug, had it towed out to the shallowest part of the Quicksands, and sank it. He not only ran it aground; he also opened up all the petcocks so that it would sit there, for good and for all. The theodolite tripod was set up in the towering wheelhouse, and the *Bon Vente* became tower number six, or perhaps seven. There had been so many by now that Fisher had lost track, if not hope.

And the seemingly hopeless magging began again.

10

Gold Fever

Fisher was a man who lived perpetually on the edge of the void. His affairs now were neither more nor less tangled than usual, and he had problems.

At this time he had only two regular sources of income: the Vero Beach wrecks, on which he still kept teams of divers in summer, and the Pirate Treasure Galleon Museum. Both were in trouble. In addition, his fleet of diving vessels was diminishing—violently—as well.

Fisher's principal vessels in the north were a small and rather decrepit secondhand launch called the *Treasure Hunter*, whose captain got drunk one night and drove it up onto a jetty; and a barge called the *Gold Digger*, which was fitted with three mailboxes, powered by three derelict automobile engines, and which remained afloat only a short time longer.

By now the Vero Beach wrecks seemed to have dried up, and in addition Fisher was being sued by Real Eight, which sought to break its contract with him. What little treasure had been found lately, Fisher's divers had found, and Real Eight wanted him out. Real Eight wanted its wrecks back.

For Fisher the climate in Vero Beach had become ugly. Storm winds blew all the time. Though he won the lawsuit, rancor only deepened, and one night someone sabotaged the *Gold Digger*. Its engines were vandalized, it was cut adrift, and winds and tide drove it up onto the beach. Fisher left it there and left the town for good. He had been commuting between his apartment in Vero Beach and a Key West hotel. Now he moved to Key West, bringing with him only Deo, the kids, their personal belongings, and two shabby houseboats he had traded gold bars for, one to live in and one to serve as a supply depot out at the Marquesas.

Meanwhile, his pirate treasure ship, leased to a land development company, was tied to a wharf in Fort Lauderdale. The galleon museum had never been successful there. Tourists driving south on U.S. 1 might spy the masts and signs and be attracted to it, but left turns onto its causeway were prohibited. It could be approached only from the other direction. Why had Fisher chosen such a bad location in the first place?

He was a disorganized man, and these things happened.

Nor was the pirate galleon lucky. First it was stuck up at gunpoint and robbed of gold coins and other treasure worth about $50,000. Later, after being vandalized, it sank.

Refloating it, Fisher had the galleon towed to a Key West wharf adjacent to the Pier House Hotel. But a view over the recently refloated pirate treasure ship was not enthralling, and certain neighbors screamed. Fisher always had an extraordinary ability to arouse people's passions. Incredibly, he always seemed completely unaware of it and blithely continued whatever it was he was doing. One night the galleon's cables were cut through with a hacksaw, and it drifted out to sea. The Coast Guard towed it back the next day. Fisher's principal reaction seemed to be amusement—there had been no need to saw through those cables, which must have been a hell of a job. The loops could have been lifted off the pilings instead. Somebody must have been blind with rage.

Fisher's talent for arousing passion extended even to the authorities. This did not appear to faze him either. State of Florida bureaucrats were furious because he rarely waited for an exploration lease to work its way through channels. He simply started searching. By the time he got his lease, that area was searched, or nearly so, and he would apply immediately for an amended lease or a new one. State officials suspected what he was doing but, short of sending marine surveyors out to pinpoint his location each day, could do nothing—except to harass him in petty ways. Certain leases began to be denied him on the grounds that he had too many already. Soon he was restricted to a single search boat and a single dive boat. It had been Holly's practice to carry dive gear aboard *Holly's Folly*, and sometimes a diver as well; in this way peg readings could sometimes be checked out at once. But now, rated as a search boat, Holly was forbidden to carry as much as a single air tank.

Other agencies were also angry at Fisher. The Coast Guard had routed his theodolite from Cosgrove Lighthouse, tower number two, and the National Park Service had done the same at the bird watcher's tower on the Marquesas, tower number three. But the man wouldn't go away. The Navy found him set up on the target ship *Patricia* and had to drive him off there.

Eventually the Coast Guard became aware of the various navigation hazards Fisher had fathered.

Tower number one still sprouted up out of the hull of the *Barbinero*, guy wires and all. Complaints reached the Coast Guard only after a ship mistook this tower for a signal buoy and ran aground nearby. A cutter sailed out to take a look; officers aboard could not believe their eyes; nor could they imagine how the tower had got there, or what it was for. They cut it down. Fisher, when he heard, only laughed. "I bet they had a job, because that tower was really built."

Next came the 125-foot derelict tug, *Bon Vente*.

Again the Coast Guard found it. Again the men aboard the cutter could not believe their eyes. Fisher was ordered to get the wreck out of there. But Fisher needed the *Bon Vente*, and so he stalled. He couldn't move it, he said, it was sunk there.

Blow it up, ordered the Coast Guard.

Fisher managed to stall some time longer. Some interesting peg readings had just been registered within the *Bon Vente*'s orbit, and he needed it there if he was to find them again.

Fisher hurriedly constructed—once more out of angle iron junk—tower number eight, and he floated it out to the Quicksands on fifty-five-gallon drums. There he mounted it on the bottom in a shallow place. It rose only ten feet out of the sea—even less at high tide—and was extremely slim. Though solid, it was as inconspicuous as Fisher had been able to make it. There was an excellent chance that the Coast Guard, unless they ran into it some dark night, would never discover it. Fisher, as he bolted on the final strut, felt proud, and he backed his boat away for a better look. From a mile distant, even at high noon, he could barely discern it, even though he knew it was there. To an approaching ship it would be invisible.

After recharting his peg readings from this new tower, Fisher hired a demolition expert, bought several hundred pounds of dynamite, and loaded divers and dynamite aboard his dive boat. They sailed out to blow up the *Bon Vente* in the midst of an electrical storm. Lightning crackled all around them. The demolition expert eyed the explosives nervously. So did all the divers. The lightning was really close now. Everyone was under terrific tension. Gallows jokes were made, but no one laughed.

At last the storm passed by. The sun came out, and everyone laughed tensely.

Two explosions were needed. In between the divers harvested enough dead fish for dinner. After the second explosion, the *Bon Vente* sank beneath the waves. Not very far beneath either. A passing ship would still ram it. But the Coast Guard seemed more or less satisfied, though from then on they would watch Fisher's every move.

To obtain the new peg readings Fisher had been casting back toward the patch reef he had examined en route to the *Barbinero* the very first day. The "Fisher Factor" had sent him signals then, but fifteen months of failure had followed. And now, as he gazed out across the water at Holly's buoys, the "Fisher Factor" was as mute as the very depths of the sea. Still, Fisher was not discouraged. There were a lot of new buoys to dive on. Holly seemed to have dropped them every three or four hundred feet.

Fisher felt an eagerness to be in the water. To dive. To search. To find. He plunged over the side.

Above him the hull of his favorite dive boat, the *Virgalona,* rose and fell on the swells. Its engines came on inside the mailboxes. The *Virgalona* seemed to lurch against its ropes, like a man in the electric chair receiving a jolt. The twin blasts of water came straight down.

The cascading water enveloped Fisher, became a bubble, swelled outward. Suddenly his vision seemed fifty times what it was. Below him a crater began to form. Some metal fish traps suddenly appeared. Well, so much for that peg reading; the *Atocha* did not carry metal fish traps. In the next hole a fifty-five-gallon oil drum was revealed. The *Atocha* did not carry fifty-five-gallon oil drums either.

Fisher came topside, and the *Virgalona* was moved on top of the next buoy. Fisher swam down again. More sand melted away. A five-hundred-pound bomb appeared, and after that a coil of steel cable.

Topside, the boys who worked for Fisher hauled on the anchor ropes, jerking the *Virgalona's* hind end into position over still another buoy. The mailboxes began hammering water down once more. Hovering in the blast, Fisher watched the sand blow away. Suddenly a barrel hoop materialized, and after that a single musket ball. Fisher grabbed up the musket ball, kicked his way to the surface and said, "This is it. We've found the *Atocha.*"

No one who knew him ever denied he was an optimist or that, despite incredible setbacks, he would persist.

An enormous anchor was found next—it was sixteen feet long with a ring that a man with a tank on his back could swim through.

That proved it to Fisher. He had found the *Atocha.* But where was the treasure?

Several days of blasting craters into the sand near the galleon anchor produced nothing, and hopes fell once more. The anchor proved little. It could have been torn loose miles from where the ship went down.

Still more craters were bored. Nothing.

A speedboat brought out some supplies and a new diver, twenty-five-year-old Don Kincaid, a photographer who wanted experience in underwater photography.

Fisher had hired him both to dive and to take pictures of the first of the treasure—when it turned up. Cameras around his neck, Kincaid swam down to the bottom. He found little to photograph. The bottom was smooth sand. Nothing grew. The *Virgalona* sent blasts of water down, which stirred up the sand; Kincaid couldn't even see. How was he going to photograph work like this, he wondered, as he swam through the curtain into the hole.

Inside, the bubble of clear water enveloped him, and he stared at the bottom of the crater at an eight-foot-long gold chain. Just lying there. Nothing dramatic about it. Kincaid decided that the chain was probably brass and that somebody had tossed it into the hole to fool him, the new guy. The water was rather green, and the chain did look like brass when he picked it up. But he thought it pretty heavy for brass. He flashed it at Rick Vaughan, the diver in the hole with him. Vaughan wasn't too impressed either. Kincaid decided to swim up with his chain. He was wondering how to behave if this indeed turned out to be a joke. But the closer he got to sunlight, as he described it later, "the golder and golder" the chain got. As he broke the surface, he could see no one on deck except one other diver, who was urinating off the bow. Still in the water, Kincaid showed his chain. The other diver nearly fell overboard. Fay Feild came up from below and let out a string of curse words. Kincaid was yanked out of the sea. Feild shook his hand, and jumped up and down. Delores Fisher came out and started jumping up and down. Fisher came out and started to cry.

Fisher's other boats were summoned by radio. One had champagne on board. Friends of Fisher who were out sightseeing for the day sped to the *Virgalona's* side. Soon there were fifty people on board a boat designed to sleep four. "It was pandemonium," Kincaid said later. "Our crew couldn't dive because all the tourists were in the water. Gold fever swept the whole boat."

The chain had links measuring about three eighths of an inch each, each link corresponding in weight to a specific unit of 1622 currency. Some rich Spaniard had been carrying his money home to Spain around his neck. Or so the jubilant Fisher said. He immediately appraised the chain at $120,000 and rewarded Kincaid with a two-escudo gold coin, equal to thirty-two pieces of eight and worth, according to Fisher's appraisal, about $2,000. Kincaid wore that escudo around his neck from that day on.

No more gold was found for five months, though the men worked every day.

Men. They were, and remained, mostly boys, with hair streaked blond by sun and salt, and bodies the color of caramel. If one of them was twenty-two, that made him rather old. Most were convinced that it was possible to go through life wearing cutoff blue jeans and thong sandals and nothing else, diving for treasure forever at $2.75 an hour, which was what Fisher paid them. Most of these boys, even after the dying began, refused to consider that treasure diving was dangerous.

Fisher anchored a barge over the wreck site, and in the months that followed, this became his principal diving platform. Because the sea was usually too rough, a good night's sleep on the barge was rare, and the divers, six or more of them at a time, used to commute from the barge to the houseboat anchored in the lagoon at the Marquesas, some eleven miles away. Sometimes one of the bigger vessels was in the neighborhood, and available as transport. More often the divers would pile into a small outboard whaler. The outboard that powered this whaler, like most of Fisher's gear, was neither new nor robust, and the boat itself was insubstantial, but each evening as darkness fell, the boys would bound across the open sea toward a low-lying atoll that they could not, being so low in the water, even see during the first third of their hour and a half voyage.

Once at the houseboat they would prepare dinner for themselves, providing supplies there had recently been replenished. If the houseboat was out of food, they would plunge into the water and spear some fish or nose along the bottom hunting spiny Florida lobsters. The houseboat, though a better place to sleep than the barge, contained no beds. One slept on mattresses on the floor. Its windows were without screens, and on nights when no breeze came, hosts of mosquitoes attacked. By dawn the boys would be covered with welts. Sleepless, as hung over as if they had been drinking, they would drop down into the fragile outboard and, aided only by a compass, head back across the open sea toward the invisible barge anchored, supposedly, over the *Atocha's* invisible treasure. The barge was hard to spy in the open sea. Some mornings they were almost out of gas by the time they finally found it.

The risks involved in diving for sunken treasure were permanent, and came in every conceivable guise, but the boys reveled in what they were doing and bragged about the risks afterward. Near downings were frequent. Each of them had had his air tank run dry on the bottom; each, encumbered by the empty tank and weighted down by lead belts, had been obliged to force his way to the surface for his next gulp of air. But this was almost the least of the risks. In June of 1972 a hurricane struck the Marquesas, catching Kincaid trapped alone in the houseboat. He saw it coming and knew it would be bad. He deployed all his anchors and lashed the houseboat to mangrove roots. Then he just sat there, riding it out. "An ordinary person wouldn't have been out there at all," Kincaid liked to say proudly.

The men and boys who worked for Fisher, like Fisher himself, had so far been extremely lucky. Not one motorboat load of divers had disappeared into the open sea as yet, no boy had been eaten by sharks, or been brained by heavy equipment breaking loose in a storm. No one had been felled by the bends or embolism. Only one diver, Gary Borders, had been killed. Becoming euphoric at a depth of about 170 feet, he had thrown off his tank and had continued swimming joyously down; he was never seen again. But Borders had been fooling around on his day off; his death, Fisher felt, could not be laid to the search for the *Atocha*. The search for the *Atocha* was still virgin.

Though not likely to remain so much longer. Treasure diving was simply too dangerous. Everything about it was dangerous. Don Kincaid liked to boast that they were cheating death every day. Clearly he enjoyed the danger as much as he enjoyed talking about it afterward. But then, Kincaid was a survivor. He would survive the entire adventure. Others would not.

At Fisher's orders Holly thoroughly magged the two sectors to either side of the anchor. If the anchor was indeed the *Atocha*'s then the *Margarita* wreckage, according to Lyon's research, should lie one league west. Or else the anchor was from the *Margarita* and the *Atocha* lay one league east. To the east, Holly found nothing. To the west a suspicious pattern of hits perhaps represented the *Margarita*.

Fisher began claiming he had both galleons but was working the richer of them, *Nuestra Señora de Atocha*. His bragging earned him a good deal of publicity—necessary if he was to attract backers—and also a good deal of enmity from other treasure hunters.

After all, there was no proof that Fisher had found any sunken vessel at all; he had found a gold chain and a galleon anchor. The average Spanish galleon had carried four or five such anchors, and something like twelve thousand such galleons had sailed past that spot along the Carrera de Indias. As for the chain, it could have come from anywhere, even—jealous rivals hinted darkly—from one of Fisher's previous wrecks.

Treasure hunter Robert Marx said, "Fisher's giving the whole business a bad name. The rest of us don't go announcing finds unless we find something."

On Plantation Key treasure hunter Art McKee said, "Knowing Mel, I think he just wants to sell stock."

11

Raising and Spending Money

In retrospect it is possible to speculate that money alone was responsible for the tragedies that were to come. If all along Fisher had had a steady amount of it, the whole adventure would have ended differently. But Fisher and money fluctuated wildly. He always had either too much, or none. The one commodity that attaches most people to reality performed no such function for Fisher. To him money itself was not real. It was here in vast quantities today, absent tomorrow, and for no reason. Money to Fisher was as romantic as childhood, as insubstantial as hope. Reality to Fisher was something else. Reality was 1622, when he had lost part of his soul, and also tomorrow, or next week when he might find it again.

It was all quite mystical and, to other people, not very comprehensible.

Fisher could not cope with money.

The badmouthing of Fisher, which soon would grow to violent intensity, was as yet quite weak. The sound did not carry beyond the treasure hunting fraternity, plus such men as the state of Florida had assigned to police the bizarre little world treasure hunters inhabited. It did not reach those places Fisher went to raise the capital he needed to continue.

Fisher came home from these money-raising trips flushed with success, his pockets stuffed with checks. He found that his desire to find treasure often evoked a reciprocal desire in other men, especially rich men, to see him do it—and to own some of that treasure afterward. It was a phenomenon he did not try to explain. All he knew was that, given enough recently found treasure to flash, he was a genuis at raising money. Even the conservative National Geographic Society succumbed to him, investing $20,000 in his search. The Society each year backed scores of projects. Some were scientific in nature, some were mere adventures. If Fisher ever found big treasure, the Society would get an article and a TV special. If not . . .

The Society believed it had done nothing extraordinary in contracting with Fisher. Fisher believed otherwise. He was ecstatic. The National Geographic, all unknowing, had just become his papal imprimatur, his Good House-keeping Seal of Approval. Now he dropped not only gold and press clippings on potential investors' desks, but the National Geographic contract as well. Then, poker-faced, he watched the sales resistance cave in.

Raising money became easy. Too easy. Don Reit, the Securities and Exchange Commission attorney who soon began to investigate Fisher, later charged that Fisher had raised more than $1 million during this period. It had all disappeared. Where was it?

He had spent it.

All of it?

Yes. Not on himself, nor on his wife and kids. The shabby houseboat in which they all lived was as shabby as ever. The furniture still wore soiled slipcovers, and there was no treasure aboard. Fisher seemed to have no notion of comfort.

But he had bought two new diving vessels. New to him, that is. He was delighted with them though they were, like all his boats, broken-down derelicts—a pair of river tugboats never built to go to sea, much less perform the jobs there that Fisher had in store for them. Though cheap as far as tugboats go, they had been expensive, and one would prove the costliest boat Fisher had ever bought.

He had also expanded his staff. Among the new employees was a young woman named Bleth McHaley, whose husband had recently been killed in a car crash. She had been an editor on one of the early skin-diving magazines and was a diving enthusiast herself. Henceforth she would be Fisher's publicity director. She would court the publicity that was so essential to the raising of money and that was so essential to Fisher personally too. Fisher loved to talk about himself, and he loved reading about himself even more. He was the most willing subject any reporter could desire. He held back nothing, and later he would be delighted by the article, no matter what it said. He sometimes suggested to reporters that they write books about him. He also wanted a movie made about his life; the role of Mel Fisher, he suggested, should be played by John Wayne. Fisher, one sometimes suspected, wanted above all else to be famous.

Another part of Fisher's new affluence sent Eugene Lyon, Ph.D., back to Spain. The *Atocha* was about to become the most thoroughly researched ancient shipwreck of all time.

And some of the money was simply frittered away.

With the *Atocha* under his boats, and the *Margarita's* position plotted (so he apparently believed), Fisher decided to go after the third of the lost treasure galleons of September 6, 1622—the *Rosario*, even though Gaspar de Vargas had completely salvaged it within a month. The *Rosario's* treasure had gone back to Spain on the very next fleet.

Fisher was aware that there could be no profit in the *Rosario*, but then he did not seem to care about profit, ever. "All money's good for," he said once, "is to start another treasure hunt with it." Another time he said, "I don't really care about treasure possessively."

The *Rosario* had gone down, according to Lyon's research, in three arms, 16.2 feet, off the last key of the Tortugas. Normally the water was exceptionally clear there. The famous reefs and shoals of the Tortugas were considered as close to paradise as a skin diver could get.

Bob Moran, for one, had, for a time, made a living taking charter diving parties out there in his seaplane.

The Tortugas were, however, a further extension of Fisher's already stretched supply lines; they were about seventy miles away from Key West, and the long trips there further strained Fisher's decrepit old boats, too. Furthermore, the hunt for any galleon was time consuming, no matter how "easy" it might seem to be. Fisher didn't have time to waste on any *Rosario*; but, with supreme self-confidence, he evidently thought he did. Fisher always gave the impression of being in no hurry. He seemed only a big, slow-moving, slow-thinking kind of man, a man of really extraordinary patience. Even when flat broke, even when rushing for a plane, Fisher always acted as if he had all the time in the world.

However tiny the Dry Tortugas might appear on a chart, the sea around them was as vast as anywhere else, and Fisher, trolling his mag, located the remnants of two dozen other wrecks (so he claimed) before he settled upon the pile that he decided must be the *Rosario*, and sent divers over the side. But the divers found nothing in that spot. Three times Fisher sent them ranging along the bottom, searching through the tangled roots of a reef, while he leaned over the rail, watching them.

One diver came up with a big iron ring. Fisher was pleased, but this didn't explain all of the tracings on the mag graph. Next a diver came up with a fire tile—a ceramic slab used in ovens. Finally one handed up a wrought-iron hull fitting two feet long. Fisher was beaming. He knew now he had a Spanish galleon. A bit later that same day a seventy-five-pound *metate*—a stone used for grinding corn—was brought to the surface.

Fisher was jubilant. The useless junk on deck at his feet had transported him back three and a half centuries. This was what he loved. Long before he was born a galleon had hit here in a screaming hurricane and splattered. In some mystical way he believed he had brought that ship and all the people on it to life once again. He had made them a part of himself, and himself a part of them.

Some days later the National Park Service, which protects the Dry Tortugas under Federal law, arranged for specialized cameras mounted in a small plane to fly over those waters. After analyzing the film, a Dr. Allen Marmelstein telephoned Fisher. The film showed that the coral reef Fisher had dived on matched the hull dimensions of a hundred-foot-long Spanish galleon. Presumably the reef had grown completely over the galleon.

"Yes," said Fisher happily, "and I know which galleon it was, too."

Fine. But this did not pay rent or salaries or advance his search for the treasure of the *Atocha*. Time was getting tight again for Fisher, not that he appeared to notice. His divers were still working the *Atocha* site, but treasure was not coming up any more. The site seemed to be petering out.

Fisher was not alarmed. The two "new" tugs were not yet ready to put to sea, but soon would be. The two new tugs would bring him to the *Atocha's* main treasure fast.

His principal digging boat meanwhile was the *Virgalona*, which had once been a mackerel fishing boat. It was a wooden, shallow draft vessel, and in rough seas it bounded around like a fumbled punt. Nor was it a very powerful digger. Its mailboxes could not cope with the immense shifting sand bar known as the Quicksands. There were pockets of sand in this area twenty feet deep. Any treasure would have settled through such sands to bedrock—you could count on it—and the *Virgalona* couldn't dig through such thick sand fast enough or, in the deepest pockets, at all. The two new boats would change that.

Fisher had found them in New Orleans—a pair of disused, sixty-five-foot Mississippi River tugboats, one named *Northwind*, the other *Southwind*. Although the sister ships were three stories high, and therefore basically top-heavy, they had huge props. Although they were not designed for stability in the open sea, they drew as much as seven feet of water, indicating to Fisher that they would ride low and heavy over the *Atocha's* bones; the divers would be able to sleep aboard, and there would be no more shuttle trips to the Marquesas. Fisher was concentrating on the pleasant details, ignoring the dangerous ones. In particular, he liked the props. He could not take his eyes off them. He was obsessed with their size, forty-three inches. He was like a man who, having his eyes fixed on a girl's oversize bosom, sees nothing else at all.

Those enormous props once fitted with mailboxes— surely they would be able to move all of the sand in the world.

Fisher had sent a crew of three, including his second son Kim, to New Orleans to sail the tugs to Key West. The *Northwind* at this time did not run at all, which mattered nothing to Fisher. The *Southwind* would tow it. Why not? It was a tugboat. That's what it was for.

A storm of near-hurricane violence struck both tugs shortly after New Orleans dropped behind the horizon. The two vessels had the low freeboards of river tugs the world over. Neither was safe in heavy seas or during storms at sea, much less when towing one another, and now the *Northwind* began to sink at the end of its towrope; meanwhile the *Southwind* was at a forty-five degree list with one engine completely underwater.

The *Southwind's* Mayday call was picked up by the Coast Guard, which sent a cutter. Seeing that both tugs were in imminent danger of sinking, it being merely a question of which would go first and drag the other down with it, the Coast Guard captain refused to send men aboard the *Southwind*. Instead, he sent over hoses attached to the cutter's massive pumps, and water was pumped out of the *Southwind* until it righted itself. The cutter then towed both boats to safety.

The voyage was completed without further incident when calm weather came.

With both tugs at Key West, Fisher went ahead with his original plans as if nothing had happened. Mailboxes were constructed and attached to the *Northwind*, and he named his oldest son, Dirk, then nineteen years old, its captain. The *Southwind* would be captained by Kim Fisher, seventeen, and Mel Fisher, instead of attaching mailboxes ordered it fitted with a deflector—an enormous windshield-shaped panel that would hang down behind the props at a sixty-five-degree angle. This was a new wrinkle on the mailbox idea, for Fisher theorized that the deflector would clear a bigger area than standard mailboxes, though of course not as fast. A rivalry now developed between the two teenage captains. Whose vessel would be ready to put to sea first? And which would find the most treasure once they got there?

The two tugs had cost, it was said, $100,000 each, but were in such poor condition that many spare parts were needed. But parts for vessels so old were exceedingly hard to find, and also exceedingly expensive. A single one of those huge propellers Fisher so dearly loved was to cost $2,500. The *Northwind* was laid up for over a year—whether because the parts could not be found or because Fisher couldn't pay for them was not clear.

At last the *Southwind* put to sea, and on September 6, 1972, it was anchored over the *Atocha's* presumed final resting place. All were conscious of the date, and as divers prepared to go over the side, the conversation turned to what had happened at that spot 350 years ago that very day. Deo and Bleth McHaley spoke of the battened-down hatches and gunports as the *Atocha* went down and about the screaming women and children trapped in darkness inside. Fisher's divers, being young, spoke of techniques, not darkness. Their predecessors had had no air tanks, of course. Worse, those first divers on the *Atocha* could barely see. Crude goggles had existed; the lenses were tortoise shells polished to an extreme fineness. The goggles had fitted inside the eye sockets themselves, and the divers had had to shave off or pluck their eyelashes because the pressure drove the lenses up against the eyeballs. They couldn't even blink. The eye sockets hemorrhaged, and so the divers had walked around with perpetual black eyes. Also, divers had sometimes plunged into the sea clutching in their mouths sponges impregnated with oil. Once on the bottom, a diver bit down on the sponge, releasing oil. With practice, he could learn to catch the rising bubble of oil in the eye sockets and sometimes, for a moment, he then could see clearly. But neither of these systems added up to a face mask. A man could accomplish a lot on the bottom if only he could see, and the face mask had been to diving a more important invention than the air tank.

Fisher was pursuing his own brooding vision of 350 years ago, How had those five survivors got out, though no one else had? The ship's officers might have been clustered in the captain's cabin in the sterncastle, and there might have been a row of windows across the stern. The officers might have smashed their way out as the ship went down. Even so, they had not survived. In contrast the five survivors had not only got out, but also had found something to cling to amidst tumultuous seas. Somehow they simply hung on until the storm abated, after which they drifted. One of them had lasted five days on a spar, Fisher said, and had survived only because a sea gull landed near him, and he was able to strangle and eat it.

Fisher was always propounding such dramatic details, but it was never clear whether these details were genuine—whether he had read them in some historical document—or whether they had surfaced out of his subconscious, out of his vast need for drama.

When lunch was finished, divers went over the side, one of them Fisher himself. The *Southwind*'s engines began to pound. On the bottom great quantities of sand blew away.

The *Southwind* drilled a hole the size of a house, at the bottom of which Fisher found a single blackened, irregular clump of metal, and he swam it up toward the surface, knowing what it was even before he broke into the sunlight.

Pleased with himself, he tossed the clump up onto the deck.

"I got a clump of coins here," he said.

The exterior faces of the coins were ruined, and could not be read. However, interior faces might still be in pristine condition.

"What do you say we knock that clump apart and see what we got?" suggested Fisher grinning at the state of Florida agent on board. By this time the state was watching Fisher closely. An agent now rode each of his boats at all times. Fisher said grinning: "And if we find a coin dated later than 1622 we throw the whole sonuva bitch overboard."

The state agent was not amused. State regulations held that recovered objects must not be altered until after the division of spoils between itself and Treasure Salvors, Inc.

"We have a right to know what we've found," said Fisher. "We need to know the date on those coins."

The state agent was adamant. The clump must remain unbroken.

But later one of Fisher's men struck it with a hammer, and it fell into pieces.

Every coin face exposed was dated 1622. The state agent was furious. They told him the clump had broken open when someone dropped it by mistake.

So ended Fisher's third year off the Marquesas, the eighth year of his search for the elusive *Atocha*. That one clump of coins stood as the year's single achievement. He had found very little else—and at vast expense. He may or may not have raised a million dollars by then. Whatever the amount, he had spent all of it. He was now not only broke, but heavily in debt. So he went back to his backers, who saw at once that his search had in no way advanced in a year's time. The location of the *Atocha's* mass, or even solid proof that this was the *Atocha* at all, these vital details were no nearer resolution than before.

Days, even weeks had been wasted reenacting previous finds for *National Geographic* cameras. The huge galleon anchor had been entirely excavated, though not raised, for the sake of film footage. When cameras were turning, when reporters were there, then Fisher was always lavish with his time, his divers—his money if he had any. The *Atocha*, he seemed to feel, lay on the bottom and would wait for him, but fame would not. A place in history would not. The press came first.

Fisher found himself unable to raise money. As winter came all his vessels were in port, and there they stayed. For the next five months Fisher was unable to pay his bills or his divers. His rivals were gleeful. This looked like the end of the Vero Beach Treasure King.

Fisher himself seemed to feel that his only hope was Lyon in Seville. It was up to Lyon, whom he also could not pay regularly, to prove that he indeed had part of the *Atocha*, and to put him closer to its main treasure lode.

12

Back to the Archives

In Seville Dr. Eugene Lyon (Ph.D.), former city manager of Vero Beach, became aware of Fisher's difficulties when the checks stopped.

Most scholars working in the Archive lived on small grants. They were poor, but they were young. Lyon was older and, now, poorer. They were alone. Lyon had a wife and four kids. "Mel makes obligations beyond his power," Lyon said, trying to explain it to his wife, "but then he carries them out anyway. Usually. He gets into vast expenditures, followed by periods of vast penury. He swings wildly." Entertainment for the Lyons was again limited to sightseeing, picnics, and organ concerts in the Cathedral. For transport Lyon rode public buses, and as much as possible he rode them during rush hours when a working man's fare prevailed, five pesetas instead of eight, a savings of approximately four and a half cents per ride. He counted the pesetas in his pocket constantly.

Most men base their lives upon the stability of their employer. His stability becomes theirs. But Lyon, forty-three-years old, adrift with a wife and four kids in a foreign country, found himself dependent upon a void.

Another man might not have been able to function at all under such conditions. Being stronger, or perhaps only luckier, Lyon found the stability he needed elsewhere—in the Archive itself. The Archive was more stable than Fisher, more stable than IBM. It was as stable as the Catholic Church, and as changeless. It was a place where time had stopped and where, therefore, everyday worries seemed small. It became a place of immense rewards for Lyon.

Often he would come home at night and say to Dorothy, "Guess what I found out about the *Atocha* today?" And he would regale her with the myriad and frequently useless details he had discovered. Of course, some days he found nothing, and his mood would turn glum; but other days there were discoveries that seemed to him stupendous, that filled him with bursts of joy.

The desperate Fisher, Lyon knew, wanted from Lyon only specific proofs: proof that he had at least part of the *Atocha,* proof that the rest was near. He wanted proof that the treasure the *Atocha* contained was equal to his enormous costs.

But Lyon was a historian. Historians started not with answers, but with questions. Lyon had reduced his questions to six.

1. What about the *Atocha*'s exact location? Were there still no maps or facts to be found pinpointing it exactly?

2. Was it possible to identify Fisher's wreck from the anchor or artifacts found so far? What ship exactly did Fisher have? The *Atocha?* The *Margarita?* Some unknown third vessel? If a third vessel, this might have been a later merchantman or galleon, or else one of the boats sent to salvage the *Atocha* and the *Margarita.* Did records of any such third vessel exist?

3. What had the *Atocha* carried in treasure, and also in armament? Not only did a case need to be made for the richness of the galleon in order to attract investors, but also, assuming Fisher sooner or later did find the treasure, he would need to know when he had come to the end of it. As for armament, Fisher needed to know how many cannons the *Atocha* had carried, how much iron shot, how many boxes of muskets or arquebuses. Why had his mag-

netometer failed to register hits on all this stuff? He
needed to know how many anchors the *Atocha* had carried too. All of the anchors off both galleons ought to be
somewhere within the area he had magged, but he had
not found them. Why?

4. The *Margarita* had been largely salvaged. Could
Lyon prove that the *Atocha* had not been?

5. Was it possible for Lyon to find enough facts and
details so that the great storm could be accurately plotted
by a modern-day meteorologist? If so, this might give
clues as to where the bulk of the galleon could be found.
Could the second storm be plotted too?

6. Was it possible to determine how many pieces the
Atocha had broken into and what they were? If so, it
might be possible to figure out which piece Fisher had, if
indeed he had part of the *Atocha* at all, and also where
the other pieces might lie.

It was impossible to research the answers to these questions in any particular order. One paged through legajos
and made notes on what was there.

Nothing had changed in the two years since Lyon had
worked here last. Each legajo was still a bundle eight
inches thick, five to eight thousand documents covered on
both sides by the quill pens of scribes dead three and a
half centuries; the faded ink was barely legible. Sometimes Lyon could discern words only by holding the document close to his rather thick glasses. That he could read
these documents at all was something of a miracle, though
he no longer thought of it as such. He had studied paleog-
raphy, the science of deciphering archaic scripts, for a
year during his doctoral work at the University of Florida.
There were a great variety of scripts in use in Spain during the sixteenth and seventeenth centuries, and Lyon had
had to learn them all. By the time the *Atocha* sailed, some
of these scripts had passed out of use. Many others, however, had not. Italic script, which somewhat resembled
modern European handwriting, had begun to take over all
court correspondence by 1620. But it was in a special
script called *procesal* that notaries wrote all official documents. This script resembled a child's drawing of waves,
or a series of rolling n's and m's, with no high points and

no lows. Meanwhile, older people were still writing the Gothic script they had learned as children during the previous century.

There seemed to have been no official spelling as yet, either. Scribes had spelled difficult words any way they chose. Especially this was true of names. For instance, one of Cadereita's admirals had been Tomas de Larraspuru, but Lyon had already found this name spelled de Laraspur, or Del Arras Puru, or Thomas Raspur. Similarly the *Atocha* was said to have sunk in the vicinity of the Cayo de Cuchiaga, or the Cayo de Acheaga, or the Cayo de Ucheaga. All these many variations in spelling cost Lyon an immense amount of time. With scores of bundles, and tens of thousands of documents to leaf through, obviously he had to move fast, looking for dates first—these were to be found at the bottom of each document, though sometimes they did not exist—and then scanning each document for flag words. Obviously "Atocha" was a flag word, but there were many others, Larraspuru and Cuchiaga among them. The free-lance spelling only made Lyon's job harder. Lyon had to adjust his mind also to an especially difficult method of writing figures because the Spaniards had concocted a system of symbols that stood for numbers. These symbols were supposed to have been harder to forge than ordinary numerals; three and a half centuries later, they were almost impossible to decipher.

Lyon had started this year's search in the section labeled "Audencia de Santo Domingo," which was where Angeles Flores Rodriguez had found Cadereita's report to the king. This legajo was a rich one, Lyon soon saw, far richer than the single document that Señora Flores Rodriguez had found and sent. That was the trouble really with all past research on behalf of treasure hunters. The Seville researchers had had no real understanding of what material would prove valuable. In the past, most had found only part of any given story, had mailed it to Florida and had then sat back waiting for a check.

The first important document Lyon found was in Santo Domingo 132—the immensely long contract between the Avería Administration and one Alonso Ferrera of Havana for the construction of four galleons, one to be named *Nuestra Señora de Atocha*.

Ferrera's shipyard was six miles outside Havana, and the oak that would go into the four galleons would be Cuban. But the anchors, twenty-four in all, would come from Vizcaya in the north of Spain, according to the contract, as would much of the iron work and some of the rigging. The masts, yards, and bowsprits were to be German pine; Lyon speculated that they must have come in by the shipload, great lengths of trees lying on deck. The sixty-four bronze cannons for these galleons had been cast in Spanish foundries and were on hand. Ferrera was to receive twenty-six thousand ducats for each ship.

Additional papers were appended to the contract, so Lyon read on.

The first three galleons had been turned over to the guard fleet in Cuba in 1619. The *Atocha* joined the fleet August 16, 1620, in a ceremony at Havana. But her maiden voyage was brief, and very nearly disastrous. A few days out of Havana she was struck by a mild storm; it snapped her main mast in two, and the falling mast destroyed a good bit of what was underneath. Most of the *Atocha*'s ten-day maiden voyage was spent staggering back toward Havana in poor condition. Lawsuits had developed out of this maiden voyage. Ferrera was accused of using poor materials, and fleet officials later seized part of the cargo of another galleon and sold it to provide money to refit the *Atocha*. At length the *Atocha* sailed again for Spain, but her second maiden voyage was not happy either, for a good many hull leaks developed up toward her bow, and once she did reach Spain, she had to be refitted again.

Lyon was amused. The *Atocha* had not been any Queen of the Seas, exactly, had she?

Lyon saw that all of her specifications were included in the Ferrera contract, but he could not decipher them. Measurements were given in *codos* and *varas,* and weights were in *marks.* In addition the seventeenth-century nautical terminology was unknown to Lyon. He could go no further with these documents for the moment. He would have to be satisfied with the one central fact he had gleaned so far—the *Atocha* had carried no iron cannons. Fisher must be informed of this. To search for them with his mag was to waste still more time.

The survivors of the *Margarita* and the *Atocha*, Lyon well knew, would have been sat down in front of a notary and interrogated.

Lyon went looking for these interrogatories. After several days he found them, and his heart immediately began to beat fast.

Quickly he thumbed through the documents, noting to his disappointment that this pile represented the sixty-six *Margarita* survivors only. Still, each survivor would have been asked where the galleon sank and one or another might have known exactly. More than a hundred questions, always the same ones, were asked of each survivor, Lyon noted. The questions were usually long-winded; the answers were almost always long-winded. In addition, each survivor was always identified first as was the official or officials taking the testimony. The usual flowery language was employed wherever possible, as if deliberately to waste Lyon's time.

Page after page, day after day, Lyon plowed through these interrogatories, for he felt himself on the verge of answering the most urgent of all Fisher's questions. Where had the *Margarita* gone down? What landmarks, if any, were visible?

But Lyon came to the end having culled not a single new detail. Every nearby island that might have been sighted was uninhabited, and most were unnamed. The survivors had no way of telling which was which, or where the *Margarita* had foundered. In the storm they had seen little. Once in the sea, terror had blotted out all other thought.

For additional days Lyon searched for the interrogatories of the five *Atocha* survivors. He never found them. He did come across a letter written eight years later by Captain Juan de Anuez, Melián's deputy, and Lyon's excitement rose to new peaks, for Anuez was writing about a map showing where the wreck site was. The map was supposed to be attached to the letter in Lyon's hand.

A map! The map Fisher had been hoping for. The map that Lyon, too—whatever his declarations to the contrary—had always expected to find.

Lyon was breathless. The document in his fingers was

too thin to have a map attached. He glanced at it, turned it over. No map. The next document in the pile, then. He grabbed it up. It was not a map. Lyon began to fumble down through the pile. No maps. Urging himself to be calm, he went back and paged steadily through the entire legajo. The map wasn't there. Grabbing up Anuez's letter, he reread it. It definitely referred to a map, and the map was supposed to be attached.

But it wasn't.

Gradually Lyon's breathing slowed, and at last he folded the covers closed, tied the ribbons up, and went glumly home to Dorothy and the kids. But all that evening he brooded about the map he had not found. It *must* be somewhere. But where?

Lyon's days rarely varied. He was at his table in the churchlike reading room as soon as the Archive opened at nine in the morning. He would take a break at eleven, walking across the street with other scholars to the cafe called the Via Veneto. From two to four, Spanish lunchtime, the Archive was closed. Lyon would go home for lunch, eat it rather quickly, and then study the notes he had made that morning until it was time to go back. He would remain at his table until eight when the Archive closed. By then, of course, it was dark, but the streets were full of Sevillanos hurrying home from work, he among them.

The cold weather came. The former city manager of Vero Beach, who owned no warm clothing, wore long-sleeved underwear under his short-sleeved shirts. On the coldest days he wore three or four pairs of socks, and he would page through the *legajos* wearing gloves.

Then it was spring. At night in the streets Lyon sniffed the odor of jasmine and *dama de la noche*. The perfume of the night-blooming flowers hung even above the cars.

In the legajo marked Contratacíon 2211 Lyon discovered the cargo registries of both the *Atocha* and the *Margarita,* and ordered them microfilmed—the *Atocha's* alone was some two thousand pages long. The microfilm went into Lyon's briefcase to be carried with him at all times. He guarded it as carefully as money, often opening the briefcase to reassure himself that it was still there. He had only glanced through it so far. The rolling procesal script promised a long and arduous translation job, and he did not have time for that now.

For he had come upon references to another map.

This map had apparently been drawn by Captain Nicholas de Cardona, who, in the winter of 1623, had been summoned from Acapulco, together with his fourteen black divers. Hopes had risen high once Cardona reached Vargas's side, for Cardona was a salvor by trade, whereas Vargas was a fleet admiral. Cardona was supposedly the technically equipped salvage engineer who could solve all problems, though he solved none that year.

But Cardona, Lyon now realized, was the link between the Vargas salvage and the Melián salvage four years later. Cardona was also the one man who knew the location of the wreck site whom Lyon had not investigated so far.

As Lyon tried to track down Cardona, references to Cardona's map became frequent, but the map itself did not turn up. Cardona had moved around a lot. He was one of the discoverers of California. Documents on him were scattered everywhere. For weeks Lyon traced Cardona's life, following him from one section of the Archive across into another; together Lyon and Cardona moved out of the Indiferente General legajos into the Audencia legajos. Together they moved also from Mexico to Panama, from Panama to Venezuela.

References to the map became so frequent that at last Lyon was able to fix its location. The map could be found in the Biblioteca National in Madrid. Lyon even had citation numbers: M S #2464, fol. 53. So he went to Madrid and searched for the map and, in a state of considerable excitement, found it.

It was hand drawn, presumably by Cardona himself and, together with other maps of the time, had been sewn into a leatherbound tome. This was as beautiful and as priceless a volume as Lyon had ever held in his hands, and Cardona's map was interesting to look at. But Lyon's only emotion, as he gazed at it, was terrific disappointment. It purported to be a map of the Caveza de los Mártires. It showed southern Florida and the keys, and it was wildly inaccurate. The peninsula came to a point, and the keys straggled west in chunks. In the ocean surrounding

the keys floated crude rowboats peopled with naked salvage divers. Apparently these boats and divers had been
drawn by Cardona, too. Cardona was no artist; that much
was clear. There were a number of such boats. No one of
them appeared to designate the only salvage site in the
world that interested Lyon, even though the map had
clearly been drawn with reference to the search for the
galleons. There even was Cardona's handwritten narrative
which accompanied it.

The Caveza de los Mártires is the southernmost part of
Florida which runs east and west, and is located on a
north-south line with the port of Havana, in more than
twenty-five degrees of latitude; which is a dangerous
place, for there have been drowned in it an infinite number of souls, and for this reason they call it the Martires,
or because of the innumerable keys which are thus joined
together; they are of sand, and changeable in the rigors
of weather. Some are large, with mangrove and other
types of trees, and there are settled in them some fisher-
men-Indians, since they have water. The year of 1623
[sic] there were lost in this place three silver galleons of
the command of the Marqués de Cadereita, and other
ships of the fleet in which perished many souls and for-
tunes. The vice flagship of Tierra Firme with more than
a million was lost, according to opinions, in nine arms;
the galleon Margarita in five on a rocky outcropping; that
of General Chazaretta on Tortuga in three arms, with
other private ships. The year the viceroy of New Spain—
the Marqués de Gelves—sent me from the port of Acapulco in the South Sea with 14 Negro divers and instruments to Havana to help to seek this treasure. I took part
in company with the Marqués de Cadereita, Captain
Gaspar de Vargas and Don Pedro de Ursua, searching
for it in the keys of Matecumbe and in the sand banks.
Even though we found the sides of the two galleons and
salvaged from them many muskets and barrels of balls,
ballast and some silver bars, we could not come up with
the main because of the bad weather, even though we
worked with the greatest of care. Later the silver of the
galleon *Margarita* was found, by means of the notices
which I gave to Pilot Govea and to Francisco Melián,

citizens of Havana, as my certifications advise, and it is certain that if efforts are made the missing silver will appear and that of the vice flagship of Tierra Firme, for it is a shame to leave for lost more than a million in so little depth as it must be.

Lyon considered. Perhaps no wreck site map had ever existed. More probably, one or several had existed, but had been purged from the filing cabinets of the day lest they fall into the hands of the Dutch.

Lyon would do better to confine his search to documents. Somewhere there must be precise textual references to the wreck site.

He knew where one such reference was, and he went back to study it again. In Santa Domingo 132 he had come across a letter from Vargas to the king dated January 9, 1623.

According to this letter, Vargas had been at the wreck site from September 26, 1622, to January 3, 1623. He had been working in water that was never clear, and that was ten, twelve, and even fourteen arms deep. The weather was always bad. A frigate stood guard over the divers. The divers were working out of seven small boats. Vargas was not permitting them to *dalacion*—dally. The divers were slaves, and Vargas knew their *dueño*—their master, well. The man really made the slaves work.

This was interesting, though of no great importance to Fisher, but presently Lyon came again to the rest of Vargas's news: he and the divers were in the habit of leaving their base camp on "this key" at four each morning. The rowers would have them on the wreck site by seven. They would then work seven straight hours, leaving the work site about two in the afternoon, sometimes earlier, sometimes later, reaching the base camp again by ten at night.

Vague as it was, this was the only clue Lyon had yet found to the distance between the base camp and the wreck site—three hours rowing to get there, up to seven hours returning at night against prevailing winds and currents.

Now Lyon asked himself three hard questions.

1. Which island was "this key"?

Answer: Surely Vargas's base camp and Melián's four

years later were on the closest possible island to the site. Surely both camps had been the same. And Melián's had been on the Cayo del Marques—the Marquesas.

2. Which way did prevailing winds and currents move around the Marquesas today, and was it certain that these had not changed over three and a half centuries? Answer: The winds and currents moved out toward Fisher's wreck site, Lyon knew. They were often very strong. Were they the same winds and currents as three and a half centuries ago? Without knowing for sure, one had to assume that they were.

3. How far could rowers row a Spanish longboat in three hours?

Lyon had no ready answer to this question, so he began searching for a similar salvage operation where rowers were employed over known distances. The closest year, previous to 1622, when a hurricane had devastated the plate fleet was 1605. The Portuguese consortium that administered the Avería that year was forced into bankruptcy. Longboats had been used for salvage, and these longboats, Lyon read, needed about one hour to row about one league. A Spanish league was three miles.

Well, then. Nine miles in three hours, more or less. Fisher's wreck site was some ten miles from the Marquesas. Fisher, it seemed to Lyon, was about where he should be.

Lyon was learning more and more about the Archive of the Indies. He was becoming able to judge in advance where he might find whatever documents he was looking for. He felt himself growing as an historian.

But he also realized that he was becoming hypnotized by these legajos. He was stopping to read bizarre biographical details. He kept getting led astray. There was Cadereita's *residencia,* for instance.

Cadereita's tenure as viceroy of New Spain had just ended. According to the Spanish system each public official's term in office was followed by a residencia, an official report on his stewardship. Anybody at all was allowed to come in and give testimony for or against the official.

Lyon knew so much about Cadereita now that the man seemed almost a personal friend. His residencia, Lyon saw, was twenty to thirty thousand pages long. It detailed every lawsuit ever filed by or against him, every fine for infractions on his ships.

Though it was crazy to wade through such a huge residencia Lyon had to force himself not to do it. Cadereita, after 1623, had had nothing further to do with the *Atocha*. Nothing at all.

Folding the covers, Lyon tied the ribbons and with great regret lugged Cadereita's residencia up to the porteros' desk and retired it. Then he stood there a moment feeling the pang. He had just said good-bye to Cadereita forever, and the man had meant a lot to him.

Other residencias were pertinent.

The search for the Cardona salvage papers had taken Lyon into that section of the Archive called Escribania de Camara where, in legajo 76-A, he came upon the residencia of Cabrera y Covera, one of the several governors of Cuba during Melián's salvage of the *Margarita*.

Melián's name was mentioned many times.

Diligently Lyon plowed through the entire residencia, hundreds and hundreds of pages of it. There had been a scandal of some kind. Ignoring the governor, who was of no interest, Lyon tried to figure out what was being said—and what was true—about Melián.

The Crown's auditor aboard Melián's vessels, it was charged, was a creature of Melián's, and had even lived in his house. The governor had appointed this auditor, and therefore was in collusion with Melián himself. Together they had smuggled the *Margarita* treasure into Havana, and then into Spain.

Lyon read specific charges: Melián "took home fifty bars of silver, eight pieces of artillery and 64,800 pieces of eight reales and nobody ever knew what happened to them."

Was it true?

The *Margarita*, Lyon knew, had carried 411 registered bars of silver. In four years Melián had reported finding 390. Although sixty-seven of these were not on the registry, meaning that they were contraband, Melián had reported them anyway.

Nonetheless, his pay had been held up. Between 1626 and 1628 he apparently received nothing—Lyon read letters in which he begged the Crown for some of the money due him. If he was not paid, he next wrote, he would not have the means to go after the *Atocha*, a recovery job dear to the Crown's heart. Part of Melián's money was still being withheld in 1630.

According to Cabrera y Covera's *residencia*, the bulk of the papers on this sad affair were to be found in the Santo Domingo section of the Archive, and Lyon went looking for them there.

Although the case against Melián seemed to Lyon extremely thin so far, he pursued it for two reasons: because of the obvious parallel between Melián and Fisher—Fisher was always being called a crook too—and because instinct told him that he was about to find a body of *Margarita* documents he had not yet seen. But he did not find them in the Santo Domingo section.

Stubbornly, he moved into other sections, and went on searching.

He found many useful documents, and paused to note their contents. Two were letters from Melián to the king. The first was dated April 22, 1627. It explained that the winter had been severe, and that the outline of the *Margarita*, due to shifting currents, was now concealed below a sandbank. In the second, a year and a half later, Melián wrote: "The opinion of the pilot-major and of the diver Antonio de Sosa is that the galleon Santa Margarita broke in half with the chambers where the silver was stored falling off to the right, and that the missing silver was in the quartel. All excess ballast of the ship was removed leaving hardly anything inside, helping us to further confirm that the majority of the silver was contained in the missing quartel, but when we finally discovered its location, it was so very buried in the sand and so difficult to reach that if God does not help us it will not be possible to retrieve anything."

Descriptions of Melián being bedeviled by sand seemed like evidence favorable to Fisher, who was on top of the same moving sandbanks.

But where were the Melián fraud papers? They must be somewhere, for more and more often, as he paused to scan some document concerning Melián, Lyon found them mentioned again.

And so he pressed on, at last discovering the public prosecutor's file on the case.

But halfway through this file, at a spot where the Melián documents would logically be, Lyon found only a gap, plus a notice that the Melian papers had been sent "forward."

Forward?

Forward where?

For a time the entire bundle of fraud papers, Lyon learned, had been in the hands of the Council of the Indies. Lyon searched the legajo that should have contained them, but again they had been removed. Next Lyon traced them to Jaen, and finally to Madrid. At the capital, though the governor's prosecution went forward, Melián's case was abruptly severed. All salvage papers relating to Melián were detached, and where they went to, Lyon did not know. There was no further record of them. They simply disappeared. Though Lyon spent weeks, he never picked up their trace again.

The case against Melián, Lyon saw, had remained to the end as flimsy as the various cases contrived against Mel Fisher so far. Success in treasure hunting seemed to have inspired as much envy three hundred and fifty years ago as now. Melián, like Fisher, was perceived by his contemporaries as a lucky stiff. He had found treasure merely by looking in the right place, without the sweat and agony most men expended in their own searches for treasure in the world of trade. Men hated him for it. Then as now, they chose to overlook the money and hope invested, the agonizing doubts, the months and years bouncing around over the wreck site in small boats.

In Melián's case the king or some other powerful person had stepped in and quashed the prosecution against him. For finding the *Margarita* he was rewarded with the governorship of Venezuela, and in 1642 he became governor of Yucatan, moving north toward what was presumably his lifetime goal, viceroy of New Spain, the plum job of the New World, the job recently vacated by the Marqués de Cadereita. Perhaps Fisher would live happily ever after also, Lyon reflected, if he could just find the *Atocha*.

As he prepared to leave Spain, Lyon recapitulated, for

later presentation to Fisher, all that he had learned during the previous academic year.

1. What about the *Atocha*'s exact location? Were there still no maps or facts pinpointing it exactly?

Maps, no, unfortunately. But there were additional facts in abundance.

According to Cardona's description, the *Atocha* had sunk in the Caveza de los Mártires, on a north-south line with Havana. The Marquesas's group lay smack on this north-south line. No case could be made any longer for Upper and Lower Matecumbe Keys. They lay a hundred miles northeast.

What else?

The Spaniards' wreck site was everywhere described as a shifting sandbar. So was Fisher's. The Spaniard's wreck site had been a three-hour row—roughly ten miles—from the base camp, and so was Fisher's.

2.Was it possible to identify Fisher's wreck from the anchor or artifacts found so far.?

Lyon now had the registries of both the *Atocha* and the *Margarita*. If Fisher were to bring up any silver bars or cannons, these would bear numbers, which could be matched against the registries; a positive identification would be immediate.

But for the moment it was impossible to say what Fisher had. He might even have—Fisher was not going to enjoy the idea—some unknown third ship.

3. What had the *Atocha* carried in treasure and armament?

Lyon had still not translated the registry. Glancing through hundreds of pages he had noted only that each silver bar—some nine hundred in all—was identified and described by weight. This weight was immense—twenty-five to thirty tons. The gold and copper was described too. The personal jewelry, household goods, and cash money of the forty-eight rich passengers was not described, but must have been enormous. Nor, obviously, did the registry note how much the *Atocha* had carried in contraband. But probably its contraband had exceeded in value its registered cargo. That was the norm for that part of that century. The Spaniards in 1622 were a cynical people.

4. Could Lyon prove that the *Atocha* had not been salvaged?

No Spaniard had salvaged it at least up until 1630, for Melián at that time was still planning to salvage it himself.

Any suggestion that Melián or any other Spaniard might have mounted an expedition and salvaged the *Atocha* in secret was, to Lyon, absurd. Havana in the 1620s was too small a place. There was no way a secret of that magnitude could have been kept.

Might someone else have salvaged the *Atocha* after Melián left for Venezuela?

This possibility Lyon could not, as yet, entirely discount.

5. Had Lyon found enough facts and details so that the great storm, three hundred and fifty years later, could be accurately plotted?

Yes. That storm had chewed up ships and towns all over the Caribbean and reports had been made. Lyon was bringing home all this data. As for the second storm, the one that bounced the *Atocha* up and down on the bottom until it broke into pieces, some of which floated away— this storm could not be plotted today. With the exception of Vargas riding it out in the Tortugas, no important ship had been caught out in it. It had skirted inhabited areas; no data on it existed.

6. Was it possible to determine how many pieces the *Atocha* had broken into, and what they were?

Possibly.

According to Melián, the *Margarita's* sterncastle had broken off, and the rest of the ship had then sectioned into two parts horizontally along the line of the gun ports. The *Atocha* probably broke up the same way. Apparently this was a flaw in the galleon construction. Salvors saw such sectioning all the time. But Lyon would suggest to Fisher that the mass of the *Atocha's* treasure would eventually be found in and among the ballast stones of the stern portion of the hull, exactly where Melián had found most of *Margarita's*.

Lyon had no idea which portion of the *Atocha* Fisher had already located. Not enough treasure and artifacts had been found to decide one way or the other—assuming he did have the *Atocha*, of course.

It was now June 1973. One by one the Latin American scholars were leaving Seville for home. Lyon gathered his wife, his children, his notebooks, his spools of microfilm, and boarded a four-engine jet to Miami. The Marqués de Cadereita was much on his mind during the flight. For three decades Cadereita had been accustomed to crossing the Atlantic twice each year. Each perilous voyage took two months or more. But eight hours later Dr. Eugene Lyon deplaned in Florida.

He arrived in Key West just in time to verify the bullion markings of the stupendous discoveries that would be made that summer, and inadvertently to cause a public uproar that almost sank Fisher, and himself as well.

13

Bouncy John

Bouncy John Lewis, drifting about the country with malice toward none, had drifted into Key West during the next to last year of the Vietnam War. In appearance he gave no hint of the role he would assume in Fisher's affairs. Long hair dangled almost to his hips. A black beard covered most of his chest. His wardrobe was on his back. In addition he needed dental work. He had a sweet and generous smile nonetheless.

Bouncy John was a hippie, and at twenty-three getting old for the job. He was of medium height. His physique was not impressive. He had no ambition. He owned nothing.

The country was either blessed or burdened—it depended on the point of view—with hippies that year. There were tens of thousands of so-called flower children like Bouncy John. They drifted about. They would not compete. Their generosity seemed insane—they shared their money, their food, their girls. Patriots denounced them. Hard-hats threw stones at them. Cops broke their heads.

Bouncy John's progression from normal youngster to hippie was in no way remarkable. He grew up in Detroit, went to college, and studied commercial art. He became an extremely skilled artist. But day by day he saw his principal object change. He and most of his male classmates had sought not to learn, but to stay in college and thus out of the Vietnam War; but abruptly Bouncy John quit college. He became first a hippie, then a garbage man. Or perhaps it was the other way around. In a crippled country, he was part of its crippled youth. He gave away everything he owned. Sometimes he gave away too much and for a time did not eat. He slept in vans, in parks, on the floors of friends' pads.

The word got round: hippie heaven was San Francisco, the promised land. With half a dozen others, Bouncy John piled into a van and they started west. Forty years after America's first westward migration of the uprooted, there was now another, though few remarked on it in those terms, or wondered if someday there would be a third, representing who knew which new national failure.

In San Francisco a hippie's life pattern seemed to be no pattern at all. In order to be able to talk about it, a whole new vocabulary had to be invented, and was. One hung out. One tripped. One shared a pad. There were no last names. They knew each other as Bill, Sally, Bouncy John. After a time, one split.

Bouncy John Lewis, more restless than most, began hitchhiking southeast more or less in the direction of Florida, conducting, as the wheels rolled under him, a personal search for anything important that might be left in his life or the world. Most goals were evil, perhaps all of them were. Only searches were—or could be—pure, or so he hoped, and without even knowing it he began looking for some specific search he could somehow adhere to. The search he would ultimately fix on was Mel Fisher's search for the *Atocha*'s gold.

Gold had strange properties, and one of them was this: it was also an ideal. Possibly the nation's entire plague of hippies could have been eliminated in an instant merely by throwing open a few gold mines.

But of the tens of thousands of hippies nationwide, only one got caught up in a gold rush: Bouncy John Lewis. Had not past searches for gold transformed the lives of millions of men? Would this one transform Bouncy John?

The enemy of violence, having reached Florida, had conceived the idea of reaching Key West: one could bound from island to island across the glittering sea. Key West was the end of the line, man; you could go no farther. Key West, someone had written, was where the land ran out on dreamers. It had run out on Fisher there. Now it would run out on Bouncy John.

Key West was less than Bouncy expected. It was only a small town, thirty thousand people. The whole island was only four miles long. There were no bright lights; it was not even prosperous. On Duval, the town's main shopping street, Bouncy saw that many store fronts were boarded up. Even the movie house had gone out of business. On the side streets there were muddy vacant lots. The tide must be in; water had collected in the streets on the low parts of the island.

Within two days Bouncy was in jail.

Though a shabby place, Key West considered itself too good for hippies, many of whom had congregated in the town. A crackdown was ordered.

Bouncy was on the beach. A hippie more agile than he was walking up a palm tree to get at the coconuts, for the hippies were hungry. The first police car screeched to a stop. Gun drawn, the first cop raced stumbling across the sand and jammed his gun into Bouncy. Spread-eagled over the police car, the unresisting Bouncy was searched, placed under arrest, and his rights read.

Bouncy asked mildy what the charges were.

"Do you have an address in this town, scum? Do you have money, scum?"

"I have some money."

The cop opened Bouncy's wallet: Sixty dollars— Bouncy's entire fortune.

"Can I ask what your badge number is?"

"Shut up, scum."

Bouncy knew he would never see his wallet again, and indeed he did not. He only vaguely understood the intensity of the cop's emotion, though he had seen such emotion many times now.

Downtown Bouncy John Lewis was thrown into jail, where he made the acquaintance of a hundred or more other hippies. The cops didn't get everybody; there had been too many hippies to bag them all. One that they missed soon arrived to bail Bouncy out, but by then Bouncy had formed a friendship with a hippie from Montreal who had no money.

"We have to bail my friend out too," said Bouncy.

"Jesus, it will take every cent we have."

"He'll pay us back. He promised me."

"I have money outside," said the hippie from Montreal. "I swear it on my mother's grave."

In the street the hippie from Montreal disappeared. Like Bouncy's wallet, he would never be seen again.

Bouncy was hungry. He and his friend began to tramp the streets looking for work. But no one would hire them, and the hippies got hungrier.

At the shipyard on the third day without eating, Bouncy was attracted by Mel Fisher's pirate galleon, which was then being refitted. As Bouncy watched, Fisher himself stepped off the vessel. Bouncy had no idea who Fisher was, but he looked like he might be a boss, so Bouncy stepped forward saying, "Hey, man, may I have a place to sleep for a while? I'll sweep your decks for you. I'll do anything you need."

Fisher looked Bouncy John over. Bouncy was a dropout. But then Fisher was a dropout too. Put them both on the same island and it became almost inevitable that they would find each other.

The Vero Beach Treasure King had no way of knowing that this ragged youth was to find him half a million dollars worth of treasure.

Fisher kept no files on people who asked for jobs. He seemed to make no effort to hire the right man at the right time. His attitude toward hiring was as disorganized as the life he led. Glancing high up in the rigging, Fisher studied it a moment. The rigging was ten stories high. Then he turned to the hippie.

"Do you mind climbing up there and putting some ropes up for me? Some rigging?"

"Yeah, sure. Sure, I can do anything. Me and my friend here are experts."

Fisher smiled. It was as always a warm and generous smile. Fisher believed that every man ought to live his life the way he felt like it. So did Bouncy John.

"Well, actually we're not experts," Bouncy said. "But we are hard workers. We'll help you put it together."

There was a good deal of the scoutmaster about Fisher. He liked to turn boys into men. One of the boys Fisher later hired was a convicted thief who, once he started to dive for treasure, was never in trouble again.

Fisher said, "Okay. It's sixty dollars a week."

"Can I stay on the boat and sleep there?"

Fisher thought about it, then said, "No. We got security guards on there, you know."

Bouncy nodded.

"You'll have to find a place to stay by yourself."

In town Bouncy bought his way into a communal pad—a group of hippies living together in a broken-down house. Bouncy would soon have money, therefore Bouncy was welcome. He was asked to give over two-thirds of his weekly paycheck—this amounted to $160 a month—toward the pad's $80-a-month rent. Bouncy was glad to do it. Any of the others, he felt, would gladly have done the same for him.

While remaining a hippie, Bouncy broke the code. He worked: he was a kind of garbage man again, this time for Fisher. He cleaned up the pirate galleon and the assorted work sheds in which Fisher kept gear. Bouncy was a friendly, cheerful worker. In his spare time he completed his first painting in years and presented it to Fisher. The Vero Beach Treasure King, who understood nothing about art or intellectual matters, took it proudly home and hung it in his shabby houseboat.

At the end of a year, Bouncy broke the code again by opting for upward mobility. Wanting to be like the elite members of Fisher's crew, he spent money on learning to dive. But he still kept his long, tangled hair and beard, and he still loaned or gave away most of his money. He still considered being a good hippie important.

He began to go to sea on the *Southwind*. He cleaned the bilges, transferred fuel from one tank to another, and kept the engines running. He waited to be asked to dive.

Bouncy's title was engineer. He knew more about engines, pumps, and fuel transfer systems than anyone else aboard—he knew almost nothing about them. The *Southwind*'s teenage captain was Kim Fisher, who knew almost

nothing about being captain of a seagoing Mississippi
River tugboat. Together, Kim and Bouncy John were
learning both their jobs and the vessel.

The boys adapted themselves to the ocean. The vessel
adapted itself not at all. At sea the *Southwind* only plod-
ded along. Under full power, carrying ten to twelve divers, it moved barely faster than the *Atocha* of long, long
ago—about five knots. To reach the wreck site or return to
Key West was an all-day trip. The tug was awfully low in
the water, and even on beautiful, warm days when the
seas were calm, it did not seem at ease. Even gentle swells
slapped over its low gunwales.

Then came the momentous Fourth of July.

Bouncy, up early that morning, was anxious to be the
first diver over the side, for problems were sure to arise
later that would put him back in the engine room. His
tank was heavy between his shoulder blades, and then he
had plunged into the water and was swimming down. The
water was about eighty-three degrees, clearer that day
than Bouncy had yet seen it, and he kicked his way to the
bottom, about twenty-five feet down. Bouncy was standing on fine smooth sand. Nothing grew; nothing showed
on the sand at all. Above Bouncy John hung the hull of
the *Southwind*, its massive unguarded propellers turning
slowly about fifteen feet above his head. The *Southwind*
surged forward, tugging against anchor ropes as its propellers bit. The propellers blasted water backwards against
the deflector, and then down.

The sand carpet beneath Bouncy's face mask began to
blow away. A patch measuring approximately one
hundred feet square—the size of a baseball diamond—was
slowly, remorselessly, being cleared of sand at the rate of
about one inch per minute. Goodies showed up as if on a
carpet, although, if the *Southwind*'s engines were then cut
off, sand hanging in suspension would settle down, covering them again.

Today Bouncy John was down inside the blast. He had
to swim hard to hold himself on station there. Though the
blast could not even lift a gold coin, it could waft a man
away, possibly proving once again that gold was more stable than people.

There was a great deal of ballast stone mixed in with

the sand here, smooth, football-sized stones, and Bouncy watched them appear one by one. The *Atocha*—if it was the *Atocha*—had staggered through here with its bowels ripped open, and this was what had spilled out. But Bouncy, who was watching the stones closely, hoping to spy treasure, had drifted too close to the edge of the blast. Suddenly it picked him up and blew him backwards, out of the hole. He was in a swirl of sand, tumbling, but in front of his mask appeared what seemed to be several red beads and the tip of what might be a crucifix. He lunged for it, and thought he had missed. But then the sand fell away and he was sitting there on the bottom holding whatever it was in his hands. An exquisite gold rosary with red coral beads. Wow!

Bouncy burst out of the water fist first crying, "Beads!"

He was dragged on board. The other boys beat him happily on the back, even as they began to strip his diving gear off him. He looked tired, they told him. He should take it easy. He had been diving all morning and needed a rest. He certainly shouldn't do any more diving.

Meanwhile, they were dragging their own gear on. Everyone was in a hurry to reach the bottom to find the rest of the gold that must be there. Bouncy was grinning and laughing, his beard parted by all those ragged teeth. He kept staring at his magnificent rosary and saying, over and over again, "Hey, ALL RIGHT!"

Behind him other divers splashed into the water. Bouncy didn't care. He stared at his wonderful rosary. It was a really exquisite piece of jewelry, it was over three hundred and fifty years old, and he knew it was worth a lot of money, maybe as much as $100,000. That was a fortune to a hippie. Or to anyone.

"ALL RIGHT! Hey, man, ALL RIGHT!"

But the ballast stones Bouncy had noted were possibly even more important than the rosary. The divers had been trying to follow a trail of ballast for days. They did not think they had the main ballast pile—the stones seemed too widely scattered and they were too small—but you never knew. And the main ballast pile was the target of this entire search. The main ballast pile should lead directly to the *Atocha's* main treasure hold.

The theory was that the main part of the hull, containing

two hundred tons of ballast stones and nearly fifty tons of treasure, could not have moved much, if at all, in 350 years. It should still be there somewhere, more or less intact. Buried, probably, but intact.

So find the ballast and you find the treasure.

Today might be the day, all the boys thought, and they plunged into the water.

14

The
Silver Bars

Later, order was restored, and only two divers—the normal complement—were down when the day's second great discovery was made.

Under the *Southwind* Fisher's third son Kane, then fourteen, and Mike Schnaedebach watched the hole. The blowers blasted into the sand, and the water pressure pushed a blanket of sand out the back of the hole. The two divers rode just on top of this pocket of sand and water. The pocket thrust backwards under their bellies—they could feel it—and they peered down, hoping to spy treasure, and then both did spy something, though neither was sure what. Both swam hard against the current, which was sweeping now into their faces, and then they broke through the wall of water into the clear bubble directly under the *Southwind's* props.

Normally the technique was to swim well ahead of whatever object had been spotted, and then drift backwards in the current, grabbing it on the way by, after which the diver could allow himself and whatever he had grabbed to be blown out the back of the hole. He would then swim up with the object.

Now both boys grabbed the thing they had spied, but they could not budge it. It was so heavy that, for as long as they hung on to it, the water blast swept them no further. Kane Fisher's first impression was: it looks like a loaf of bread. It was black, smooth, and enormously heavy for its size, and the boys had to get help to lift it to the surface.

By the time other divers got down with ropes, two more "loaves of bread" had been uncovered.

The first loaf thumped down on the deck. Then came the two others. Everyone knew instantly what they were, even though no one had seen anything like them before.

After an awed silence, the black patina was scraped from one of the loaves: silver. Solid silver. And they had three bars of it.

Word was radioed to Key West. Three bars of solid silver. Heavy ones. Too heavy for two boys to swim to the surface. Yes, all bore discernible serial numbers.

Now the awed silence was Fisher's. The *Southwind* must be on top of the main ballast pile after all. The three silver bars must have tumbled from the *Atocha's* burst strongroom. The rest of that strongroom must lie slightly to one side. It must be only yards away; in an hour or a day they would have it. The long search was nearly over.

There was hysteria on the *Southwind*; there was hysteria inside Fisher's office on the pirate galleon, too. The air conditioning was out again. The heat was nearly unbearable. People were slapping the jubilant Fisher on the back. Sweat ran down his breastbone as he cried, "Get Gene Lyon out to the wreck quick. Tell him we got some silver bars off the *Atocha* for him to identify."

In Key West everybody raced for speedboats. By noon there were more than two dozen visitors aboard the *Southwind*, all giggling and laughing and banging each other on the deck. Forgotten was Bouncy John's magnificent rosary. It was worth far more than any of the silver bars. But the silver bars were all anyone wanted to see; they proved or seemed to prove that the end of the search was near. How many more silver bars were they about to find? Nearly a thousand, was it? Bouncy John, hair and beard glistening with dried salt, was grinning as happily as anybody. Bouncy John, hippie or not, was a team player. The team's success was far more important than his own.

The *Southwind* began to be crowded with newsmen and photographers. Everyone was waiting for the arrival of Eugene Lyon, whose briefcase would contain the last and most vital answer. The numbers on these bars—were they listed on the *Atocha*'s registry, or not?

In Key West, the tall, skinny scholar was put aboard the speedboat of a man named Preston Shoup. Although everyone else would remember the sea that day as flat calm, Dr. Lyon's impression was otherwise. To Dr. Lyon it was a choppy day. The forty-mile ride out took just over an hour. The speedboat, constantly in the air, bounded from wave top to wave top. Each time it slammed down, it knocked Lyon's glasses askew. It jarred him to the roots of his teeth. It wound his watch. He was hanging on tight all the way.

As the speedboat nosed against the *Southwind*, Lyon ached all over. He had brought his briefcase with him, though what for? He was not going to be able to make an instant identification. The *Atocha* registry alone was two-thousand pages long, and these bars probably came off the *Margarita* anyway. He felt ridiculous climbing aboard the *Southwind* into all that hysteria with his briefcase in his hand. The briefcase felt ridiculous. What must the half-naked divers think of him? Everybody on board was in a state of jubilation that closely resembled drunkenness. Fisher began pounding Lyon on the back. Lyon gave a weak smile.

Crouching over the silver bars, Lyon carefully took the numbers and markings off each. A reverent hush enclosed him. He glanced up into all those expectant faces. There was nothing he could tell them because his rolls of micro-film out here were useless.

The celebration resumed; people were pouring beverages over other people's heads. The scholar, feeling out of it, asked to be returned to Key West. So his briefcase was handed down to him in the speedboat, he pushed his glasses firmly onto his nose and Preston Shoup started back at full throttle.

Limping, sore, with a ringing headache, Dr. Lyon went directly to the library and began threading his microfilmed copy of the *Margarita's* registry into the machine there. Since the bars had been found in approximately twenty-five feet of water, Lyon was sure—whatever Fisher might think—that they had not come from the *Atocha*. Twenty-five feet was *Margarita* depth, not *Atocha* depth, so these must be *Margarita* bars. Or else they came from some unknown third wreck. Either way, it was a defeat for Fisher, who would lose his shirt. True, there would be some *Margarita* treasure left, but not much. And any third wreck could only be a small one, one that had gone down, so to speak, without a splash.

Dr. Lyon began searching.

Although each of Fisher's bars bore plainly discernible numerals, there were no corresponding numerals written out anywhere on the *Margarita's* registry. On 1622 registries, figures were written out in words, and the script used was the supposedly unforgeable and virtually indecipherable procesal.

There was a separate entry for each bar for Dr. Lyon to plow through, and each entry was twenty or more lines long. It gave the pedigree both of the bar's owner and of the bar itself. The pedigree was followed by the five sets of numbers (all written out full-length) that identified each bar: serial number, fineness, weight, value, and the amount of tax due on it. There had been 411 registered bars on the *Margarita*. Lyon couldn't scan now. He had to decipher all twenty lines of each of the 411 entries. He had to attempt to match the numbers stamped onto each of the three bars out there on the *Southwind* to one of the five sets of numbers in each entry.

The hours passed. His shoulders stiffened up, then his neck. His headache got worse. Night came and the library closed. Lyon went home. The next morning he was on the stoop when it opened. He worked all day. He worked until his vision began to blur. The amount of concentration the job demanded was awesome. Again he found not a single entry matching any of the three bars.

The former city manager of Vero Beach worked altogether five days at the library microfilm machine. By the time he had come to the end of the *Margarita's* registry, his mind felt permanently blunted, though less than half his job was done. The bars were not on the *Margarita*'s registry. To Lyon this meant the bars were off a third ship. He would search the *Atocha*'s registry for them, but only as a formality; they would not be on it because the water was too shallow. He was bitterly disappointed. He felt terribly sorry for Fisher, and he felt sorry for himself too. Even the *Margarita*, though Melián had pretty well stripped it by 1630, would have been a richer prize than whatever nameless third ship Fisher actually had. Fisher, in all his bragging, had always admitted that he might have the *Margarita*. He had left open that faint possibility. But some third ship so insignificant no treasure hunter had even heard of it . . .

Fisher would look like such a fool. A bankrupt fool, too.

Lyon threaded the first of the *Atocha* rolls into the microfilm machine.

More hours began to pass. The *Margarita*'s registry had born 411 silver bar entries. The *Atocha*'s was more than twice as long. Dr. Lyon counted them up: the *Atocha* had carried 901 bars.

Lyon's eyes began to give out. More and more often he was obliged to remove his glasses and rub the pain away, after which he would have to wait several minutes blinking until vision returned. Sometimes he would decipher an entire entry, only to realize his attention had wandered completely. He would have to go back and decipher the entry all over again. Reading procesal never got any easier. The more he read it, the more every word in every line resembled every other.

Once more he rubbed his eyes, waited blinking until he could see again, then plunged into the next *Atocha* entry.

In Cartagena, 27 days of the said month of July in the said year the accountant Benito Marques Vellido, in name of the said Jacove de Vreder, silver master of the said galleon confessed to having received from Senor Francisco de Reboledo and accountant Don Alonso de Corral de Toledo, official judges of the royal treasury and of the royal chest in their charge in which is deposited the proceeds from slave licenses, the silver bars and coins following. Item: a bar number four thousand five-hundred and eighty-four, fineness two thousand three hundred and eighty, weight one hundred twenty-five marks three ounces. It is worth two hundred and ninety-eight thousand three hundred ninety-two maravedis, from which should be deducted six thousand seven hundred thirty for the senoraje—

That was it. Bar four thousand five hundred eighty-four was one of the three Fisher had. Lyon began to grin, though he did not know it. After copying out the entire entry in English, Lyon moved on through the registry. Nineteen folios later he found Fisher's second bar, and three folios after that the third one. But how had the bars got into such shallow water? Lyon still couldn't explain it.

Lyon rolled the microfilm back onto its spool, fitted it into its box, and placed the box into its precise spot in his briefcase. Fisher would be very pleased. Lyon was very pleased too. Fisher had found the *Atocha* after all, and Lyon rushed through the streets of Key West to tell him so.

Fisher's excited reaction was to call in the *Southwind* at once. He wanted to hold the most dramatic press conference of his life. He could barely wait to announce to the world this formal proof that he had found the *Atocha*. Every TV news crew around would want to film this press conference, he chortled.

Lyon cautioned Fisher not to announce his finds so promptly. The bars really ought to be weighed first. The matching serial numbers did not constitute really conclusive proof. The Spaniards had cast millions of bars of silver. There could have been duplications in such serial numbers. There must have been.

"Notice that the weight of each bar is given in the registry," said Lyon. "If the weights also match, we would be doubly sure."

But Fisher never double checked anything.

"There could even be duplicate serial numbers on the *Atocha*," Lyon said. In fact, even one of Fisher's three silver bars was a duplicate, though Lyon didn't know this yet.

"The weights will match," said Fisher confidently.

"It doesn't cost anything to be sure before you make your announcment."

"Tell you what we'll do," said Fisher, and a broad smile came onto his face. "I'll announce that we have the *Atocha* today, and then when the *Southwind* gets in we'll weigh the bars in front of the press and TV, and that will prove it."

"But suppose the weights are wrong?"

Fisher only smiled.

Caution was not part of Fisher's makeup. His confidence was, as always, astonishing, and he convoked the press while the *Southwind* was still at sea, the three bars still aboard her, still unweighed. He also ordered a freight scale brought around and lugged up onto the pirate galleon's deck.

Press and TV crews were waiting there as the *Southwind*, bright yellow and three stories high, chugged into Key West harbor and was moored alongside the galleon. Cameras were already turning as the three silver bars were carried up onto the weather deck.

"If the weights don't check out, that will really be something, won't it," whispered Fisher to Lyon, and he laughed heartily at his joke.

About fifty people crowded the galleon's midship well. Nearby stood a garbage can full of beer and crushed ice. It would be a beer celebration, should the weights check out. Though the summer had just started, Fisher was almost out of money and was too poor to afford champagne. He would have to raise more money soon. Today's publicity would help.

The crowd had formed a semicircle and stood well back from the freight scale. Everyone was tense. The heavy, upright scale stood isolated against the rail. Anxious glances touched it and moved away. The scale dominated all thought, all conversation. The scale dominated the deck: it stood there, ominous as a guillotine. It could behead all hope.

On a calculator Lyon had converted the bars' registry weights from Castilian marks into American pounds. This had been no easy job. He had had to trace Castilian weights and measures forward in time until the Spaniards themselves converted to the modern metric system. Thus he learned that each Castilian mark equaled in weight 230.5 grams. Since each U.S. ounce equaled 28.35 grams, each Castilian mark worked out to 8.11 U.S. ounces. There were 8 Castilian ounces to the mark.

Lyon's calculator showed, therefore, that bar No. 4,585 (125 marks, 3 ounces) should weigh 63.59 pounds; bar No. 794 (124 marks, 1 ounce) should weigh 62.95 pounds; and bar No. 569 (136 marks, 6 ounces) should weigh 69.36 pounds.

Bar No. 569, the heaviest, would be weighed first.

"We've preset the scale," Fisher announced confidently to the crowd. "We've set it at sixty-nine pounds six ounces. That's what this bar No. 569 is supposed to weigh, according to the *Atocha*'s registry. If the weight checks out, it proves we've found the *Atocha*. If it doesn't—"

And he grinned.

As Lyon approached the scale with the heavy silver bar, Deo Fisher, her face drawn, passed her tongue over her lips. Bleth McHaley turned away, unable to look at all. But Fisher gazed straight at the freight scale. His eyes were bright. This was what he loved. The gambler was again risking all his winnings so far. Every chip lay piled on one number on the table, because that was the only way that life made any sense to Fisher.

Lyon placed the silver bar on the scale. The crowd on the weather deck leaned forward tensely.

Lyon's hand moved away from the silver bar.

The scale's balance lever moved half an inch or so and hovered there, moving neither up nor down: Sixty-nine pounds six ounces, exactly.

There was a scream, then a shriek, followed by another scream.

"Ladies and gentlemen," said Fisher, "We have found the *Atocha*."

There was no possible doubt now, or so it seemed to all of those present. Fisher's claim went out onto the news wires and the airwaves. In his euphoria the future seemed paved with gold. There was no sign anywhere of the slander, the legal actions, and the anguish that now lay just ahead.

15

The Bank of Spain

It was the most glorious summer of Fisher's life, though a short one. It ended after about three weeks.

The *Northwind* had still not put to sea, but its nineteen-year-old captain, Dirk Fisher, diving off the *Southwind,* recovered a bronze astrolabe. Astrolabes had been the principal navigation instruments for the early Spanish galleons, and this one still worked. It was an artifact of extraordinary value. From its markings Professor DeSolla Price of Yale tentatively identified it as having come from the workshop of one Lope Homen, a Portuguese cartographer and instrument maker who worked between 1517–1565. There were said to be only a few such astrolabes in the world, all from the same workshop, and it was possible that this instrument could be sold at auction for $100,000 or even more. It was worth $300,000. Fisher immediately claimed, further infuriating the cabal that was beginning to form against him.

But the *Atocha's* strongroom was not to be found in or near the hole that gave up the astrolable, nor did they find any more silver bars there.

Yet triumph followed triumph. About twenty arquebuses were found. Presumably they had been deeply buried in sand almost from the moment they were plunged into the sea, for once uncovered, they were seen to be in a remarkable state of preservation. Some even had their stocks intact.

One day the prop blast, after blowing away surface sand, began to cut into what appeared to be soft, blue clay. It wasn't clay at all, but the remains of bales of dye, an extremely valuable cargo in 1622—the *Atocha,* according to Dr. Lyon, had carried tons of indigo dyes. Now the seawater turned deep blue in all directions. When the divers surfaced, their bodies and faces were also stained blue, and they were laughing their heads off. But they were hurriedly sent back down again, with instructions to watch carefully while all that dye dissolved and drifted away because, as Dr. Lyon had made clear, unregistered treasure was often secreted amidst dye. Dye was one of the best hiding places for gold and gems that anyone could think of in 1622. The stuff was so messy that customs agents hesitated to stick their hands into it.

However the *Atocha's* main treasure lode was not to be found in the vicinity of the dye, either.

Morale was so high, and the divers were finding so much, that some stayed working on the bottom for up to eight hours in a single day, using up ten or more tanks of air. There was no danger from the bends—the water wasn't deep enough—but there was also no reserve supply in a tank. The divers became so preoccupied with their own success that they never worried about air. A diver learned his tank was empty only when he sucked hard at his mouthpiece and got nothing.

But this seemed an extremely small risk when compared to the glorious excitement of surfacing with an important piece of treasure. They found gold chains, pieces of silverware, and clumps of coins. Kim Fisher found a gold chalice, and this was the second most valuable item yet brought to the surface. Divers who had found something valuable commonly went into a state of near-shock. They tended to wander around the boat in a daze. Some of them still wore glazed grins—and full diving regalia—when it was time to go to bed.

They found cannon balls and bar shot, pottery shards

and many more ballast stones, but no further evidence that the *Atocha's* strongroom was nearby.

It was the *Virgalona's* prop blast that cut into the "Bank of Spain." The crater had not deepened very much before it was seen that its walls were chock full of coins. They were spilling down off the sides to the bottom of the hole. Silver pieces of eight. In mint condition. It was incredible—some were still shiny. Like the arquebuses, they had been so deeply buried in sand that three and a half centuries on the bottom of the sea had not touched them at all.

As per instructions from Fisher, those coins that showed were gathered up, the *Virgalona's* blowers were turned off, and the hole was marked with a buoy. No more digging was to be done at that spot until the TV crews got out there.

Usually, loose coins signified that the contents of an entire chest had been discovered. The chest might long since have vanished, but the coins would still be in a pile. Depending upon the size of the original chest, there might be hundreds or even thousands of similiar coins in the same spot. Most chests in use in 1622 had held about three thousand coins. That's how many Fisher expected to find now, three thousand—minimum. With seventy-five other chests nearby, for that's about what the *Atocha*, according to Lyon, had had aboard. Once again he was convinced that he was within a few yards of the main strongroom.

Fisher thought always in terms of film and in terms of leaving a permanent record of himself and his accomplishments. He wanted TV cameras out there filming him and his divers as they brought up three thousand coins—and also as they crashed into the *Atocha's* strongroom.

While awaiting the arrival of camera crews, the *Virga-*

Facing page: *Mel Fisher studying solid silver pitcher—to a collector worth thousands of dollars —which his divers brought up from the wrecked galleon* Atocha *after 350 years on the bottom of the sea near Key West.*

Above: *The astrolabe, found by Fisher's son Dirk in 1973, was the principal navigational instrument used by the seventeenth-century Spanish fleet. This one, still in working order, is the most valuable single item so far recovered.*

Right, bottom: *More than thirty-five gold chains were found; crustaceans had built homes around several, including this one. Rich Spaniards wore such chains not simply as ornaments: each link had a specific money value.*

Right, top: *Gold bullion was shipped in small, heavy bars. This one, found in September 1974, bears official stamps showing that the "Royal Fifth" tax had been paid. Bars were extremely valuable and easy to hide, and unstamped ones—divers found several—were undoubtedly contraband.*

AUTHENTICATION
I.D. NUMBER
35
This historic artifact was
salvaged from the Spanish
Galleon "NUESTRA SENORA
DE ATOCHA"
Sank in 1622
Salvaged in 1975 by
TREASURE SALVORS, INC.
100 Margaret St.
Key West, Florida

inscribed with Roman numerals indicate
each ship's cargo. The markings on the
rough metal used on a barge from
... that silver shipped in bars, or ingots,
... loud was minted into coins at Spain.

Left: *Don Kincaid, who found the first treasure, and who survived the whole adventure.*

Below: *A page from the registry of* Nuestra Señora de Atocha *listing certain of the 901 silver bars she carried. One of the bars, weighing almost seventy pounds, is at right. It was Dr. Eugene Lyon, after years of research in the Archive of the Indies in Seville, who found and deciphered documents such as this one, written in 1622 script, and who pointed Mel Fisher and his divers toward the final resting place of the sunken galleon.*

Below: *The Atocha carried twenty richly decorated bronze cannons such as this one. They weighed 3,000 or more pounds each, and were engraved with their weights, together with other identifying numbers. These same numbers had been listed in official documents, which were discovered by Dr. Lyon in Seville. As each cannon was raised from the deep, it was matched against the* Atocha's *registry by (left to right) archeologist Duncan Mathewson, Mel Fisher, and Dr. Lyon.*

Right: *Bouncy John Lewis, the former hippie, who found more at the bottom of the sea than any other of Fisher's divers.*

UPI

Below: *First of the nine bronze cannons from* Nuestra Señora de Atocha *is being hoisted aboard the tugboat* Northwind. *This cannon carried the royal crest of Philip III of Spain, and was dated 1607. The numbers chiseled into it match those listed in the registry, and were final proof that the galleon had been found. That day, July 18, 1975, was a joyous one. Two days later the* Northwind *joined the* Atocha *on the bottom of the Gulf of Mexico.*

Left: *Jim Solanick escaped from the sinking tugboat through a ten-inch porthole. Some of his shipmates were not that lucky.*

Below: *At the bow of the* Southwind, *sister tug to the unhappy* Northwind, *stands Mel Fisher. Behind him are his sons Kim and Kane, his wife, Deo, and his daughter-in-law, Angel Curry Fisher.*

Right: *Diver Tom Ford, who brought up Angel's body.*

BOB HALL

ROBERT DALEY

Left: *The late Dirk Fisher. The first two cannons had just been hauled aboard the* Northwind, *and Dirk, six feet two and twenty-one years old, was happy.*

Below: *Dirk's grief-stricken father.*

Below: *Panama-born Demostines Molinar, captain of the* Virgalona, *was one of those rare divers who regularly accorded the sea all the respect it deserved. It was he who found and rescued the survivors.*

The Virgalona, *shown left top, in port with its mailboxes up, and below, digging in a rough sea, was the workhorse of Fisher's boats, but this time it reached port bearing bodies, not treasure.*

ROBERT DALEY

ROBERT DALE

With the Northwind gone, Fisher sent the derelict Arbutus to anchor over the remaining cannons. It is shown here as a change of crew arrives on the Virgalona. Severe winter storms battered the former buoy tender, which had no engines and could not be moved out of the way; several times it too nearly sank. But Fisher, right, refused to be discouraged, and the search for the treasure of the Atocha went on.

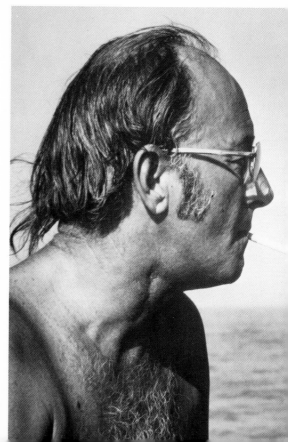

lona was winched to one side, where it began to dig more holes—there was no sense wasting time, and the strongroom must be close.

But hole after hole was dry.

To the divers it was bitterly frustrating work. They had already worked months and years on dry holes. Now they were forced to work still others, though a rich vein of silver lay only a few yards away.

On the bottom, Spencer Wickens, twenty-one, unable to resist the lure any longer, swam away from the latest dry hole and into the shallow crater, where he began fanning the sides with his hands. Sand rose into suspension. His hands moved like those of a lover, cupping, smoothing, caressing. Sand drifted away. Coins began to fall out. Wickens, after gathering a double handful, thirty to forty pieces of eight, kicked his way toward sunlight.

Demostines Molinar, captain of the *Virgalona*, had been standing at the stern watching the surface. Suddenly he had noticed a trail of bubbles moving away from where the divers were supposed to be.

When Wickens's head broke the surface Molinar asked, "Where have you been?"

Dumping his coins onto the deck, Wickens replied, "I've been to the bank."

From then on that hole was known as the Bank of Spain.

Next day the TV crews arrived, and so did the *Southwind*, which Fisher ordered positioned over the Bank of Spain, for he wanted to uncover whatever treasure was there as fast as possible.

Once its anchors were in place, the *Southwind*'s engines began to thunder. Water cannonaded against the deflector and bounced downward.

The small crater that the *Virgalona* had bored disappeared. It was replaced by a vast depression which soon became littered with silver coins. Everybody dove. Kim Fisher, on the bottom with both hands full of coins, suddenly spied a solid gold disk measuring about four inches across and about an inch thick. He threw away one handful of coins and grabbed it. Then he spied a solid gold rod about as thick as a curtain rod—it was about twelve inches long and bent nearly in two—and he threw away the second handful of coins to grab up the second bar; then he realized he had thrown away, probably, $1,000 worth of coins, and he began trying to gather them up again without losing the two pieces of gold—he was stuffing coins into his gloves. Excitement made him clumsy. He could not control all the gold and silver—escaping coins were spinning back to the bottom, and he swam to the surface, threw everything on deck, and dove back down again.

At times there were eight divers in the water at once. They swam around scooping up coins and dropping them into mesh gear bags. They filled the mesh bags so full that it took two or three boys to swim one to the surface.

The system was to blow away about thirty inches of sand at a time, after which the blowers were left idling so as to keep suspended sand from drifting down again while the divers picked up coins. In the course of the first two days, during which about three thousand coins were recovered, the divers' moods changed perceptibly. At first it was fun to fill the so-called goodie bags, and it was much more fun to muscle them up from the deep than to drop a rope down attached to a winch.

But in time the divers tired, both mentally and physically. Recovering treasure was hard work, and instead of swimming up with individual loads they began merely to pile coins in the center of the hole.

Finally bedrock was reached, but still coins showed. However these proved to be stuck firmly in place, and it was necessary to pop each of them off bedrock with a screwdriver—in most cases the coins left behind perfect impressions of themselves.

In all, six thousand coins—two chests worth, probably—came out of that dune, too many even to catalog all at once, much less evaluate. But certain of them, it was seen, had come from the Santa Fe de Bogotá mint, whose existence as early as 1622 had not previously been known. There were at least eight of these coins, perhaps more. They were unique in the world, and the amount of money collectors might pay for each of them was incalculable.

The Bank of Spain yielded treasure worth about half a million dollars. However, it did not lead Fisher's divers toward the main strongroom or toward any more silver bars.

Fisher was so flushed with success that he rented Dr. Lyon and his family a house on Big Pine Key for the summer—that way Dr. Lyon would be near by to identify any further finds. Surely the *Atocha's* strongroom had to be close to all this other treasure. Finding it could only be a question of time. A few more days, no more.

Fisher's largess was boundless. He called a stockholders' meeting. Its site was to be the Marquesas Atoll, and he ferried a hundred or more people out and kept them there living on boats all weekend. They swam, sunbathed, spearfished. They dined on Florida lobster, crawfish, and groupers cooked over open fires on the beach. At night they sang around the fire. There were trips out to the wreck site, where Fisher took his more adventurous stockholders down to the bottom to watch the divers work, to watch, hopefully, that strongroom appear.

Fisher had long ago perceived that most of his investors were seeking vicarious adventure. Though sedentary persons, they wanted to imagine themselves participating. Having shrewdly recognized this emotion, Fisher regulary mined it, with Deo his always willing accomplice. One of the previous stockholders' meetings had been held on uninhabited Ballast Key on Easter weekend. Fisher had brought a minister out. After an Easter Sunday sunrise service, there had been an Easter egg hunt. The eggs Deo had decorated herself, and the prizes to the winners had been pieces of eight.

This year Fisher organized a treasure hunt for the bow of the *Atocha*. It had probably fetched up on this beach here, Fisher told his stockholders, and he set them to digging. The sun beat down. Eventually some pottery and some rotten timbers were unearthed. Fisher said this was the *Atocha's* bow and congratulated everybody.

Among the stockholders was Eugene Lyon, Ph.D. The scholar was not a stockholder by choice. Fisher, from time to time unable to pay Lyon's salary, had paid him off in stock instead; Fisher paid everybody in stock or in treasure whenever possible.

Nor was Lyon an eager participant in this stockholders' weekend. He was not a physical person. He did not dive. He could not see a thing underwater without his glasses. The three days on the beach at the Marquesas seemed to him endless. He was sunburned, insect bitten, caked with salt and sand. What he wanted above all else was a bath. At one point he and his wife ran out of water. Fisher and Deo were living on the supply houseboat anchored in the cut between the tower island and the next island north. Fisher had water, Lyon supposed, and so he climbed into a rowboat to row across the cut. But the tide was flowing out. Lyon was attempting to cross a river flowing out of the atoll's lagoon at four to five knots, and suddenly he understood what Vargas had been trying to describe in his letter to the Crown dated January 9, 1623. Lyon himself was in danger of being borne out to sea, and he laid to his oars with all the energy he had, while at the same time visualizing the Spanish longboats as they tried to regain this beach each night after the seven-hour, ten-mile row in from the wreck site. Lyon, still only halfway across the cut, was already exhausted. How exhausted the Spaniards must have been, pulling against this current in the dark, aiming toward a bonfire, probably, unable even to see the island getting closer.

When the so-called stockholders' meeting ended, Lyon returned to civilization, to his notebooks and his microfilm. But for him the shipwreck of the *Atocha* had now become a physical experience as well as an intellectual one, and he realized how totally committed he had become to this search for sunken treasure. Possibly he was more caught up than anyone else. For most of the others—especially for most of the stockholders—this treasure hunt was a search for money, neither more nor less. But for Lyon it was a search for other lives, another century. He felt he knew certain of these long-dead Spaniards intimately. He had read their words, handled documents they had handled, he knew their signatures. Now he had rowed against a current Vargas had fought; he had lived on a beach Cadereita had walked; he had handled silver bars that had been part of the *Atocha's* cargo.

Back in Key West the tall, skinny scholar volunteered to aid state agents who were counting out pieces of eight and bagging them for the trip to Tallahassee—now Lyon had even handled the Spaniards' money. Tourists coming aboard the pirate galleon stopped to watch Dr. Lyon work. Fay Feild, standing over Lyon, said, "Well, it looks like you were right about where the *Atocha* went down, and all the others were wrong."

Lyon could only nod.

In mid-July about five hundred pounds of treasure, including 1,172 silver coins, three silver bars, Bouncy John's gold/coral rosary, Kim Fisher's chalice, Dirk Fisher's astrolabe, and an assortment of spoons, plates, and other items were packed into three beer coolers which were then filled to the top with seawater. Seven armed guards escorted the beer coolers to Tallahassee, where they were lodged in a subbasement drunk tank in the Leon County jail pending formal division between Fisher and the state of Florida. Fisher had sent similar shipments to Tallahassee in the past, and would send additional ones in the future. The Leon County drunk tank was full of beer coolers and would get fuller. But Fisher couldn't touch any of this treasure yet. State regulations stipulated that formal division could not take place until all salvage on the *Atocha* had been completed, even if this took years. Emotionally Fisher was in a state of euphoria at this time. Financially he was not much better off than he had ever been.

At the moment he did not seem to care. Surely the treasure found this summer—and especially the publicity it had generated—would make the raising of additional capital easy. He did not know that the Security and Exchange Commission was about to clamp all his financial arteries shut, nor that favorable publicity was almost at an end.

By midsummer Fisher was celebrated, and so was the *Atocha*. Pleasure boats flocked to the wreck site to watch the divers go down. On weekends whole flotillas of pleasure boats anchored nearby, even though treasure diving was not a visual spectacle. Events beneath the sea had occurred in secret since the beginning of time, and, to ordinary human beings, were secret still. From the surface nothing could be seen. Fisher himself brought newsmen and investors out to whatever vessel was anchored over the site. Usually it was the *Southwind*—and he took down anybody who wanted to go down. Above their heads, the *Southwind*'s 600-horsepower engines thundered. The uncaged bronze propellers churned the sea to froth. Tons of water bombarded the deflector and bounced to the bottom of the sea. Those huge tugboat props sucked water in and spat it out, and could do the same to limbs or people, but had not done so—not yet. The menace of those props was obvious to all. The divers entered and quit the water off the stern, using the deflector as a dive ladder. It was understood that no one was to enter the water forward. The props did not worry Fisher, but then nothing worried Fisher. His operation was covered by Workmen's Compensation. That was obligatory. He carried no other insurance.

The discoveries thus far that summer had been so glorious and so numerous that the *National Geographic* had stationed one of its star photographers in Key West indefinitely. His name was Bates Littlehales, and he had even rented a house on Dey Street for himself and his eleven-year-old Nickie. Littlehales was divorced, but he had borrowed Nickie to share his assignment with him, for the little boy loved the water and was a strong swimmer.

At sea Littlehales donned diving gear and readied his cameras. Nickie wanted to dive too. Fisher had no objections. Fisher often let children dive, and a twelve-year-old would later be involved in an even worse tragedy than today's.

And so Bates Littlehales and little Nickie Littlehales went over the side.

It was Nickie Littlehales who got sucked into the *Southwind's* props.

A body cut to pieces by a ship's propeller does not turn the water blood-red. There is presumably not enough blood in the human body to do so—certainly not in the body of a child. In any case it escapes too slowly.

Attempts were made to revive Nickie Littlehales on board the *Southwind*. The Coast Guard log afterward showed that the *Southwind's* call for emergency assistance was received at 4:22 P.M. A helicopter was dispatched from Miami and lifted the child directly to the Naval Air Station at Boca Chica Key. A waiting ambulance raced him to Florida Keys Memorial Hospital but he was dead on arrival. The county medical examiner later noted six or seven deep lacerations in the left thigh, which had severed the major arteries. There were deep lacerations also in the other leg, the abdomen, and the buttocks.

The captain of the *Southwind* had been Kim Fisher, age seventeen, though his father had been aboard that day also. The *Southwind* reached Key West the next morning. The sheriff and Coast Guard officials were waiting for it at the pier, and they conducted official interviews with the crew, probing for all the grisly details. Then came interviews with reporters.

In the log of the *Southwind* Kim Fisher wrote, "The past two days have been nightmarish. Sorry we can't wake from them."

Fisher himself seemed visibly shaken by the tragedy. As he answered questions his voice was unsteady and his eyes were red-rimmed.

But he sent the *Virgalona* out less than two hours later. It began digging as soon as it reached the site, and before the day ended its divers had brought up some pottery, various encrusted objects, a silver candlestick holder, an arquebus, twenty-two silver coins, and nine and a half inches of gold chain.

16

Fisher Accused

The Securities and Exchange Commission investigation of Fisher had proceeded quietly for a time. Fisher knew about it. At last public announcement was made: Fisher was under investigation for the alleged sale of unregistered securities. The public was allowed to make of this what it wanted. But the words sounded like fraud. Big fraud. Fisher was ordered to cease all stock sales pending the outcome of the investigation. He had done so—voluntarily—the moment he had learned of the SEC investigation, he said. A lawyer would have told him that this was too big an admission already, and to keep his mouth shut. But there was an innocence about Fisher no lawyer could cope with. "I may have stretched the law a little but I don't think I broke it," Fisher added.

Fisher's stock sales over the years had taken, principally, two different forms.

One was the "investment contract." The buyer purchased a specific share of a specific wreck's yield during a specific period—for instance, a 1 percent share of the *Atocha*'s yield for calendar year 1970; during 1970 the *Atocha* had yielded nothing. Or a 1 percent share for calendar year 1973; during that year the *Atocha* had coughed up treasure worth more than a million dollars.

Any cop could see possibilities for manipulation here. If Fisher so chose he could deliberately direct his search away from known treasure until many or most such "investment contracts" had expired.

However, it was Fisher's habit when selling stock or contracts to hand the investor pieces of eight, or other treasure, whose value, according to Fisher exactly equaled the amount invested. If the wreck site failed to produce a profit during this specified period, then the buyer was allowed to keep the collateral.

So technically, these transactions were not investments, but outright sales. Or so Fisher and his attorney—he had many attorneys over the years—believed. Fisher's legal bills were regularly astronomical. These bills he also tried to pay whenever possible with treasure or with stock. But most lawyers demanded money.

Fisher's second method was to sell stock in Treasure Salvors, Inc., or in one of its wholly owned subsidiaries. There were a number of subsidiaries. One was Ocean Search, Inc., which owned the magnetometer patents and leased mags to other treasure hunters for $1,000 a month or sold them outright for $14,500 each. The SEC investigation was not interested in Ocean Search, Inc., but rather in one of Fisher's other subsidiaries, Armada Research, Inc., the company that conducted the actual searches for galleon carcasses, turning them over for salvage to Treasure Salvors, Inc. Most of the stock in the parent company Fisher held himself; stock in Armada Research was what he mostly sold investors, and one of the charges against him now was that Treasure Salvors and Armada Research were identical: same officers, same offices, same personnel, same vessels. In other words, Armada Research did not really exist, since prior ownership in most of its assets was already vested in Treasure Salvors.

To the despair of his lawyers, who wanted him only to shut up, Fisher saw no need to do so. He had nothing to hide.

"That's a ridiculous charge," explained Fisher, who thought he had nothing to fear, either. "We don't even keep a separate set of books on the two companies."

Precisely.

As for these books that Fisher mentioned so proudly, they proved to be, as might have been expected, a mess.

Don Reit, the SEC attorney, found that hundreds of people had handed money to Fisher over the years. Some had invested substantial enough sums—$2,500 had bought a 1 percent share of one or another of the wrecks that had preceded the *Atocha*. But Fisher, always broke, would take whatever he could get. In 1970, according to Jack Fay of Vero Beach, Fisher had sold Fay a $500 stock certificate for $20 cash. "You can pay the rest later. I got to have the money," Fisher was said to have told Fay.

The investigation of Fisher proceeded. SEC agents went over his books—such as they were. They traced down and interviewed his investors. They added up prodigious amounts of money and wondered where it all had gone.

They found no one who had ever made a profit out of an investment contract with Fisher.

Meanwhile, Fisher tried to go on with his search for the *Atocha*. There was only one way he knew to conduct such a search—to spend money. His payroll was about $200,000 a year. It was true that his divers earned only $2.75 an hour, but he was maintaining three crews at once, and at sea he paid his divers for ten-hour days. The *Southwind* at sea for ten days with a crew of ten thus cost him $2,700 in wages, plus however much money ten healthy young men ate up in groceries. Meanwhile a second crew was usually at sea on the *Virgalona*, and ashore a third crew still struggled to refit the *Northwind*, which had yet to spend a single day over the wreck site. The office staff and the pirate-galleon tour guides also had to be paid.

But Fisher's payroll was almost the least of his expenses. Fuel bills were enormous. A vessel like the *Southwind* consumed vast quantities of fuel. All day its mighty engines drove seawater against the deflector while other engines on board powered compressors, pumps, and generators. Parts and gear had to be replaced constantly, for the sea destroyed all; and Fisher's gear, being in such wretched shape to start with, the sea destroyed even faster than normal.

Fisher used up money so quickly that even when he was flush it could not last for long.

He was not flush now.

In the past nearly all his costs had been covered by the investment contracts. But the SEC had closed that door, and his principal source of capital was gone.

He had never needed money more than now, when the bulk of the *Atocha*'s treasure seemed so close. He had three silver bars. The other 898, he felt certain, must be only yards away. A few more days or weeks. That's all he needed.

But where was operating capital to come from? He could not sell any of the *Atocha*'s treasure. That was locked up in Tallahassee. He could not even borrow on it lest the SEC, misinterpreting, order him arrested.

What else did he have to sell?

Well, he owned certain rare coins that he had salvaged years earlier in the northern keys off elements of the 1733 galleon fleet. These so-called Pillar dollars were the first round, stamped coins ever minted in the New World. They were so very very rare that they might be expected to sell at auction for $10,000 or more each.

Fisher had been holding them back for an emergency. The emergency was now. If he could raise $100,000 he could complete the present diving season.

The coins were worth that much money. Maybe more. The coins would save him, he believed.

Optimistic as always, Fisher began the excruciatingly quiet search for a showcase that would both attract major collectors and confer a seal of authenticity on his coins.

Fisher found the rare coin show he was looking for in Boston, and his coins went on display there to a buzz of excited conversation. Collectors who began to look them over were dazzled, but certain expert appraisers were not.

One coin was particularly rare. Indeed, no one had ever seen a coin like it before, and this fact was about to put Fisher in worse trouble than ever. The coin was dated 1732 and bore the initials *MF* of the original assayer. These same initials had shown up previously, but never on a coin dated as early as 1732. Experts attending the show examined the coin and were skeptical. At length Clyde Hubbard, considered one of the foremost authorities in the world on Spanish colonial coins, pronounced the coin false. A second expert, Virgil Hancock, a past president of the American Numismatists society, concurred.

The rich collectors melted backward into the crowd.

Forced to withdraw his coins, Fisher began searching for some other place where he could offer them. But major auctions do not happen every day, and three months passed before he found an auction in New York conducted by a dealer named Hans Schulman. To Schulman Fisher consigned only three of his rare coins. Schulman planned to call for an opening bid of $10,000 on the first *MF* coin, and if this price was successful, the next coins would start even higher.

But Clyde Hubbard, learning of the auction, protested so strongly that Schulman withdrew the coins.

Feeling his own integrity questioned, he also announced that he would hold no more auctions of coins recovered from galleons. "I would refuse even if the sellers offered to pay for the catalog, advertising and all related expenses."

Two months later Fisher consigned two coins to a Florida dealer for sale at only $1,500 each. But because of the controversy around them, the dealer would not take any others.

Frantic now, Fisher consigned several dozen coins to a Houston dealer named George Vogt, who promptly turned two of them over to Virgil Hancock for authentication. Hancock's report suggested that the coins had been chemically aged to simulate two hundred years underwater. After peeling away the encrustations that covered one of them, he had examined the bare silver with a thirty-power magnifying glass. Hancock said, "The surface has an absolutely regular pattern, like extremely fine sand paper. I've never seen anything salvaged with such an extremely regular surface."

So Vogt, too, refused to handle any more coins from Fisher.

Hancock at this time was columnist for a collector's magazine called *The Numismatist*. He was sharing his opinions of Fisher—and they were murderous—with every coin collector in the country. "I wouldn't buy a coin from Mel Fisher if you gave me the money," said Hancock.

The final authority was considered to be the American Numismatist Association Certification Service. Its director, Charles Hoskins, said publicly, "I think what Hancock said about chemical aging was absolutely correct. We haven't seen one of these coins yet that we consider genuine." Hoskins, Hancock, and Hubbard were all known to each other. All were present or past American Numismatist Association officials, and their entire world had been confounded not once but several times by the rare coins that Fisher had found in such profusion—coins which he brought forth only one by one when desperately short of money. That is, the appearance of Fisher's coins corresponded only to his emergencies, never mind theirs. Fisher regularly traumatized their lives. They didn't like him.

Now Hancock began to hammer away on the subject of Spanish gold bars. They were usually fake, too, he wrote. They were worth bullion value and not one cent more. In an article called "Featuring Fakes" in *The Numismatist,* Hancock referred to the circular stamp which most gold bars bore. "See if you can locate any eight escudo or any eight reale pieces from an identical die," he wrote.

Fisher, who had several such bars to sell, produced Eugene Lyon, Ph.D., whose opinion it was that the die in question had never been used to strike coins of any type. It was a royal seal, and that's all it was. It was for bars only.

But Lyon's opinion, since he was in Fisher's employ, convinced no one. Fisher found he couldn't sell his gold bars, either. Where was working capital to come from?

Fisher's problems, grave as they were, got worse.

A collector who had bought a coin from Fisher filed a formal complaint with the Florida attorney general's office, claiming the coin was fake. He had done so, he later admitted, on the urging of Virgil Hancock—indeed, Hancock had sent him the necessary forms to fill out.

The attorney general announced that a special prosecutor had been appointed to investigate Mel Fisher for the possible sale of fraudulent coins.

Denied access to investors, unable to sell coins or gold bars, investigated on all sides, Fisher floundered. As his money ran out, the *Atocha's* treasure seemed to run out too.

Behind the SEC, and the Florida special prosecutor, and the numismatists, came the archeologists, the environmentalists, and the rival treasure hunters, all also attacking Fisher.

Archeologists and environmentalists wanted him stopped because, in his relentless search for gold and treasure, he was said to be ruthlessly destroying Florida's priceless archeological heritage of ancient shipwrecks. Fisher's technique was described—wrongly—as ranging from dynamite to bulldozers, and ordinary Florida citizens, it was charged, were being ripped off from the heritage handed down to them by the Spanish conquistadors.

A book by rival treasure hunter Dave Horner entitled *The Treasure Galleons* had appeared. It contained an entire chapter on the *Atocha-Margarita* shipwrecks, and was documented from original sources in the Archive of the Indies, some of which even Dr. Lyon had not yet found. Horner could not read archaic Spanish script, and most of the research had come to him from Robert Marx, also a treasure hunter, and the author of a new book called *Shipwrecks of the Western World*. Marx's research had in turn come principally from Angeles Flores Rodriguez in Seville—the same stale research Fisher had worked from for five years. Neither author had taken note of Dr. Lyon's discoveries. Both still placed the *Atocha-Margarita* wreck site off the Matecumbes, and Marx, together with his partner Tom Gurr, was still actively searching there.

Unfortunately Marx, like Virgil Hancock, had a forum— he was a contributing editor to *Argosy* magazine. In his articles and personal appearances over the next several months Marx managed to suggest that Fisher did not have the *Atocha*, that Fisher's principal object seemed to be to raise money, that Fisher was perhaps not to be trusted.

The Miami *Herald* now published a two-part "exposé" on Fisher in which a reporter named Robert D. Shaw reiterated all the old charges and added some new ones, principally that Fisher's silver bars were not from the *Atocha* at all.

Shaw had found treasure hunter Bert Webber of Annville, Pennsylvania, vice-president of Continental Exploration and Salvage. Webber had a copy of the *Atocha's* manifest, and had checked the markings on Fisher's silver bars against it. These markings, Webber insisted to reporter Shaw, did not match. But Webber had not studied Fisher's bars. Nor did Shaw identify Webber as a direct rival of Fisher. He merely quoted him. In addition to its serial number, Webber said, bar 569 was supposed to be branded with the interlocking letters *JZ.* The brand was plainly marked in the manifest Webber owned. But on Fisher's bar the curved base of the *J* was missing. As for bar 794, according to Webber it should have been branded *MB.* But Fisher's bar bore no such brand. Bar 4584, according to Webber, was supposed to carry no brand at all. Whereas Fisher's was quite clearly branded. The implication was clear. Fisher was either honestly deceived, or he was a crook.

Even as readers digested this information, new headlines rocked the treasure hunting world. Rival hunters Art Hartman and Teddy Tucker claimed to have found evidence that an English captain named Seymour had salvaged the *Atocha* in the seventeenth century. The treasure Fisher was looking for wasn't even there any more, and investors who were told otherwise were being defrauded.

It seemed incredible that a man as simple and as unsophisticated as Fisher could provoke hostility on this gigantic scale.

Fisher said nothing vituperative in return. Stockholders urged him to sue certain of his detractors, and so did family and friends, but he always refused, adding with a smile, "Maybe tomorrow is the day we find the gold."

With bankruptcy near, only two questions preoccupied Fisher: (1) Where was he to get money to continue operations? and, (2) Where was the *Atocha's* main treasure?

All the rest, including criminal investigations into his conduct, he ignored. He looked right past them. The only criticism which appeared to reach him was this one, delivered with scorn by a rival treasure hunter, "If he's found navigation equipment, he must have found the captain's cabin. He must be over the main site. Where's the treasure? He ought to be blowing coins out of there like seashells. Why the hell isn't he?"

This reasoning made sense to Fisher. He was as puzzled as anyone. After three silver bars and six thousand coins— nothing. The *Atocha* had carried a quarter of a million coins and twenty-seven tons of silver bullion. Where could this stuff be? Why hadn't he found it?

His money ran out.

Unable to pay his divers, Fisher called them together and announced that the search was over. He would have to lay them off. He had no other choice.

But the search was not over because Bouncy John, Don Kincaid, Spencer Wickens one by one said they were staying. So did most of the others. Bouncy John said, "You can't lay us off, Mel. You haven't been paying us anyway, and we refuse to go."

And they moved out of their shabby furnished apartments onto Fisher's decks, and the diving went on.

17

Expert Testimony

At last the *Northwind* put to sea. It proved a far more powerful digging tool than anything the divers had experienced so far, but it took getting used to. Its mailboxes hung down so far that in some places they hovered only seven feet off the sand, and those tugboat engines produced such thrust that the divers couldn't stay in position. They would get blown upward or outward each time, and there was danger of their bouncing up into the propellers, though these were encased in mesh cages now.

Once the *Northwind's* crater began to form, the divers had an easier time. The new technique was to swim in between the two cannonading columns of water and to hover in the lull above the saddle of sand that formed in the middle. The diver had only to avoid drifting to one side or another; if he so much as touched the edge of one of the columns, it would suck him in, blast him bouncing and tumbling down into the hole and then out of it. Not only could he miss any treasure revealed in his absence, he could get hurt. Divers took to wearing extra weight for added stability under the *Northwind*.

The *Northwind* was a horse for work, but like Fisher

himself its luck was bad. On September 16, positioned over the Quicksands, it began to punch holes through twelve to fourteen feet of sand. Twelve holes it dug that day. The next day it dug ten, and the next ten more—thirty-two holes in three days. But not a single item relating to the *Atocha* was found in any of them. On October 24 it dug ten holes and scored one chunk of pottery. On November 16 it was able to dig only three. All went to bedrock. The first cut down through twelve feet of sand, the second through eighteen feet, and the third down to bedrock through between twenty-two and twenty-five feet of sand. It was incredible that a single device of whatever kind could move that much sand in a single day in the depths of the sea. Everyone exulted in the *Northwind's* accomplishment. "Yeah, *Northwind*," wrote its proud captain, Dirk Fisher, nineteen, in his log. But there was nothing in any of these holes either, and after the last of them the *Northwind* was out of fuel and had to stand to until the *Virgalona* could come out from Key West with more.

Through the gradually worsening weather Dirk Fisher persisted. Autumn waves smashed coldly over the deck, coming aboard sometimes faster than the pumps could pump, until the former Mississippi tug listed dangerously. Since it was always fixed into position by four or five spread-eagled anchors, it could not be turned into heavy seas easily, and sometimes there was serious question whether the anchors should be cast off and the tug turned before it sank. Once, when the boys had delayed too long, it almost did sink. Just in time they quit diving, raced to the lines, and began the slow, laborious job of yanking the old tug around. Once the seas no longer washed over its low freeboard, the pumps could handle their job well enough, though the boys watched carefully as, like a man straightening up under an enormous load, the *Northwind* slowly, painfully righted itself.

With each immediate crisis averted, no one worried overmuch about the next one or considered that the *North-wind*—both tugs in fact—were congenitally unsafe in the open sea. Instead the boys rated them only tempermental. The tugs were filthy things; they were rusty and cranky, but they were lovable. They were not dangerous if you learned to understand them, and the many crises had

alerted everybody to one of their idiosyncracies: they had
to be made ready for rough seas well in advance.

But the question of safety became an academic one.
With Fisher totally out of money, all his boats went into
port, and the diving stopped. The SEC investigation had
at last smothered him.

Fisher's only income now was the ticket money tourists
paid to go through the pirate galleon, and if a hundred
came aboard in a single day, that was a big day.

To Fisher the SEC was at the root of all his problems.
If the SEC would just go away, he would again be able to
sell coins and raise money.

There were endless conferences with his lawyers. As
winter came—the investigation had started the previous
July—there seemed to them three possible outcomes. The
first was total exoneration. Though this was what Fisher
confidently expected, the lawyers told him not to count on
it.

The second was indictment and criminal prosecution.
That's ridiculous, said Fisher. Don't be too sure, said the
lawyers.

The third was a compromise of some kind. The lawyers
were trying to work it out. There was a chance that they
could, provided Fisher did nothing in the interim to make
Washington mad.

In six months the investigators had taken testimony
from scores of witnesses, some of whom had agreed to testify against Fisher in any criminal trial. By Christmas the
investigators had come back to Washington from the field,
and in January the evidence against Fisher was sifted by
SEC lawyers.

There was not very much of this evidence. Fisher, as a
stock salesman, could be accused—and convicted—of pan-
dering to what most Americans considered the basest of
human instincts, man's lust for gold. However, this was
not a crime. Fisher could be accused—and convicted—of
having discerned the exact outer limits of each sucker's
greed. However, this was not a crime either.

He could be accused of sloppy bookkeeping, and this
was potentially a crime—provided criminal intent could be
proved. But Fisher's entire operation was sloppy, and it
would be difficult, probably impossible, to convince a

jury that his sloppy books indicated special intent of any kind. The jury would be more likely to believe that, for Fisher, sloppy was normal.

There was no evidence that any of the enormous sums Fisher had raised had stuck to him personally. The investigators had searched for secret bank accounts, but had not found any. They had searched for evidence of high living, but Fisher's shabby houseboat and dented car seemed to prove quite the opposite.

There was no evidence that Fisher had exerted any significant control on treasure coming up from the bottom of the sea. Always finds had been noted immediately in log books and had been raised promptly, and those Florida state agents who now rode all Fisher's boats had attested to this.

There was no evidence that Fisher had counterfeited any coins, though SEC agents had looked for such evidence. The Florida attorney general's office had jurisdiction over this anyway, though its investigation of Fisher seemed to be going nowhere also.

The dossier on Fisher was many inches thick, but added up precisely to zero.

However, any investigation as long and expensive as this one always acquired a momentum—a cutting edge—of its own. To investigators the subject became, inevitably, a wrong guy—it was necessary to believe this in order to justify all the time and effort that had been spent. The next decision therefore became inevitable also. So much time and effort must not be wasted: Let's nail the bastard for something.

The SEC agents assigned to the Fisher case at length reached their joint decision. They could not bring him to trial because they had nothing significant on him. But they could damn sure put him out of the investment contract business.

And the call went out to Fisher's lawyers.

Between the lawyers for both sides the matter was settled quickly. But after that Fisher's lawyers had to deal with Fisher.

The suggested compromise was this: a civil complaint would be filed against Fisher in Federal Court; Fisher

would answer it the same day—neither admitting nor deny-
ing guilt—by signing what was called a consent decree.
The consent decree in this case would bind him to cease
all possibly illegal stock sales and to conform to all securities laws in the future.

His lawyers imagined he would never sign such a thing.
Fisher proved surprisingly docile.

"You mean if I sign this, the case is over?" said Fisher.

His assembled lawyers nodded.

Fisher hardly saw the document. He saw only that all
his boats were in port.

He signed.

Now to raise new capital quick. But how?

Fisher at this time still held personally treasure he said
was worth $2 million. Using this treasure as collateral, he
had sometimes—though not recently—been able to borrow
up to $600,000 from banks.

Fisher decided to put half this treasure—according to
him, a million dollars worth—up for sale at $300,000.

Fisher's target was Mel Joseph, a fifty-three-year-old
Delaware road builder. Joseph would buy this treasure,
Fisher told his associates. Joseph would save him. And
Fisher went looking for the fellow.

Joseph was a rough man, usually roughly dressed. He
sometimes appeared at official functions wearing a wind-
breaker, looking like a man who had just stepped down
from one of his earth-moving machines. He claimed to be
a millionaire, and he did not mind talking about financial
killings he had made in the past, mostly in land development. Now another killing was being offered to him, so
Fisher claimed.

Joseph, who had a fifth-grade education, was involved
in highway construction and mobile homes, owned part of
a race track, and was trying to develop an automobile engine that would answer the country's pollution problems.
But he kept all his business in his head. He wrote nothing
down, because anything written down sooner or later had
to be read, a job he detested. "I do the figuring for bids
and that kind of thing in my mind," he liked to brag.

Joseph had run away from grade school when he was
ten, and had joined a traveling carnival. That was it for

books for him. He had started in business for himself with three trucks. By the time he dealt with Mel Fisher, he was rich all right. His offices and his imposing brick home adjoined each other on U.S. 113 near Georgetown, Delaware. Out back was Joseph's private airstrip on which waited his personal twin-engine turboprop.

Joseph had been dabbling in treasure since meeting in 1962 a man who called himself Captain Leo Barker. After firing Joseph's imagination with tales of sunken gold, Barker had flashed a "genuine" Caribbean treasure map. It purported to show where galleon wrecks could be found. Joseph saw that it was "written in old language," and that it bore official-looking stamps and seals. To Joseph such details proved absolutely that the map was authentic, so he bought it, formed his own salvage company, and went after some of that gold.

Such conduct continually amazed people foreign to the treasure-hunting mentality. How could such a hard-nosed, otherwise successful businessman behave that way? The answer was that, where treasure was concerned, such men behaved that way all the time.

Also, the word got around. Everyone in treasure hunting knew who such men were.

The map was genuine, Joseph always maintained later. It was just that he himself had not been able to devote his full time to exploiting it.

At a Daytona Beach construction project in 1965 Joseph had been sitting up on top of a huge earth machine. He had been happily pushing tons of earth around. Fisher, who had some gold coins to sell, had heard that Joseph was in town, and he walked out into the mud and introduced himself.

Joseph climbed down from the bulldozer. Joseph listened to Fisher's sales pitch, and he smiled a lot; but he had been burned once, and he did not buy any coins from Fisher, nor did he invest in any of Fisher's companies.

But Fisher was not the man to let such a prospect get clean away; he kept in touch with Joseph over the years, and Joseph had purchased, at about the time the three silver bars were found, a small interest in the *Atocha* salvage.

The investigations of Fisher, and the terrible charges

against him, had offended Joseph's sense of justice. Joseph knew an honest man when he saw one. "All I know is, you can't make wrong from right," he said. "Right is right."

And with that he decided both to save Fisher and to make himself a tidy profit. He seems to have imagined himself buying money at thirty cents to the dollar. For approximately $300,000, Mel Joseph purchased treasure allegedly worth a million dollars and took it home to Delaware and stashed it in a Sussex Trust Company vault. Fisher personally helped him load the beer coolers on the plane. Joseph said, "I just know cotton-picking well that Fisher's not smart enough, and neither am I, to do some of these things people have been talking about." As for himself, he said, "After thirty-five years of building a company, several companies, and a name, a man don't team up with somebody who's not for real." Then he added, "I don't want the people I respect to laugh at me."

From then on Joseph considered himself Fisher's principal backer—Fisher allowed him to think this, though apparently it was not true—and he was sometimes on the phone to Key West three times a day. He claimed that he had brought to Fisher not only cash, but also his business acumen and his knowledge of moving sand. The addition of Joseph's own temperament would not hurt, either, he said. "Mel Fisher never raises his voice, whereas I've been known to scream a little. Once in a while you need a screamer to get things stirred up."

Or a man with $300,000 to spend.

That Joseph had saved the search for the *Atocha*—for at least one more year—was unquestionably true. Fisher took the $300,000 and paid all his bills: He paid his lawyers, his divers, and his taxes. He filled up the fuel tanks on all his vessels, and sent them to sea, and they began their fifth year of hammering additional interlocking craters into the floor of the Gulf of Mexico ten miles west of the Marquesas.

They were still concentrating their search in the Quicksands, and the pattern of craters had begun to form a corridor about half a mile long and about two hundred yards wide. Every piece of treasure found so far had come from within this corridor, which was bounded on one end by the Bank of Spain and on the other by the galleon anchor.

Any digging to either end of the corridor, or to either side, had so far turned up little or nothing. There were those around Fisher who suggested that the time had come to range well outside the corridor in search of the main ballast pile and the *Atocha's* strongroom. But Fisher vetoed these suggestions. He thought both ballast pile and strongroom were inside the corridor somewhere, and he did not want to move until every square inch had been searched. Each crater, after all, was only about thirty feet in diameter; and many virgin patches of bottom remained to be excavated.

Besides, the divers were still finding gold. Bouncy John Lewis was finding more of it than anyone else.

Diving off the *Northwind*, Bouncy had watched two gold chains suddenly materialize. They lay in a single two-and-a-half-pound pile. He swam to the surface clutching gold in his fist—it was escaping in all directions. Grinning, he cried out, "I GOT SOMETHING FOR YOU!"

The former flower child was probably the most popular diver, and he was Fisher's favorite, after Fisher's own sons. Bouncy was good. Better still, as far as Fisher was concerned, Bouncy was lucky. He was still a hippie. He worked more than his share, and on payday loaned or gave away all he had. He sometimes went a month without a day off, riding one tug back to Key West for fuel and groceries, switching to the other one, and riding back out again.

The two chains were stretched out on deck—each was six feet long. Of course, Bouncy hadn't found them stretched out full length, and as he brooded over what this detail implied, his exhilaration began to fade. The two chains had lain in such a compact little pile that they must have once been contained in a pouch, which meant that they had belonged to some real-life person who, in terror and panic, knowing that the *Atocha* was going down, had grabbed up his pouch and, probably, tied it to his wrist. Perhaps it was the man who had the two children with him. Perhaps he was trying to save his two children, and he had thought to save some gold too, so as to sustain them all for a time, if they survived the shipwreck. He had not survived it, of course, and the gold chains were all that was left of his body. Bouncy, sobered, felt a bit like a grave robber. He had found not the king of Spain's treasure, but some ordinary person's treasure.

The divers kept punching holes into the ocean floor, holes that proved rich in personal jewelry. Gold chains, rings, and such kept coming to the surface clutched in the fists of grinning divers. But personal jewelry gave no clues as to where the *Atocha's* strongroom might lie. Meanwhile, no more silver bars were found, nor any more chests of coins. Fisher appeared calm. His optimism bordered on complacency. The man's faith in himself, in the search, in what can only be termed his lucky star, continued to baffle everyone who came near him. It was as if there was this flaw in his character: normal human anxiety had been left out. He seemed to have received a double quotient of serenity in its place. Panic, fear, outrage, and most of the violent emotions were unknown to him. It was as if he had created his own world—which in a sense he had. Within it he lived at peace.

He did not choose to worry about the Florida attorney general's investigation of him. He would be exonerated, he said, and presently he was.

He did not choose to worry when Florida decided to hire the renowned numismatist, Dr. Albert Pradeau, to check the authenticity of the *Atocha* coins. Instead Fisher began to wait eagerly for Pradeau's report.

But suppose Pradeau ruled the treasure fake?

In fact, Dr. Pradeau spent five days in Tallahassee, and he examined, according to his report:

Three large silver bars; one gold ingot, oval shaped; a holy water vessel, somewhat crushed, gold metal; several gold ornaments of various sizes and a gold chain, several feet in length with one end embedded in a calcareous mass, this last item of superb workmanship, hundreds of links of unbelievable similarity; many gold coins of various denominations in perfect condition but of contemporary crude stamping or coining, polygonal or clipped planchets (Macuquina type) with only portions of marginal inscription, many of the Philip III period (1598–1621) but undated; 698 silver coins, mostly of the eight real (dollar) denomination of which 260 specimens were rechecked for verification. . . .

It is my opinion that the material examined had been immersed since 1622. In the lot there were no specimens that could be attributed to a posterior date. From a numismatic standpoint the silver coins could be sold for about $50,000. This estimate is based on a minimum restricted auction sale, where the purchaser, competing with interested parties, might increase the bidding phenomenally. As to the gold specimens they could easily be appraised at from $300 to $500 each, subject of course to the whims of the bidder who may offer much more.

As he read this report, Fisher began chortling. Pradeau, whose reputation was that of a conservative man, was appraising 698 silver coins at a minimum of approximately $71 each—and Fisher had more than six thousand such coins, not to mention the few extremely rare ones.

What had anyone ever been worried about?

As the official investigations closed, and as the authenticity reports became available, Fisher became so confident that he spent all that was left of Mel Joseph's $300,000.

Not only did he keep all of his vessels perpetually blasting away at the Quicksands, but also he hired two new scientists who, together with Dr. Lyon, might be able to tell him where the *Atocha*'s main ballast pile and strong-room lay.

The first was Duncan Mathewson, a marine archeologist. By laying out an archeological grid on the bottom of Fisher's treasure corridor and by taking test borings of the stratification of the sands, Mathewson might be able to tell Fisher which patch of sand to search next. At the very least, Fisher reasoned, Mathewson would silence those who charged that all treasure hunters—and Mel Fisher in particular—simply destroyed these galleon wrecks, with no concern for their archeological importance at all.

The second scientist was Commander John Cryer, a navy meteorologist with two decades of professional exposure to Florida weather. It would be Cryer's job to plot the direction, duration, and intensity of the storm that had destroyed the *Atocha* and the eight or nine other vessels of the 1622 fleet. It was possible that Cryer, working with all of the information Dr. Lyon had compiled so far, would be able to point Fisher in some new direction.

As for Lyon, Fisher wanted additional proof that he had found at least part of the *Atocha*—proof not to convince himself but to silence, for good, all critics, and he sent Lyon back to Seville. Fisher was also asking Lyon to prove, if he could, that the *Atocha* had never been salvaged in the past.

The very least gain Fisher could expect from the richness of detail these men would provide was this: they would make the *Atocha* the most famous, most romantic, most glamorous Spanish galleon that ever sailed—with a corresponding rise in the market value of her treasure. And with a corresponding increase in the fame of Mel Fisher, too.

Next Fisher decided to lay permanently to rest charges that he had counterfeited over a hundred rare 1732 and 1733 coins. This was going to be extremely costly. The best expert he knew of was Xavier Calico of Barcelona, who would charge at least $130 per coin, and there would be high laboratory fees as well, but arithmetic was not the field Fisher excelled in.

Gathering together 122 pieces of eight dated 1732 and 1733, all from the Mexican mint, plus three other coins which the sea and the centuries had cemented to an iron key, plus a silver ingot weighing 953 grams, Fisher sent this package to Barcelona.

Calico's eventual report read in part:

> Having examined the items referred to, and having compared them among themselves as well as to the three coins united to the iron key—despite the fact that these last were covered with a heavy incrustation of corrosion— we come to the conclusion that all were the same, or very similar, and that they have the same origin, which is demonstrated by the composition of the patina.

But what was this origin?

The Calico Laboratory turned over to the Barcelona Provincial Archeological Museum the group of three coins welded to the iron key. A long series of scientific tests ensued, and the museum report, when issued, was many pages long. Fisher must have read this report with considerable impatience. It spoke of electrolytic reduction, of immersion in dilute ammonia, of the use of microcrystalline waxes. Fisher was interested in the last paragraph only, which stated that "one is dealing with an authentic item, sufficiently eroded and whose products of corrosion correspond completely with the vicissitudes through which it has passed."

Happier, though much poorer, Fisher went out to sea to watch his divers work.

In the sector adjoining Fisher's to the east, salvage boats belonging to John Berrier now appeared. From the heaving deck of the *Virgalona*, Fisher, his feet spread for balance, trained binoculars on them. His alarmed divers clustered around him, waiting for his verdict.

Taking the glasses down from his eyes, Fisher said nothing. The binoculars began to pass from diver to diver. One by one each studied the newest and most dangerous rival yet.

Berrier's boats and divers could be seen quite clearly with the naked eye. The binoculars merely brought them up painfully close. Berrier's mag boat on its programmed search patterns plowed carefully back and forth. Berrier's divers went down and came back up again. Vessels and gear appeared brand-new, and far more expensive than Fisher's. Obviously Berrier had spent a great deal of money. His financial backing must be substantial. They must be confident.

Berrier and his partners owned four leases. It didn't show yet, but they had Fisher's sector practically surrounded. Berrier was using Bert Webber's newer and more sophisticated magnetometer, and he was working with a document Jack Haskins had found in the Archive of the Indies, which laid the wrecks out in sequence. According to this document, the *Rosario* had grounded on the last key of the Tortugas (this much Dr. Lyon knew, too). The *Margarita* had then sunk sixteen leagues due east of that point, and the *Atocha* one league further east than the *Margarita*. Berrier had worked it all out on charts. If the Spanish measurements were accurate, then the *Atocha* lay precisely within the variance that Berrier was working.

He expected to turn up the *Atocha's* carcass any day.

Was it possible that Berrier, because of newer and better equipment, could find the bulk of the *Atocha's* treasure in an area that Fisher had mag-searched years ago? The underwater detection of treasure was not an exact science, after all.

Fisher, who remained calm all day, was amused that his divers kept staring pensively across the intervening water. "I've already searched that spot, and it's not there," he told them.

For years treasure hunters had been searching behind Fisher. No one had ever found anything yet.

"Forget about Berrier," said Fisher with a smile, and he stepped blithely down into the speedboat and bounded back to Key West across the waves.

But everyone else worried. References to Berrier began to appear in the logs. A *Virgalona* entry read: "We watched them all day and they appeared very close. Charter-boat captain timed the distance at 2,500 yards from the galleon anchor. Boxes had been down since 1:45 P.M. that we noted. They have two boats—one for digging, and one magging, and no state agent aboard."

The absence of a state agent was puzzling, for Fisher was obliged to carry one at all times. In fact they were harassing him, presumably on orders from Tallahassee. One night the *Virgalona* arrived from Key West with stores for the *Southwind*. It was ten at night before these were transferred. Although the *Virgalona* carried no diving gear, the *Southwind's* state agent ordered the *Virgalona* to return to Key West at once, which it was obliged to do, reaching there at three o'clock in the morning.

Three and a half months later Berrier's boat was still there, for Dirk Fisher wrote in the *Northwind* log: "Saw Berrier's boat come out—approach very close to our wreck site. He is 0–10 degrees now due north."

Berrier's brand-new boats stayed on the site day after day, whereas Fisher's old tugs were plagued by breakdowns.

During the latter part of August both were in port for extended repairs—the best weather of the year was being wasted. By September the *Northwind* was out again, and a new gold detector that Fisher had leased was tried out.

But the *Northwind's* engines were still overheating, and at a depth of only twenty-five feet the new gold dectector sprang a leak.

The fifth year on the wreck site was drawing to a close. Although it had started late and was finishing early, it had been successful. Many additional coins, both gold and silver, had been recovered. So had a quantity of silver candlesticks, some swords and daggers, and gold chains of varying lengths.

Berrier's divers had found nothing yet, but might at any time find the main pile.

In addition, much pottery and ballast stone, hundreds of encrusted objects, and a good number of stone and iron cannon balls had been found. But it was clear by now that this stuff was only secondary scatter. The main portion of the hull was somewhere else—probably outside the corridor. But how far outside and in which direction? There were no clues, and it had become entirely possible that someone else would find this pile before Fisher did.

18

The Vindication of Eugene Lyon

Dr. Eugene Lyon, at the height of the controversy that raged around Fisher, had heard himself called Fisher's prostitute—Fisher's whore would say anything Fisher paid him to say. The words had stung them, and still did. The former city manager had quit politics because he could not bear the abuse and vituperation that was so much a part of it. He had opted for a scholar's life instead.

As a scholar Lyon had found, for a time, all the peace he had hoped for. But with the raising of the three silver bars Lyon's peace had ended. Suddenly his name had appeared in headlines again, and he was being called worse names than before. Rumors spread that Fisher was going to jail for fraud—and Eugene Lyon, Ph.D., was going to jail with him.

In the midst of all this the academics of Florida had abandoned Lyon. They had refused to rule on his scholarship. They had refused any comment at all.

Lyon had been a director of the Florida Historical Society; he had considered himself a personal friend of every man on the board. Lyon had also been appointed to the

Saint Augustine bicentennial project—he knew every historian involved in the project. But when he needed them, not one came to his support.

The state of Florida was safeguarding the treasure Fisher had found; it also, Lyon felt, ought to be safeguarding the historical data—Lyon's data—that went with this treasure. But it was not doing so. It was not even asking to see Lyon's data. In Lyon's opinion the state people—both the politicians and the academics who sat on state committees—should be giving definitive answers as to which ship Fisher actually had. But they said nothing. They were afraid of controversy.

Because of their silence, rival treasure hunter Robert Marx continued to write in *Argosy* and elsewhere that Fisher's evidence—meaning Lyon's—was inconclusive and misleading. Marx, as Lyon saw it, had put himself in a ridiculous dialectical position. Marx was saying that Fisher couldn't have the *Atocha* off the Marquesas because he, Marx, had it up north off the Matecumbes, when in fact Marx had yet to find anything. Nonetheless, he was being believed. One day a magazine editor had said to Lyon, "Why should I believe you? I don't know anything about you. You're nobody. Bob Marx has seventeen cards in the Library of Congress."

But it was the failure of the academic community in Florida to support Lyon's position that upset Lyon most, and it was those people, rather than the public at large, that Lyon now set out to impress. He meant to document the *Atocha*'s identity in a manner no one could dispute. By the time he returned to Florida in the spring there would be no unanswered questions, not one.

There had been archives all along that Lyon had not searched. One was at Simancas, near Valladolid. Lyon rode up there on the train from Madrid. The walls of El Escorial, that vast fortress home of a whole series of Spanish kings, began to pass outside the train windows. The Valley of the Fallen came into view, its colossal cross jutting up in the saddle between two mountains; beneath this cross, so it was said, was the tomb in which General Franco would one day lie. The walled city of Avila appeared; there St. Teresa had lived out her life of self-denial. Lyon could feel the history of this stern country all around him.

The Archive of Simancas was in a chateau that loomed over the village. Once this chateau had been a royal prison, and then under Carlos V it had been converted into the Royal Archive. The Indies documents had first been housed in this archive before being moved to Seville, and the job Lyon set himself was to find some legajos that might have been left behind during the transfer two centuries ago. So he searched, but he found nothing.

He returned to Madrid, where there were two other archives to search, first the National Library and then the Royal Academy, which was housed in an old church on Calle Leon, just off Atocha Street and about two blocks from Atocha Station. Our Lady of Atocha was a Mexican saint, Lyon knew, yet here in the capital of the mother country, as in Lyon's life at present, the name had him surrounded. Our Lady of Atocha and the Child of Atocha had become known as the patron saints of travelers, and over the centuries they had been credited with many remarkable miracles. But no miracle had saved the travelers who rode the galleon *Atocha*. As it sank, everybody aboard was probably praying to the two saints. Their prayers were not answered.

In the Royal Academy, as in the National Library, Lyon found nothing useful relating to the sunken galleon.

So Lyon went on to Seville. He was alone, and already lonely. He missed Dorothy. He missed his four kids, especially the two littlest girls. But Fisher was not paying him enough to bring them over. He took a room—it was little better than a cell—in the Escuela de Estudios Hispano-Americanos on Calle Alphonso XII. Room and board would cost only seven dollars a day—he had, as always, so little money. In his new room he put his suitcase down on the floor and looked around: a cot, a table. Good shelf space, though. He had reached Madrid brimming with confidence, but that confidence was already gone.

Downstairs in the lobby, he met some of his fellow students. Later he would get to know all of those with whom he shared this building: three American students in their mid-twenties, two Spanish lawyers, two Spanish philosophers. Only rarely did visiting scholars, passing through

Seville, choose to live here. Two Argentinian priests and a
Mexican historian would be the total for the year. Lyon
went out into the small garden. He stood amid palm trees.
Outside the iron gates moved the traffic and pedestrians
of the city.

Lyon went to the Archive of the Indies. He passed
through the great wrought-iron doors and climbed the vast
marble staircase. Nothing had changed here. At the top of
the stairs, as always, stood the great bullion chest in which
treasure once was stored during the two-month voyage between the New World and the Old. The chest on display
was four feet long, two feet wide, two and a half feet
deep. It gaped open now—the better to dazzle tourists—
showing the fourteen teeth around the edges of the lid,
with which it was locked. All fourteen of those spring
locks had opened simultaneously with a single key, but
this key, it was said, was so big and moved with such
difficulty that horses were required to turn it. This was all
to the good, since there were no such horses aboard ship. At
sea, treasure was safe. None of the categories of men who
sailed the Carrera de Indias, from sailors to nobles,
could get at it. The storms could, though . . .

Lyon went into the reading room and began the last
and most difficult leg of his own personal search for the
Atocha.

How do you prove that treasure came from a specific
sunken galleon? Fisher's three silver bars had seemed
proof to Lyon, but that proof had been widely rejected.
What other proof was available to buttress it?

If one could assume that everything Fisher had recovered so far did come from a single galleon, and it was
difficult to imagine that more than one had sunk within
the narrow corridor Fisher was searching, then perhaps it
might be possible to exclude all other possible galleons
one by one, until only the *Atocha* was left.

Because so many newly minted coins dated 1622 had
been found, Lyon reasoned, all wrecks prior to this date
could be excluded. No coins newer than 1622 had been
found, not one out of more than six thousand, and this
seemed proof enough that Fisher's wreck had sunk either in
1622, or very soon thereafter. Since Lyon had found
records of no other galleon shipwrecks in the vicinity of

Fisher's wreck site during that entire decade, then obviously Fisher's materials had come either from one of the nine or ten ships that sank in September of 1622 or from some other vessel that sank while trying to salvage one or more of the 1622 wrecks.

Lyon's first job was to learn in detail exactly what the *Atocha* had carried, and he separated this search into three categories: arms and equipment, cargo, and people. The first category alone sent him into three different sections of the archives and consumed weeks.

Lyon learned that the *Atocha* was, for its day, armed to the teeth. It had carried 20 bronze cannons, 1,200 pounds of match cord, 7,000 pounds of gunpowder, 540 iron cannonballs and 60 marble ones, 300 yards of linen for cartridge cases, and 60 harpoonlike bar shots.

If an eventual attacker could not be repelled at a distance by this artillery, the job of defense passed to the infantry company aboard. The *Atocha*, like all of the guard galleons except for the flagship, which carried more, had also been loaded with 60 muskets; with powder flasks packed in chests; 25 pikes; 25 lances; 100 pounds of lead balls; 1,700 pounds of arquebus shot, and 500 pounds of musket shot, the above to be packed in six barrels; and (an addendum that Lyon was not sure he properly understood) "two hundred pounds of musket balls in branches for spares in case the men don't make enough balls."

As for the smaller pataches, their manifests showed that they had carried no mortars or stone cannon balls at all. They did carry from Spain fifty muskets each, but their orders had been to leave twenty of these from each patache at Margarita Island as they passed by it. Thus, Lyon reasoned, when the hurricane had struck the pataches, sinking two out of three, those which sank could have been carrying only thirty muskets each.

But Fisher had already found thirty-six muskets. He had also found a number of stone cannonballs.

This seemed to rule out any possibility that the shipwreck he was working was not the *Atocha* at all, but one of the lost pataches.

Alonso Ferrera, the builder of the *Atocha*, had been obliged to furnish it with five anchors, each weighing 2,200 pounds, plus one stream anchor weighing 500 pounds.

Lyon wished he knew how much Fisher's one anchor weighed. Maybe it weighed 2,200 pounds exactly. Fisher had not tried to raise it. How do you raise something that huge, and what do you do with it once you have it on board? Fisher had no vessel big enough to receive it. It was still down there, and would stay down there for a considerable period to come; there was no way even to estimate its weight. But Lyon was satisfied that it weighed plenty, that it was far too large to have come off any of the frigates, barks, or longboats used by Vargas, Melián or any of the other salvors of the 1620s.

Lyon now noted down all the numbers off the bronze cannons that the *Atocha* had carried, though this data was of little use to him. Fisher had found no cannon yet. Why hadn't he?

Lyon forced this question out of his head. It led, for the moment, nowhere.

Adding up the weight of cannons aboard the *Atocha*, Lyon found that this sum came to twenty-seven tons. The *Atocha* had carried exactly as much weight in cannons as in silver.

Wondering what such cannons looked like, Lyon walked through the streets of Seville to the Torre de Oro, that gorgeous crenelated tower on the banks of the Guadalquivir which, over the centuries, had served as a dungeon, as a repository for treasure from the New World, and, now, as a museum. Two bronze cannons stood on their cascabels, there, flanking the entrance door like tall, thin sentries. They must have looked murderous in their day—certainly they had been designed for slaughter. But today they merely looked beautiful, and the bespectacled American historian stood gazing at them. Lyon noted how each gun was decorated: just below the shield was inscribed the gun's weight in *quintales*. A quintal, in the seventeenth century, was a hundred pounds.

One inch above the base ring of the barrel was inscribed the date of the year in which it had been cast. The location of the numbers was important. Fisher should be told where to locate the identifying numbers once his divers began to find cannons—with a momentary surge of hope, Lyon was confident that these cannons would begin to emerge from the Gulf of Mexico any day.

If the *Atocha's* cannons were found, Lyon reflected wistfully, this would furnish the definitive identification Lyon longed for. Of the *Atocha's* twenty cannons, Gaspar de Vargas had salvaged two. That left eighteen still down there. Surely Fisher would begin to find them soon.

And once he had the cannons, then directly underneath, or very close to the side, would be found the silver bullion and the bar copper. In any case, that's how the *Margarita* had lain, when it had given up its treasure to Melián.

The *Atocha's* shoulder weapons, Lyon saw, had been packed in chests, ten to a chest. Fisher had evidently found four chests worth, thirty-six muskets and arquebuses in all, with four missing. Perhaps in the swirling undersea sandstorm those four had simply been missed by Fisher's divers. Or perhaps they had been in the hands of sentries when the galleons went down. Fisher had found no pikes or lances or helmets or armor yet, though this stuff was iron and should have scored reasonably big hits on the magnetometer.

The *Atocha* had sailed fully equipped with the most vicious weaponry of the day, and for a moment Lyon found his thoughts straying to the strange situation in which the Spaniards had found themselves in 1622. The *Atocha's* sole purpose was to protect the king's treasure from the hard, mean power of the Dutch. The Spaniards were involved in trade. The Dutch were interlopers. Heavily loaded with cargo, it was the Spaniards' job to go from Point A to Point B over a well-known and unchanging route.

The Dutch, who had only recently come onto the high seas, had no such responsibility. The Dutch ships were fighting ships. The Dutch had tremendous money power—almost all of which was directed toward privateering. The West Indies companies gave out charters for privateering. It was legalized piracy. It was because of the Dutch threat to Spain's lifeblood that the *Atocha* had been built—it was because of the Dutch that it had sailed so late in the year at the tail end of such a cumbersome convoy. To a large extent it was the fault of the Dutch that the *Atocha* had sunk.

From arms and armament, Lyon turned to the *Atocha's* cargo. He had on hand the *Atocha's* registry from all three ports at which it had touched: Porto Belo, Cartagena, and Havana. The *Atocha*'s more than 250,000 coins (mostly pieces of eight) had weighed approximately one ounce each, a total of about ten and a half troy tons of silver coin. The 901 silver bars seemed to average between sixty and seventy pounds, for a total of approximately twenty-seven tons. According to the registry the *Atocha* had also carried a great quantity of worked silver—candlesticks, pitchers, etc.—and although some of these items were described in the registry individually, most were simply lumped together by weight. Lyon saw no way to relate any of the worked items that Fisher had found specifically to the *Atocha*. Nor unfortunately, did any of the 161 gold items relate specifically. They ranged in size from 2 to 107 ounces, but not one was listed by serial number. Some registry entries were identified only as *unos trozos de oro* weighing so much, contained in a box. Presumably the box had once borne the owner's brand mark. Perhaps certain of the individual pieces of bullion did as well. There was no way of knowing now.

Gold was selling for approximately $160 an ounce, and so Lyon did some rapid figuring in his notebook. If Fisher were to find all of the *Atocha*'s 216.5 pounds of registered gold, and to sell it for bullion value alone, this would bring $554,027. In addition, the *Atocha* had probably carried almost as much again in contraband. In other words, Fisher could hope to find over $1 million worth of gold bullion. Of course it would be insane to sell the *Atocha*'s gold for bullion. Each piece was a precious artifact and could be sold for many times bullion value. It was the same with the 901 silver bars which, as bullion alone, would be worth today almost $3 million. As artifacts they should be worth much more too.

Before leaving behind the silver and gold portion of the *Atocha*'s cargo, Lyon was obliged to delve into the Santa Fe de Bogotá section of the Archive to try to trace down the background of the eight *Atocha* coins bearing the Bogotá stamp. Until now it had been believed that this mint went into operation only in 1627, and no coins of earlier date had been known. Of course that made Fisher's eight coins unique—and also so extremely valuable that counterfeiting by Fisher was sure to be charged. It was up to Lyon to prove that this mint had begun operating as early as 1622. The only 1622 mint previously known had been in Cartagena, and so Lyon went back into its records, finding that because of a series of audits and scandals, the mint had been shifted from Cartagena to Begotá. By 1622 it was firmly established there; and Lyon microfilmed a number of documents that would prove this to potential buyers of the coins.

What else had the *Atocha* carried?

When her hull had been completed a mixture of sand and gravel had been poured in on top of her keel as ballast. Planking went down over this, and then had come approximately two hundred tons of ballast stones. Directly on top of the ballast stones, assuming that the *Atocha's* hull was dry enough, would have been loaded the 525 bales of tobacco that went aboard in Cartagena and which weighed in total approximately twenty-five tons.

At Havana, the *Atocha* had taken on 350 chests of indigo. Because Fisher's divers had found indigo, Lyon began searching through the registries to find out which other of the wrecked ships had carried indigo. None of the lost pataches had. One or another of the lost merchantmen might have. Lyon could not, from the available documents, be certain. Among Lyon's problems when searching these registries was that often he could not tell by its name alone which ship he was reading about. A single *Nuestra Señora de Atocha* had sailed with the 1622 fleet, but there had been five ships named *Nuestra Señora del Rosario*, including *Nuestra Señora del Rosario y Buen Viaje*, and *Buen Jesus y Nuestra Señora del Rosario*. There were also three ships involved, including a small Cuban coast guard vessel, called *Nuestra Señora de Candelaria*.

One helpful note did emerge from Lyon's study of indigo—once immersed in the sea it was considered worthless. The presence of indigo on Fisher's site seemed to Lyon to exclude the possibility that Fisher was working not over the *Atocha*, but over some shipwrecked salvage vessel. No salvage vessel would have bothered to lift aboard chests of sodden indigo.

Next Lyon considered the copper that Fisher had salvaged.

According to the registries, copper had not been loaded onto Cadereita's pataches or merchantmen. Copper was Crown property. It was loaded, like the silver and gold, only on the guard galleons, and a portion of it had been loaded aboard all three of the galleons which were to sink: *Rosario, Santa Margarita,* and *Nuestra Señora de Atocha.* But Vargas had got all of the copper off the *Rosario.* Most of the *Margarita* copper had been salvaged by Melián; it was returned to Spain between 1626 and 1631. Of all of the vessels sunk by the 1622 hurricane, the only other one to carry copper was the *Atocha.*

The gold chains which Fisher's divers had brought up in such profusion—this was personal jewelry. So were the rings and reliquaries, Bouncy John's gold rosary, and Kim Fisher's gold chalice. Lyon began studying the *Atocha's* passenger list, and after that he studied the passenger lists of the other vessels in the armada. The pattern Lyon had suspected soon began to emerge. The rich passengers had sailed on the guard galleons. The fleet pataches and the merchantmen carried few passengers or none at all; no name renowned at the time was to be found on their passenger lists.

Clearly the personal jewelry Fisher had found pointed to this hypothesis: He was salvaging a vessel on which many wealthy persons had perished, and not the remains of some smaller ship carrying more ordinary men.

Lyon now amassed what he called location information, gathering together every clue to the *Atocha's* grave site that he had unearthed during the last five years. He marshaled his arguments like an army, references to Caveza de los Martires in one column, to Cayos de Matecumbe in another, to Cayos de Tortuga in a third, to Cayos del Marques in still a fourth. Now the archival citations stood in orderly rows, neat as soldiers, and it was possible to see in what ways all of the names and all of the sunken ships of the 1622 armada related to each other. What had long seemed obvious to Lyon would now seem obvious to all: every reference to the wreck site—by whatever name that site was known—pointed to the exact same spot, and this was the approximate spot Fisher had been diving on for the last five years.

In his notebooks, and in the scholarly paper he now began to prepare, Lyon noted down what were to him irrefutable conclusions.

1. The analysis of the more than 6,000 coins Fisher had salvaged on site 8MO141 (the variance designation conceded by the state of Florida to Fisher) bore out the provenance of the wreck from mainland South America in 1622.

2. The site could not be the wreckage of a 1622 fleet patache, or the wreckage of the Cuban patrol vessel *Nuestra Señora de Candelaria,* which was lost at the same time, or the wreckage of another *Candelaria,* the salvage vessel that disappeared in 1625 in that same area. The reasons: None of these ships carried stone cannonballs, copper, or indigo; moreover the anchor found by Fisher was too large for them.

3. The site could not be one of the two, possibly three, missing merchantmen for the same reasons. It could not be some later salvage vessel, because no such salvage vessel would have bothered hoisting aboard the worthless indigo.

4. All location data amassed so far pointed toward the wreck being either the *Atocha* or the *Santa Margarita.*

5. Tentative identification as one or the other was supported by all of the finds to date—the rich personal jewelry, the thirty-six shoulder weapons, the indigo, the copper, and the stone cannonballs.

6. To differentiate between the two, one had only to examine the three silver bars. Their pedigrees existed. Lyon had traced them back to the mine at Potosí they had come out of, through the tax office where the 20 percent royal fifth was paid. They had been loaded aboard the *Atocha* at Cartagena.

Lyon could go no further. The three silver bars proved that Fisher's wreck was the *Atocha.* One either believed Lyon's research and therefore his arguments, or did not. The lure of treasure was a mystical thing. One could explain it only so far. Faith was a mystical experience and could not be fully explained either. In the final analysis one had to want to believe.

Lyon sent his scholarly paper off to be read by a colleague to members of the august Florida Historical Society, and he waited to learn of whatever furor it might create.

There were additional details to be cleaned up. Lyon went on working, returning to his cell of a room as late as possible each night, using work to hold off loneliness.

Some young American scholars shared the archive with Lyon; so did some important professors from important American universities. In contrast to the youngsters who liked to have fun, the professors seemed determined to bring to their research in Spain the unbending demeanor and concentration that, in their opinion, serious scholarship demanded. One professor from Duke always appeared wearing jacket and tie—he wouldn't cross Duke campus dressed any other way, he explained in a sonorous voice, and he did not see why he should lower his standards in Spain. The young scholars addressed such men as Doctor, or Professor, and listened to their scholarly advice. "Don't write articles, write books," the professor from Duke told them. "Keep your notes on file cards in shoe boxes. When you have two and a half pairs of shoes, write a book."

Dr. Eugene Lyon seemed more scholarly than any of these men, but there was nothing forbidding about him. The younger scholars called him Gene. But Lyon in his loneliness was so preoccupied that occasionally he did not respond to their greetings, until one day Grady Hardy, a master's degree candidate from Louisiana said to Lyon, "I'm sorry if I've caused offense by calling you Gene. If you would rather I call you Dr. Lyon, or Professor Lyon, I'd be glad to do so."

"Oh no," said Lyon, shocked. "Please call me Gene."

Lyon befriended all the young scholars, helping them find documents, sometimes deciphering documents they could not decipher themselves. Although the proctors in their blue smocks were quick to silence young scholars who talked or joked in the study hall, Lyon was older, and when they caught him whispering to a younger colleague, they only threw him baleful glances. The most baleful proctor had no teeth, and so the younger scholars called him Fang.

One day Grady Hardy whispered in Lyon's ear, "You know how the Spanish could never spell a name right?"

Lyon nodded.

Hardy pointed at the document he was studying. "Look how they spelled Lord Cornwallis."

The name was written "Lord Cornballs."

Lyon laughed. The porter glared. "Don't worry about Fang," said Hardy.

The young men continued to make Lyon laugh. Hardy, leaning over Lyon's table, showed a royal order he had just discovered: henceforth all documents sent to the Crown should be enclosed in envelopes. Too many were getting rained on in transit, and could not be read. Hardy pointed to the last line in this royal order: "Therefore see that this order about envelopes gets . . .

The rest of the document was illegible. "It's been rained on," giggled Hardy.

At the Escuela de Estudios Hispano-Americanos, Douglas Inglis, twenty-four, and Lyon lived in adjacent cells. "If these documents are so difficult for us to read," said Inglis one day, "how do you suppose Philip IV ever read them? He couldn't even write his name. He had to have a stamp made. I can just see Cadereita arriving back in Spain and being ushered in to see the king. Cadereita says: 'Of course you've read my dispatches, Sire?' The king says, 'Yes, yes. But I want to hear it from your own lips.' "

Lyon was laughing.

"Or else," Inglis continued, "the king points to Cadereita's dispatch saying, 'I want you to explain one thing to me, what does this chicken scratching mean? Oh, you've just lost nine of my ships and two million pesos, is that what it means?' "

These young people, these future professional historians, were engaged in the kind of leisurely, untroubled research that Lyon had always supposed was the lot of all historians, but which so far was foreign to him.

Christmas neared. It was the first time in twenty-two years Lyon had been away fron his family at Christmas time. One day he looked up from his table in the archive and Hardy heard him mutter, "I'll never do this again. Never."

In Florida, Lyon's paper was read to the state historical society. There was no furor. There was virtually no reaction of any kind. Lyon's only hope for vindication rested apparently with Fisher. Lyon had put Fisher onto the wreck originally; it was up to Fisher by finding the missing bullion and artillery, to save Lyon's reputation as a historian and his future in academic circles.

Lyon, unable to stand it alone any longer, had scraped up the money to send for his wife and their two smallest children. He met them at the airport—a joyous day. Lyon had found and rented a "modern" apartment in downtown Seville. It was going to cost more than he could afford, and the rooms were not only too small but also were jammed with overstuffed furniture. Hoping Dorothy would overlook such details, Lyon threw open the apartment door.

Dorothy said nothing.

A huge, overstuffed, red satin couch, and two huge red satin overstuffed armchairs entirely filled the tiny living room. The tiny bedrooms were equally crowded.

"The Spaniards don't seem to mind small rooms," said Lyon.

Dorothy began to laugh. "We'll rearrange the furniture," she said.

The next day they jammed one of the huge armchairs into the bedroom between the bed and the wall. This liberated the living room, but now no one could get into the bed from that side.

Every morning Dorothy Lyon got the school books out and taught her class of two. Weekends, often joined by Grady and Barbara Hardy, the Lyons would ride buses out into the country, there to climb a tree, feed a burro, or eat a picnic lunch under the trees. They rode to Penon, a high rocky place with a sixteenth-century shrine, and sat on the lawn there under umbrella pines. Far below huddled a primitive village. Beyond it a range of hills rolled toward Portugal.

They rode a bus out to the Necropolis Carmona on the road to Cardoba, once a Roman burial ground, and walked through a museum of Roman artifacts. Afterward it began to rain. They stood with plastic sandwich bags over their heads waiting for the bus back to Seville.

In the Archive of the Indies a happy Lyon began the last two jobs left to him: first, to prove, if he could, that no one until Fisher had ever salvaged the *Atocha*; and second, to learn all of the *Atocha*'s measurements so that Fisher might know better the exact dimensions of what he was looking for.

How did one prove the *Atocha* had never been salvaged? How did one prove a negative?

In 1630 Melián had gone off to Venezuela still promising to come back and salvage the *Atocha* next. Had he done so? Other people had made attempts. In Santo Domingo 135, Lynn discovered an order dated January 26, 1639, by which the governor of Havana dispatched an expedition to the site. But this expedition must have failed, for Melián's former deputy Juan de Anues made a try in 1643, and also another after that in 1647; Lyon found records of these expeditions in the same legajo. It was incredible that, more than twenty years after it sank, the *Atocha* was still on everybody's mind. In 1643 Melián himself had planned what was to have been his last and greatest salvage expedition. His contract was approved in Spain, for Lyon found the order in Contratacíon 5175 dated May 12, 1643.

The order would have reached the New World at the end of summer. The expedition could not have sailed until the summer of 1644 at the earliest. Had it ever sailed at all?

Melián had been governor of Yucatán by then, and so Lyon turned to the Mexico section of the archive where in legajo 469 he found a document dated July 6, 1644, which noted Melián's recent death. Obviously any expedition scheduled for that summer had died with him.

Now Lyon began to range forward in time and altogether he recorded, he saw from his notes, sixteen separate attempts to salvage the *Atocha* before 1650, and others afterward. In 1681 a Portuguese named Beyra had obtained a salvage contract from the king of Spain. However Beyra was arrested for smuggling, and his contract was annulled. Finally in 1688 a kind of census of past shipwrecks was taken. Lyon found reference to it in a legajo labeled Indiferente General 2699, and this document, as far as Lyon was concerned, sealed the matter once and for all. The Spanish, sixty-six years after the *Atocha* sank, had considered it still unsalvaged.

Could it have been salvaged earlier than that by the Dutch or some other power?

Dutch warships had chased Melián's crew away from the *Margarita* often enough, and Lyon had once found this ominous line in a 1627 letter that Melián had written to the king. "Again we found iron chains attached to the wreck."

Obviously the Dutch with a few quick dives might have grabbed some of the *Margarita's* treasure. The *Margarita* was in relatively shallow water and plainly marked by buoys. But the *Atocha* was not marked, it was fifty-five feet deep, supposedly, and it was buried in sand. A quick grab there seemed out of the question; anything other than a quick grab would have been noticed, Lyon felt. The Spanish themselves were almost continually on the site, or at least watching it, until mid-century. Even after that Spanish ships continued to sail fairly close, for the wreck site lay, after all, at the edge of the Carrera de Indias. Could somebody simply have sailed in, scooped up 901 silver bars, and sailed away again? It had taken Melián five years to salvage the *Margarita*. Fisher, equipped with every modern device, had himself been working five years at the site. The idea that some seventeenth-century captain might have done the job so quickly as to escape notice was preposterous.

Lyon was satisfied that the treasure was still down there.

In some ways the years in Seville had not changed Lyon at all. He still ate oatmeal every morning for breakfast. He still didn't eat bread crusts or egg whites. He still drank Fizzies for the Vitamin C content, and when he washed up the dishes for his wife at night he always finished by pouring boiling water over them. He still read to his little girls at night and one of the books he read them during this period was *Treasure Island*—he came to know this book so well that he once quoted its last chapter from memory to Grady and Barbara Hardy.

Lyon's final job—and it was among the most difficult he had yet tackled—was to prepare, gunport by gunport, mast by mast, an exact physical description of *Nuestra Señora de Atocha*. At any moment Fisher might find part of the articulated hull structure, and it would be essential to know which part so as to decide where the strongroom might lie. But more than this Fisher wanted to construct a scale model of the *Atocha*. So did his divers; so did Lyon. All wanted to see a physical representation of the elusive galleon for which they had been searching for so long.

But how was Lyon to put together such a description? Although the shipwright's contract with the avería administration gave most of the specifications according to which the galleon was built, the nautical terms and measurements employed had passed out of use—one did not, after all, sail galleons across oceans anymore. He had consulted modern Spanish dictionaries and the modern nautical ones, but these were no help, and now he was obliged to delve into obscure ancient books. The one that helped him most was called *Instrucción Práctica de Navegar;* it had been published in Mexico in 1587, no doubt on one of the earliest printing presses to reach the New World. By studying this tome carefully, Lyon was at last able to grasp the meaning of terms that had baffled him—terms that, although commonplace to the youngest cabin boy aboard Cadereita's ships, had probably not been spoken aloud in centuries.

The nautical measurements of 1622 were a separate problem. What was *codo*, what was a *vara*? For answers Lyon returned to research he had done in the archive in Simancas. While searching there in a section labeled Guerra Antigua 3146, he had come upon a curious 1613 document, copies of which had supposedly been sent around to every ship in the fleet that year. Apparently an attempt was being made by the navy department to standardize as much as possible various units of the mightiest fleet afloat. The Spanish navy was going off the vara standard and onto the new codo standard. The new codo was to equal two thirds of the Castilian vara, plus one thirty-second of a two thirds vara.

It was complicated. Lyon got out a calculator and began to work out the measurements for the *Atocha*. Its keel was 86.48 feet long, but to this, he saw, was added a bow overhang of 17.86 feet and a stern overhang of 6.11 feet— a ship of those days bulged outwards in all directions. This gave the *Atocha* a total length of 110.5 feet on the weather deck. The ship was widest one deck below that—

the main deck—32.9 feet. Apart from forecastle and stern-castle, the galleon had only two complete decks, the main deck and the weather deck. The depth of the hold from keel to main deck planking measured 15.91 feet.

The masts must have been astonishing things, thicker than full-grown trees, for the main mast, Lyon saw, measured 69.9 inches in circumference where it went through the weather deck. It was just under 70 feet high—the height of a seven-story building. The foremast was about as thick and about as high. The mizzenmast—the mast farthest aft—was smaller, only 53.58 inches in circumference at the weather deck, and rising into the air only 42 feet 9 inches. As for the bowsprit, it too was enormous, 75.2 feet long, and 57.6 inches in circumference where it passed through the weather deck.

The *Atocha*'s hull had been of oak, its masts of pine, but a good deal of cedar deck planking had been used. In the event that Fisher's divers discovered intact wood, even though such wood might have the consistency today of wet cardboard, still it would be possible to determine what type wood it was, and theoretically possible therefore to determine which part of the ship it had come from. This would be especially true if it still contained nails. For instance, the the *Atocha*'s gunports had measured 28.2 inches square, and each gunport had hung from three hinges, each half of each hinge being planted with three nails.

During this time Lyon searched in vain for architects' plans or drawings of the *Atocha,* or of any other galleon of the same type, but he found nothing, and a visit to the Naval Academy in Barcelona proved equally fruitless. Even museum paintings of galleons were vague, for most were stylized battle scenes romantically obscured by smoke. Though the galleon as a type served Spain well for 250 years and though it was quite possibly the most famous ship type in the history of the world, still it had evidently made little impression on the artists of those days, and Lyon found himself wondering why. The rich noblemen who commanded the galleons had only themselves painted, not their ships. Perhaps the galleons had been constructed in such numbers as to become common-place. Another possible explanation was that each galleon lived an extremely brief life. Those that survived the hurricanes, the sea battles, and the pirates were eaten by worms in a very short time. Had not one of Columbus's ships, around 1503, been sunk by worms before he could get back to Spain? Probably not a single galleon ever lasted long enough or completed enough voyages to become famous on its own account.

It was now Holy Week in Seville. From their tiny apartment the Lyons could hear drums from the nearby churches as the floats left for the cathedral. They could hear the songs being sung in the streets. April 9 was Lyon's forty-sixth birthday. Barbara Hardy made Lyon a mini-legajo tied with old ribbons and labeled "Real Diferente."

Back in Florida the paper Lyon had prepared for presentation to the historical society, and certain other papers that he had prepared for Fisher, had begun to achieve some circulation. Scholars had had time to study them and to become impressed with the massive research project Lyon had undertaken and accomplished. His theories were so precise, so carefully and copiously documented, that the vindication he had sought was at last coming his way. A TV special was being prepared on the *Atocha* salvage; cameramen who came to Seville to photograph Lyon rented an apartment across from the Archive of the Indies. From their balcony they photographed the historian entering and leaving the building. Additional footage was made from street level. There were close-ups and three-quarter shots. It took all day. The other scholars stood around watching, and Lyon grinned, feeling embarrassed.

Arrangements were made to bring cameras into the archive itself, and in the vaulted reading room a track was laid down so the camera could dolly back and forth. Once again Lyon sat alone over Contaduría 1112, the worm-eaten record of Melián's salvage of the *Margarita*, Lyon's first clue to the Marquesas' site. Along the track the camera dollied in, reaching over Lyon's shoulder to focus lovingly on the wormholes and the faded, archaic handwriting. Alternately awed and irreverent, the other scholars watched this film star who had once sat among them. Lyon himself felt silly. It occurred to him that these TV people were spending more money in Seville in a week than he himself had spent there in three academic years.

But when the camera closed up on his face and the hard question was asked him, Lyon spoke the words that were in his heart. Why, the reporter asked, had a scholarly man like himself got involved with Mel Fisher and the treasure of the *Atocha*?

"Where else," replied the historian after a pause, "could a man like me find adventure?"

With the approach of summer, professors of Latin American history on forty-five-day excursion fares began to arrive from America to visit the famous Archive of the Indies. A number of them had heard of Dr. Lyon's work and wanted to meet him.

The Hardys, Douglas Inglis, and the other young students watched this with awe. To them these professors were world-renowned scholars, yet here they were, lining up to shake Gene Lyon's hand.

Once again it was time to return to Florida. Lyon gathered together Dorothy, the two little girls, his stack of notebooks, which now stood almost four feet high, and his spools of microfilm totaling now eighty thousand pages. As he said good-bye to the overstuffed apartment on Calle Abad Gordillo, Lyon had only one nagging worry. Suppose Fisher did find the *Atocha*, all of it—but there was no treasure there. . . . Lyon thought of it like the scene from *Treasure Island*: Long John Silver steps to the edge of the hole, and it's empty. Long John's line was, "Dig away boys, you'll find some pignuts and I shouldn't wonder."

What would Lyon's line be?

19

All Precautions Taken

That winter the division of
spoils between Fisher and Florida had suddenly taken
place. Never in any hurry, Florida had intended to perform this division the next summer, or perhaps the next
year, moving the date up only because it feared a Supreme Court ruling, due any day. Suit had been brought
against nine coastal states that claimed ownership of tide-
land oil rights. If the states lost, then this ruling would
also apply to Fisher's treasure. Ownership would revert
solely to Fisher.

But when Florida decided to divide at once, Fisher was
agreeable. His lawyers told him Florida would lose in the
Supreme Court, and to wait. But Fisher couldn't afford to
wait. He needed the *Atocha*'s treasure right now. He
needed to flash it if he was to raise new capital, and new
capital he simply had to have. And so, in effect, he was
willing to pay a 25 percent commission on his own gold
and silver in order to take possession of it at once.

The division of loot took a solid month of extremely
hard work. The approximately 918 solid objects and approximately 6,240 coins that Fisher's divers had brought

up were all assigned points, and these points were supposed to represent their relative value. For instance, cannonballs were rated at between 1 and 5 points, depending upon their condition and whether or not some other object had become fused to them during the centuries in the sea. But bar shot, chain shot, and split shot went for 50 points each, as did the stone cannonballs—because these things were curiosities. The best of the swords and arquebuses went for 200 points. The most valuable item of all was judged to be Dirk Fisher's astrolabe, which was assigned 20,000 points. Second was Kim Fisher's gold chalice—18,000 points. Bouncy John's gold rosary got 6,000 points, as did three of the gold bars. The longest and heaviest of the more than thirty gold chains went for up to 6,000 points each. The three silver bars whose markings Dr. Lyon had found on the *Atocha's* manifest were assigned 4,000 points each.

Not all the coins had yet been cleaned. Those that bore legible markings were studied under magnifying glasses and microscopes to determine in each case the mint, reign, assayer, denomination, date—and any other unusual characteristics—and this data was checked by both sides against every available reference. A few badly eroded coins were then assigned as few as 1 or 2 points. The great majority were awarded around 20. Of the eight unique coins from the Santa Fe mint, the two best were awarded 750 points each, five others got 500, and the last of them, being badly eroded, 50 points. The coins were judged within the *Atocha* collection, rather than by what was known to exist among collectors and dealers in the outside world.

On March 5, 1975 the state made its choice from among four roughly equal piles—the one containing Dirk Fisher's astrolabe—and the division was over. State officials refused to assign any monetary value to the state share, though reporters begged for even a rough estimate. Fisher was not nearly as reticent. "Six million bucks," he said, plucking a figure from the air. The grateful reporters put the figure in headlines.

Twelve days later the Supreme Court ruled against the coastal states. Florida had lost jurisdiction over its tidelands, including jurisdiction over the *Atocha*, and Fisher had lost—needlessly—25 percent of his treasure. Florida did not offer it back. Fisher would have to sue to get it, which he could not afford to do. Lawyers would cost much of what the treasure was worth, and politically he would commit suicide. Should he ever want to move back into Florida territorial waters, he would wait a long time for his variance.

No, 25 percent of all treasure raised so far was gone forever.

In Tallahassee, Fisher's share of gold and silver was sealed into bank bags and transported by Brink's truck to the Cape Coral Bank. All other artifacts, still in padded containers filled with seawater, were sent by bonded mover to a bonded warehouse in Fort Myers.

Fisher now called a stockholders' meeting at the Cape Coral Country Club. It was his idea to hire away from the state of Florida its conservator, an environmental biologist named Austin Fowles. Fisher wanted to put Fowles to work cleaning the rest of the coins. These coins had been nearly a hundred years longer in the sea than any ever cleaned before, and their condition was delicate. Fisher wanted Fowles's laboratory set up inside the Cape Coral Bank itself, for in this way evidence of authenticity would be maintained. Fisher didn't say so, but he didn't want any more charges that his coins might be counterfeit.

There was only one difficulty. Fowles wanted a salary of $27,00 a year, and fully aware of Fisher's reputation, he wanted that year's salary placed in escrow in advance.

So Fisher now asked his stockholders to subscribe the money to hire Fowles. The stockholders were in a good mood. Fisher was expansive and confident, and so were they. This would be the last season needed, all were convinced. By September the divers would have brought up most of $600 million—mention of this incalculable sum still intoxicated everyone. And so Fowles's salary was quickly subscribed.

But Fisher was short a good deal more money than this. Whatever the actual worth of the treasure raised so far, there was no way Fisher could sell all or part of it at high prices quickly. In the meantime taxes had to be paid, and the Internal Revenue Service, as always, was taxing him on seven times the bullion value of gold items, and three times the bullion value of silver ones.

In addition the vessels had to be refitted and sent to sea. The new season would drink up money as fast or faster than past ones, and Fisher set out to raise it.

The SEC consent decree signed a year previously had changed Fisher's technique—and his success—only slightly. He was now required to provide each new contract investor with access to his books, and also with a so-called Black Letter which each was required to read and sign before investing.

The Black Letter made for stern reading. In it the investor confirmed that he had been advised of the following by Fisher:

1. There was no assurance the *Atocha* had been located, none that treasure existed, would be found, or could be sold at a profit.

2. The company might have violated antifraud provisions of various federal and state laws governing the sale of securities; the company might have misrepresented the value, source, authenticity and title of collateral given to previous investors; the company might therefore have contingent liabilities in excess of its assets.

3. The SEC had alleged that the company and Fisher had violated the registration provisions of the federal securities laws; the company and Fisher had consented to an order enjoining them from making offers or sales of unregistered securities.

4. The company had not maintained customary accounting records, and could not guarantee either the state of its assets, or that disbursement of past funds was for proper corporate purposes.

5. The company could make no representation as to the value of treasure already recovered. The company did not have the money to continue in operation during the term of the contract and might not be able to obtain such money.

In signing this document, the investor certified that he knew the risks, could afford to lose his money, and wanted no further information about the company. Further, he certified that he was aware that his investment contract could probably not be resold by him without violation of the Securities Act of 1933. In other words, he could not get his money back, except in treasure.

Fisher's Black Letter seemed designed for the sole purpose of scaring away any reasonable investor. But then treasure hunters were not always reasonable people, and there is no evidence that this Black Letter scared away anyone. Instead, each investor allowed himself to be dazzled by the gold ornaments Fisher flashed and to be swamped by Fisher's sales talk. The Black Letter, when Fisher whipped it out for signature, appeared to be written in a foreign language. Signing it and his check, the investor handed both back to Fisher, and the Vero Beach Treasure King went on to the next prospect.

And so Fisher's divers lugged their gear onto Fisher's vessels, and the boats put to sea, and this "final" season of the search for the treasure of the Atocha got under way.

As he watched his yellow tugboats sail out of Key West Harbor, Fisher could congratulate himself on many counts. He had enough money for several months, and as treasure came up surely he would be able to raise more. What seemed more important was that he had now surrounded himself, his company, and his operation with some of the finest scientific and academic talent in the country today: Feild, the electronics wizard; Lyon, the historian; Mathewson, the archeologist; Cryer, the meteorologist, whose plotting of the direction and violence of the 1622 storm would perhaps show divers where to look next; and Fowles, the conservator, whose skill would enhance the value of everything found. As for Fisher himself he stood at the head of the most serious and important marine salvage effort of modern times.

He had taken precautions against nearly everything, except for the terrible tragedy that was soon to engulf him.

20

Sharks

Man's senses are fragile things, and one of the most fragile among them is his sense of danger. Prolonged use dulls it. Overuse may blunt it completely. It is as ephemeral as the sense of smell; after a time even the strongest of stimuli ceases to react on the human brain.

Fisher's sense of danger was dim, or perhaps it no longer existed. He may have feared going bankrupt from time to time; fear of an intellectual nature perhaps still reached him. But physical fear did not. At sea he was not afraid for himself and he was not afraid for others, either. What could possibly go wrong?

The same thing was happening to his divers. They no longer feared the dark heavy depths at which they worked or the predators with which they shared those depths; sharks and barracudas had become harmless shadows. They did not fear the props churning the water to froth overhead. They did not fear storms. They did not fear drowning. They began quite literally not to know what fear was.

When the mailboxes were working, a four-foot-long barracuda liked to share the hole with the divers. They called him Ralph, considered him their mascot, and fed him chum so he would stay.

Bouncy John met Ralph on one of his first dives. Ralph swam in under Bouncy's arm and hung there. Bouncy lunged for the surface and screamed, "There's a barracuda down there!"

On deck everybody laughed. Bouncy, unable to bear the laughter, rejoined Ralph on the bottom and began to study Ralph's habits. He decided Ralph was playful, like a cat. Ralph liked to appear unexpectedly. Ralph liked to freak divers out, but didn't like to be freaked out himself. Ralph could have torn a chunk out of any of them at any time, but they pretended this wasn't so.

Ralph liked to follow divers to the surface. Once Spencer Wickens tossed chum into the water close to the surfacing Bouncy John, just to see what Ralph, excited by the chum, might do. Ralph attacked Bouncy John and ground his jaws on Bouncy's flipper, that's what Ralph did. This was considered hysterically funny. It had everybody laughing until tears came.

Sharks were fun also. Everybody had seen them, some divers had been attacked by them, but no one feared them much, and certain divers apparently did not fear them at all.

Dave Hargreaves and Pat Clyne had once crewed on commercial shark boats. They had butchered sharks by the hundreds. Every day had seen them lathered in shark blood, for commercial sharkmen wasted no part of a shark except the eyeballs which, Hargreaves liked to tell people, were as hard as glass and could be bounced like golf balls.

The *Atocha* had sunk in waters that abounded in sharks. Don Kincaid, the photographer, once made an aerial photograph near the wreck site in which could be counted approximately three hundred sharks of various sizes and species. Kincaid was one of those who professed to be unafraid of sharks. He had seen so many, he once remarked, that he simply went on automatic when one appeared. There was really nothing to fear, Kincaid said. A shark's every movement was totally controlled by instinct; sharks were interested in eating only other fish, not people.

Once, driving the little outboard whaler across the open

sea, Kincaid had seen what looked to him like two dorsal fins cleaving the water, one following the other. Just for fun he decided to drive between them. "I'm going to scare the shit out of those two sharks," he told himself.

And between those two fins he did drive, but when he looked down he realized that only one fin was a dorsal; the other was a tail. Beneath him nine feet of shark head stuck out on one side of the boat, and ten or twelve feet of shark tail on the other. It was an enormous hammerhead. It was twenty-two to twenty-five feet long, the biggest shark Kincaid had ever seen, and it was six inches beneath him.

Feeling the little whaler on its back, the mighty fish reacted. Violently bumping and scraping, it swirled out from under. The whaler tilted and rocked crazily from beam to beam. But it did not capsize nor did Kincaid fall into the sea.

Kincaid told this story for months, and got laughs every time.

For laughs Pat Clyne liked to tell about the day when, wading in shallow water trying to free a boat that had run aground, he had stepped on a shark. Hargreaves had a funny shark story also. He had once slit open the belly of a pregnant shark, finding unborn young swimming in sacks inside. What did he do? Yo, ho ho. In full view of everyone he slit open each sack and dumped all those cute shark babies into Key West Harbor, that's what he did. The spectators were horrified; they were furious.

"Don't worry," smirked the teenage Hargreaves. "When they get older they'll all swim out to sea again."

Usually Fisher's tugboats stayed anchored at the wreck-site for ten days or more. When food ran low and the meat was gone, divers plunged over the side with spear guns and went hunting for dinner. Sometimes there were sharks hunting for dinner also. The closest place to find fish was at the reef that had sunk the *Atocha*. It was rarely more than five hundred yards away, and the water over it varied between seventeen and twenty-five feet.

Clyne, Kincaid, and Bouncy John, having anchored the whaler on this reef, free-dove down. Kincaid and Bouncy carried arbalette spear guns. Clyne had a big pneumatic gun; the divers called it a bazooka. When fired it made an explosion that sounded underwater like a stick of dynamite. Sharks, as all the divers well knew, are attracted by explosions. The three men separated and ranged deep. Above them floated their boat, empty.

Presently Clyne spied and stalked a fifteen-pound grouper. He fired. An explosion occurred. The instant the spear hit the grouper, an eight-foot lemon shark hurtled out of the gloom and grabbed the impaled grouper. Clyne, the former shark fisherman, recognized the shark as a lemon by its brilliant yellow eye.

Lemon sharks are listed as maneaters in U.S. Navy dive manuals, and this one was a good deal bigger than Pat Clyne. It was shaking its head, the way sharks do, trying to cut the grouper in half for an easy swallow. But the spear was in the shark's way. Frustrated, the shark jumped clean out of the water, still shaking its head. With a tremendous splash it re-entered the water—losing the grouper. It appeared to search for the grouper but could not find it, and in any case, it now seemed to be entertaining the idea of an alternate meal—Pat Clyne.

Clyne was not wearing a tank. He was paddling around on the surface while the shark circled ever closer underneath. When it got too close he gulped a breath and went down to meet it. It made a pass at him. He threw his bazooka at it. It retreated, but Clyne was now unarmed. It made a large circle, then a smaller one, then swooped in at him. He kicked at it. And missed.

Suddenly it was gone. Clyne hung with his face in the water, waiting for it to come back.

Some yards away was Bouncy John. He had not seen Clyne spear the grouper, nor had he seen the shark take the grouper and leap out of the water. And he saw nothing now. Bouncy John was still looking to spear a fish for dinner.

The shark made a rather vast circle, looping around Bouncy John, and it then came in with a rush at Don Kincaid. Kincaid saw the shark-shaped shadow coming at him. He held his gun out and fended the shark off with it. He poked it in the nose with his spear. He didn't shoot it because he didn't think the spear would penetrate. If it did penetrate, the shark would get mad, and then the best Kincaid could hope for was that he would lose his gun.

The shark began circling Kincaid. Twice it circled around. Then it came in. Again Kincaid poked it. Again it swam away, as if to think things over.

On the surface Pat Clyne was screaming, "Shark!" Bouncy John, underwater, heard nothing. Kincaid, on the surface, knew all about the shark. Kincaid wished only that he was wearing a tank. A man on the surface had too many limbs dangling under water.

The shark returned again and again. Each time it came close, Kincaid jabbed it.

The shark then disappeared. The three divers swam for their boat. One by one, watching for the shark carefully all the time, they climbed back into it. They never saw the shark again. Bouncy John, in fact, had never seen it at all.

In the whaler, to reassure themselves, they regaled each other with their knowledge of sharks. The shark was after the speared fish, said Clyne. "This shark was not interested in us."

"He had been excited by the vibrations of the grouper," agreed Kincaid, "and could no longer find the fish. We were on the surface looking out for him, and not swimming in a normal smooth pattern, and he was just reacting to instinct."

"There was never any danger," said Clyne. "You have to understand sharks and the way the animal reacts."

By the time they reached the tug the experience had become a rather funny story that they were anxious to relate to the other divers—who would no doubt be green with envy at what they had missed.

Any time the seas got up to six feet high more or less, it was too rough to use the mailboxes, and it was sometimes impossible even to remain anchored in one spot. So a great deal of time was spent—and had been spent during more than five years—anchored in the lee of the Marquesas waiting out rough seas, and the Marquesas was real shark country. The divers saw two or three every time they rode the little whaler into the beach. This did not stop them from swimming or spear fishing in those waters. They merely kept their eyes open, and they were careful to stay out of the water at night. Their theory was that the only dangerous shark was one you couldn't see.

To anchor off the Marquesas pleased each of the divers

each time. They were all tough kids, and very young. Yet none was immune to the rather stark, silent beauty of the Marquesas. It was the quietest place any of them had ever known. But at the same time excitement—the sharks— could be had any time they chose.

Leaving one diver behind to prepare dinner, the rest liked to step down into the little whaler and motor ashore, there to wander barefoot along the beach admiring the random patterns of the seaweed. There was always sea flotsam new since the previous time, and incredibly delicate shells, some of which were extremely rare. A number of divers had begun shell collections.

Later they would climb the high wooden birdwatcher's tower. From high up one could see over the mangrove trees into the lagoon that filled the center of this atoll. The beach had been a good place to listen to silence. The tower was the place to listen to the screeching of the birds, and to watch them soar and dive in incredible profusion as they hunted: the long-winged frigates, the pelicans with their heavy heads and ponderous dewlaps, the reddish egret, the purple gallinule, and the great long-legged herons with their yellow or blue crowns. There were swooping ospreys, the so-called fish hawk that was really a kind of eagle and the only sea bird that hunted with its talons rather than with its beak. Sometimes the boys even caught a glimpse of a flock of pink roseate spoonbills, and these they talked about for days.

The tower was also a good place to wait for sunset. Some nights the sun seemed to bleed to death into the sea. At sunset in the tower, sharing a joint with comrades— there was no better time and place to savor this great adventure they were living: they knew they would remember it all their lives.

And after dinner would come the sharks.

Fisher's vessels were never clean. He never spent a cent on paint, or worried about rust, and all his boats swarmed with cockroaches. Nonetheless, dinner was usually quite good, partly because the sun had been so hot and the air so pure all day, and partly because these were healthy young men and they were hungry. Those among them who did the cooking relied heavily on prepared sauces and canned goods. Fisher, when he had money, did not stint on buying food, and there was always beer, although when he was broke he did, and there wasn't. Sometimes, though not always, there was hard liquor, usually rum. In good times and bad the divers foraged in the sea for food, and they ate a good deal of fresh-caught lobster, groupers, and jewfish.

Besides, fish for dinner meant sharks for fun later on. In the lee of the Marquesas the kitchen garbage always went directly over the side, the better to attract sharks to the boat and to keep them coming back. As soon as it got dark a shark hook was thrown out. The hook was big, four inches across, and its leader was heavy link chain. The fish line itself was a length of anchor rope. The bait was the head, tail, and carcass of whatever grouper or jewfish had been eaten for dinner.

As it slowly got dark, the diving vessel rocked gently at anchor. There was usually a guitar on board, and as they waited for a shark to hit the line, the strumming and the soft singing would begin. Other nights, a nickel poker game might start. Ordinary rules of poker were rarely observed. Before long everyone was cheating and laughing so hard they could barely speak. Sometimes the game ended with somebody flinging his hand overboard rather than show the aces he claimed he had, and although this could be funny, it meant no more card games until the next trip.

Still waiting, they would read the latest magazines, a selection of which always came on board with the groceries. This selection was narrow, *Playboy* and its imitators for the most part. *Playboy* this year most divers considered too modest. They much preferred *Playboy*'s raunchier imitators, especially *Hustler* and *Gent*. They referred to these as crotch books and kept piles of back issues around for six months or more.

If no shark hit, then lights out came early—the vessel would return to the wreck site at dawn. There was rarely enough cabin space for everybody. The *Virgalona*, for instance, slept four, but there were usually eight or nine on board, and it carried nine foam rubber mattresses. These reposed in stacks in the forward bunks by day, but beginning about nine o'clock, each boy would go below and come back carrying a slightly damp mattress, a rather filthy pillow, and a rather dirty sheet. He would lay the mattress down on the deck, pull the sheet over himself, and gaze up at the stars until the motion of the boat rocked him to sleep.

Sleeping out on deck in the lee of the Marquesas could be a thing of unutterable tranquility. Totally refreshed, one awakened usually while it was still dark and counted the stars again—there really were billions of them. Far beyond the low islands the sky glowed above Key West. Closer by, Cuban shrimp boats had anchored, and individual points of light showed where they were. As the dawn began to come up one could hear activity aboard them. The sounds carried clearly across the still water. Their engines came on, and they motored away.

If the divers had found treasure during the day and if it did not rain at night at the Marquesas, then there was no finer life than this anywhere, and clearly the divers wanted it never to end.

But some nights it rained. All eight or nine divers and their soggy mattresses crowded into the little cabin. For the rest of the night they caught what sleep they could standing up. Life was a tough place after all, and idylls were temporary—as each rain storm might have warned them.

At dawn the sky would turn deep blue long before it was really light on deck. Overhead wheeled flights of frigate birds with long crooked wings. The boys stood up yawning, then climbed onto the gunwales and urinated into the sea. The surface of the water was usually flat calm that early in the day. The boat hardly moved at all, and the air was already hot. The damp mattresses and damp, dirty pillows were carried below and shoved into the bunks. The damp, dirty sheets were balled up and thrown into corners.

In the galley, water was set to boil for coffee, and whoever was cook that morning began whipping up scrambled eggs and bacon. Then the shark line was hauled in. If there was nothing on it, then the engines were started, and the boat moved toward the wreck site, toward whatever fabulous treasure they might find that day. As they waited for breakfast, the boys, working meticulously, got their dive gear ready.

The shark line was sometimes ignored by sharks all

night. The hook, hauled in next morning, still wore the head, tail, and backbone of the grouper or jewfish that had served as bait. Other mornings there would be something else on it.

Once it was the head and half the body of a lemon shark. The head was as wide across as a man's arm was long. The rest of the shark was gone—presumably in one bite.

Usually the bait was hit at dusk. The boat began to respond to the violent jerking. The boys would jump up from their guitars or their poker game or their crotch books, run to the stern, haul in the shark, and transform it into a sacrificial victim. One shark they shot five times in the head with a .38 caliber revolver. The shooter was standing on one of the shark's flippers and trying to pump bullets into its head and not through the hull or through his own foot, while the shark squirmed and bucked. Another shark they beat with clubs and axes. When they had beaten it half to death, and cut its head half off, they dropped the shark back into the water and began shooting at it, laughing uproariously all the while.

Sometimes while a still-alive shark was on deck, one diver or another, on a dare, would attempt to take the hook out of its maw, while a colleague stood on the shark's pectoral flippers to hold the brute steady.

Night after night they treated the sharks to as much terror in their domain as most men experienced in the sharks'. It was a way, no doubt, of sublimating the knowledge that their work each day was dangerous, that the bottom of the sea was not where man belonged. It was a way of sublimating fear of death itself. Sharks seemed to represent to them the unknown darkness waiting at the end of life, and so they baited them just as prehistoric man once baited other great beasts. They used sharks to prove their invulnerability, their fearlessness in the face of fear, and their manhood in front of other men. There was a tremendous camaraderie among these divers, a warmth and love found often on football teams, or among soldiers in face of the enemy. This camaraderie was never closer than when they had death on deck and were massacring it.

Their biggest shark was a tiger that measured twelve to fifteen feet in length. They did not get it on board. They knew it was a tiger, and that it was big because they saw it: the shark, holding the bait in its mouth, leaped clean out of the water beside the boat.

Everybody had jumped up. Somebody said, "Goddam, look at that."

It was well hooked. They could see the hook through its jaw. Smashing back into the water, it began to drag the stern of the boat sideways.

Such strength and ferocity provoked not fear but awe. For once, no one was laughing.

Surging alongside the boat, the shark leaped again. It was tailwalking like a billfish. It tailwalked past the divers at eye level. Its malevolent glare seemed to flick from face to face.

But where sharks were concerned the divers could never keep hilarity off for long. The black Panamanian, Demostines Molinar, forty-three years old and captain, now ran to the fartherest corner of the boat, where he pretended to cower in terror, saying, "Did you see that shark look at me? That shark got a good look at me, man."

"He's coming on board to get you, Mo."

"He won't be able to recognize you, Mo. You people all look alike to a shark."

They were all laughing. The great tiger shark was still yanking their boat this way and that, but they were hysterical with laughter.

The shark gave one last leap. They saw the anchor chain leader hanging taut from its jaws. The chain was attached to a three-eighths-inch, two-thousand-pound test, polyester rope, but the shark gave one last shake of its massive head, and the rope snapped. The boat stopped shaking. The shark was gone. The boys pulled in their rope, and stared at its frayed ends.

"Goddamn, look at that."

Sharks were on Fisher's mind all the time, too, and he talked of them constantly, whether to exorcize old ghosts or new ones it was impossible to say. Perhaps he was only trying to titillate or impress his listeners, who very often were either reporters or investors.

In the days when Fisher still owned Mel's Aqua Shop he was also filming sharks whenever he could and selling the footage to a TV agency for ten dollars a foot.

For unusual shark footage, a competing agency would pay more. "Unusual" to Fisher meant footage of himself attacking sharks or being attacked by them. In the Caribbean, Fisher had arranged to film himself and three other men spearing a tiger shark that measured, Fisher later claimed, twenty-three feet. One of the other divers was Robert Marx, later to become a marine archeologist, an author, and one of Fisher's most outspoken critics.

On signal the four swimmers closed in on the great fish, and fired their spears.

Like all previous sharks Fisher had speared, this one went into convulsions. It turned itself into a hoop and began snapping at its own tail. Then it rolled into a hoop in the other direction. Its jaws were snapping reflexively. Then it began rolling itself up on the spear lines. In effect it was reeling in the four divers at the other ends of those lines, reeling them closer and closer to its sandpaper skin and its great toothy smile. The other divers either let go of their guns, or else their spear lines broke, until only Fisher was still attached to the shark. He could not let go of his gun because his thousand-dollar movie camera was bolted to the frame. He hung on. The shark reeled him closer and closer. He had his hand on its body. His hand was practically in its mouth. Then the shark died. End of story.

Fisher told his shark stories with great amusement. Anyone who dined with him regularly over a six-month period would hear the same ones several times. He enjoyed telling them; he enjoyed the memories they brought back.

Most of these stories Fisher's wife Deo listened to with a patient smile. But others—the ones she had been part of herself—made her grimace in advance. The memories were not fun for her.

Once with two friends, they had gone spear fishing off a Caribbean island called Frenchman's Cap. The water around it was as clear and blue as had been promised, and Fisher took movies of his friend Doc Mathison spearing a thirty-pound parrot fish. The speared fish was thumping the spear that impaled it. Sharks are often attracted by such vibrations. Spotting a six-foot mako shark approaching from below, Fisher swam down to film it. Then he saw another mako and photographed it also.

Fisher, as he neared the surface, spied Doc's thirty-pound parrot fish drifting, when suddenly a huge mako hit the parrot fish and cut it cleanly in two with a single bite.

Fisher wanted footage of the half parrot fish. It would show how lethal a shark's bite could be. As he was filming, another shark swam up out of nowhere and snatched the remaining half—and was immediately hit and gutted by a third shark. There was a cloud of blood and guts. Chunks of white meat filled the water in all directions.

Suddenly there was a frenzy of sharks all around Fisher. The sharks were eating each other. Fisher was swimming frantically toward shore—except that shore here was a sheer cliff face. His wife and the two other men had their backs to the cliff. They were scuttling sideways, trying to find a place to climb out of the water. Fisher got his back to the cliff too. The cloud of blood drifted toward them. It was filled with frenzied sharks. Their feet found an underwater ledge. They stood on it, still waist-deep in the sea. Fisher stood guard while the others attempted to scrabble up the cliff wall. Blood and foam spilled against Fisher's waist. Out of this foam rose shark fins that darted in all directions. One shark, back awash and jaws agape, swam straight toward Fisher. Fisher's only weapon was his camera. He held it at arm's length, hoping to ward the shark off. He was prepared to give up camera and arm in exchange for the rest of himself. The shark, still coming straight for him, swam into the bloodiest part of the froth and was lost from sight. In an instant Fisher expected to feel its snout, its teeth.

But it must have veered or dived. Nothing happened.

Before it could come back, Fisher too had scrambled up the cliff face, spilling forward on top onto his belly. Only then did Fisher realize that he had clambered across a bed of sea urchins. So had the others. Fisher started to laugh. The four of them sat there picking sea urchin spines out of each other, laughing their heads off.

Fisher, telling this story, always seemed to expect his audience to chuckle appreciatively. But it was not a funny story. One night, as if puzzled by the absence of laughter, Fisher appended the following postscript, "When I had Mel's Aqua Shop, our whole business used to change every time the papers carried news of a shark attack. We would get people who wanted to dive not because it was fun, but because it was dangerous. They were a whole different class of people." He gave a giggle before adding, "And I was one of them."

A photo of Fisher once appeared on the cover of a man's adventure magazine. Armed with a knife, he was shown riding on a shark's back stabbing it to death.

21

The Cannons

The "final" year of the search for the *Atocha* had started.

The divers hovered in the craters. Sand abraded their flesh, collected inside their gloves, inside their fins, their ears, their swimsuits. By day it invaded their bodies and by night their dreams. Some, particularly the new divers, continued to stumble into the steely grip of the mailbox blast. Cannonading down, the high-velocity water rolled men into the bottom of the hole, bounced them, hurled them spinning and bounding out into the calm depths of the sea.

This always produced great mirth among onlookers, if any. Again this year the pretense was being kept up that this quest for gold was not really serious, much less dangerous, and no one would get hurt. Never mind that gold in the past had always imposed terrible sanctions on those who sought it.

The divers wore full wet suits all spring as the water warmed up, and usually half wet suits even in summer, though water temperature was over 80° F. by then. Human body temperature however is 98.6° F., and an hour's work in the bottom left even these strong eager boys chilled and fatigued. The sea drained away calories, as well as money and faith.

Fisher planned an all-out assault, and there were many new divers.

Jim Bradley, twenty-two, called Spaghetti, was from Buffalo. He had reached Key West with a beard, a guitar, a stash of grass, and a desire to catch a boat farther south into the Caribbean. But when Fisher hired him he stayed. Bradley was both a diver and a welder. Fisher always needed welders. Fisher's entire world was held together by welders.

Bruce Wisely, twenty-one, an Oklahoma University marine biology major, had never dived in anything except creeks, streams, and flooded mine shafts. He had nothing in common with the other divers, except his love of diving. "When you dive down 120 feet in a mine shaft it's pitch black. It feels kind of crazy. When you dive so deep that you can't see, it becomes a whole new world."

Tim March, twenty-three, was from York, Pennsylvania. He had curly red hair and the physique of a weight lifter, and he liked to lift anchors out of the water single-handed, muscles bulging. He loved diving. "Until this year I had never done anything in my life worthwhile. Diving is a whole new world. It's the nicest natural high I've ever experienced. At sea you can relax and get your head together." March's mother had died when he was three. The child was placed in a home and left there for six and a half years. A good many of Fisher's divers were what might be described as lost souls, waifs like March wandering about the world. In Fisher such boys seemed to think that they had found something solid they could hang on to.

Joe Spangler, twenty-three, was a doctor's son from Columbus, Ohio, and he found gold almost at once. At a depth of about twenty-five feet, hovering with Pat Clyne on top of ten to fifteen feet of sand, he watched the mailboxes bore toward the bedrock. Visibility was so bad Spangler could barely see his own hands. How could anyone find treasure in murk like this? But suddenly Clyne scooped two pieces of gold chain off the bottom. When Clyne held this close to Spangler's face mask, Spangler was stunned. Finding gold must be easy.

They went up to change tanks. It was getting dark, but Spangler wanted to go down again and find his own gold. While Spangler swam along with his nose close to bedrock, Clyne illuminated the scene with a dive light.

Suddenly Spangler grabbed up what seemed to be a gold penknife. Clyne shone the dive light on it. It was a boatswain's whistle on a double strand golden chain. But it was a kind of penknife, too, for it opened out into a fingernail cleaner, a toothpick, and an earwax scoop.

Spangler, on deck, had his hand wrung by everybody. He stood grinning, trying to blow his whistle. Out came seawater and sand. Finally it tweeted. The other boys began begging to blow his whistle, whose sound, all were aware, had not been heard by men's ears for more than three and a half centuries.

Fisher was fascinated by the boatswain's whistle, too, and for a while wore it around his neck to meetings that he addressed, piping on it from time to time. It made a mournful sound, and seemed to have a morbid fascination for everyone. Fisher was fond of saying, "The last guy who blew this was a sailor who's still down there."

The whistle would sell for $50,000 or more, for it was an exquisite piece of jewelry. It must have been extremely valuable in 1622 too, and doubtless had belonged to no ordinary sailor. An officer or wealthy passenger must have owned it, and probably the man went into the sea with the whistle around his neck.

Gold remained pure after being immersed for no matter how many centuries, but nearly everything else the divers found was burly with encrustations. However slim itself, each object had become as unrecognizable as a man in a heavy overcoat. One had to watch carefully. The older divers knew what to look for—principally any sort of geometric pattern that did not exist in nature, especially straight lines.

In theory new divers found nothing, though this spring the opposite seemed true. Soon after Spangler's whistle, Tom Ford, on only his second trip to sea, found a bar of gold bullion.

Ford represented another of Fisher's ingenious solutions to a vexing problem. Technically Ford worked not for Fisher but for the Key Security Agency. Technically he was not a diver but a security guard, and it was his job to catalogue and authenticate any recovered treasure. Later the Key Security Agency would supply certificates (countersigned by Tom Ford) attesting to the authenticity of each item, and these apparently impeccable pedigrees would accompany the treasure when it went on sale. Certificates from an independent outside agency were vital. Buyers were not going to pay high prices for treasure unless convinced it was authentic.

The only trouble was that Ford was not really an independent outside agent. He was really a diver, just like the others.

Formerly the state agent on board had served to authenticate Fisher's treasure. Now that state agents rode his boats no longer, Fisher had had to find a substitute. Key Security had seemed the answer. When the agency had asked, "Which of our guards do you want?" Fisher had replied, "I want you to hire a fellow named Tom Ford, and assign him to me."

Ford had come to Fisher for a job as a diver. Seeing that he was a superb one, Fisher, had sent him first to Key Security, and then to sea—as diver and authenticator both.

Almost the first treasure Ford had to authenticate was his own gold bar. The tip of one end was peeking out of the sand, twinkling at him and he grabbed it. He was not impressed by it or himself, thinking that finding gold was what he was there for. And he swam up and thumped the bar down on deck.

The reaction of everybody on board astonished him. Elation spilled over into hysteria—with a good deal of jealousy mixed in, he noted. He had never in his life observed such silliness and glee.

That was when he realized how rare gold was.

Few divers remained who had seen the first treasure come up almost four years before: Don Kincaid, John Brandon, Bouncy John Lewis, Pat Clyne, Hugh Spinney, Spencer Wickens, one or two others.

Of these Wickens, twenty-three, had never found any gold at all until suddenly he too, after three and a half years of diving, plucked an eight-inch-long bar of gold bullion out of the sand. It caused one of the biggest adrenaline rushes of his life, he said later. He thrust it so close to his face mask that he nearly broke the glass. He couldn't believe his eyes. He showed it to John Brandon who was in the hole with him. Wickens realized his bubbles were flying in all directions. So were Brandon's. Brandon clapped his hand to his face mask and pretended to swoon.

Instead of thumping the bar down on deck, Wickens stuffed it inside the sleeve of his wet suit, and started up the dive ladder. When the others came close he peeled the sleeve back slightly, letting the gold peek out, and letting himself grin at last as everyone began screaming and hugging him.

Then a reaction set in that Wickens was totally unprepared for. He began to tremble as if he had just had a car crash. He was sucking in fresh air as if through a regulator. It took him five minutes to calm down enough to go back under. But there was no other gold in that hole, or in any other he was to dive in that day or any day.

Treasure diving was a continual intellectual puzzle. One asked oneself why there was only one bar of gold in Ford's hole, or Wickens' hole. How did it get there? Had some Spaniard had it in his pocket? Were these divers finding nothing but corpses?

Similar questions could be applied to Fisher's entire search. It was now the summer of 1975. Fisher had been searching this spot for more than five years. A 600-ton, 100-foot long galleon had disappeared here, a massive thing. Fisher couldn't seem to find it. Where were the *Atocha*'s eighteen bronze cannons? Where were the 898 remaining silver bars? Assuming that Fisher had found two chests of pieces of eight and that the *Atocha* had carried around eighty chests in all, then where were the other seventy-eight chests? Why had he found swords, but no pikes or armor? Why only one anchor, but not the others? Why dyes, but no tobacco? Where were all the tons of copper? Fisher was finding only bits and pieces of the *Atocha*, and widely scattered bits and pieces at that. Where was the rest of it? The gold bars were far smaller and fewer than the silver bars, yet he had found eight gold bars and only three silver ones. Why? The whole thing was crazy.

The Fourth of July. Fisher came out to the *Northwind* in a speedboat bringing guests, and a box of distress flares with which to conduct a fireworks display.

Dinner was fresh lobster, fresh speared grouper, and roast beef brought out from town. This holiday feast, cooked by Dirk Fisher's wife, Angel, was washed down with plenty of beer and rum. "Eighteen for dinner," noted Angel in the *Northwind's* log.

After dinner distress flares began to blossom in the night sky. Flares were shooting up from all over the sea. They were being fired from the flimsy, angle-iron tower two miles distant, on whose tiny platform stood three tipsy divers and also from the whaler which was out there in the blackness somewhere, putt-putting around. They were being fired from various decks of the *Northwind*.

It might be argued that distress flares are not firecrackers. The shell leaves the muzzle with enough velocity to tear off a man's head and, once alight, blazes fiercely. It might even be argued, to those of a mystical bent, that distress flares should be reserved for distress, and that Fisher was using up too many cries for help in one night. Such arguments, if he thought of them at all, did not deter the Vero Beach Treasure King.

A flare attributed to Pat Clyne, with all of the open sea to land in, came down blazing on the *Northwind's* deck. It missed the various fuel drums lashed into place there. It did not land on and consume any compressors or hoses or dive gear. Nor did it cause any air tanks to explode into shrapnel or set fire to anyone's clothes or hair. There was no general conflagration in which the *Northwind* sank. The *Northwind* was not destined to sink for another fortnight. Clyne's blazing distress flare caused no distress at all. It was considered to be hysterically funny, though it had to be extinguished, of course.

After this was done the conviviality, the hilarity, and the flare shooting resumed as before. Over and over again black night exploded into brilliant, eyeball-searing color. It was indeed very beautiful.

Nine days later the *Northwind* was still out there, and Dirk Fisher, waking up and stepping out into the early morning sunshine, saw calm seas, the start of a bright hot day. He also saw that the *Northwind* had dragged anchor during the night, for the tug's position in relation to the buoys had changed. That would have to be corrected.

Dirk was not aware that this was the start of the most glorious day of his young life.

It was Sunday. They had worked eleven hard hours the day before, but had found nothing. No one was in too much of a hurry to work this morning. After a leisurely breakfast, Dirk donned mask, fins, and tank, and plunged over the side to find the half-dug hole they had started last night. Angel got out the log and noted the hour: 11:25 A.M.

Dirk Fisher, twenty-one, had been a married man almost exactly two years. He had been captain of the *Northwind* for about two years also. There were those who said afterwards that he was a mature sea captain, as mature as a man twice his age, but others were of the opinion that he had been pushed by his doting father beyond his capabilities. In his father's eyes Dirk could do no wrong.

He had been, as a teenager, prone to fads. He had been at one time so passionately religious that his friends called him a Jesus freak, but this was all right with his father, who was a churchgoing man himself. Then Dirk had discovered marijuana. He got stoned a lot, but his father did not protest. Once, stoned on marijuana, Dirk and another diver, also stoned, had climbed to the top of the pirate galleon's mast in the middle of the night. The top of the mast was 125 feet above the water—about twelve stories high—and, like their vision, it was wavery.

In personality Dirk was very much like his father. There was a shyness about both of them, and both were low-keyed. The shyness did not extend toward machines. Like his father Dirk abused machinery. He had little respect for equipment of any kind. The idea that gear needed care had not occurred to him. Like his father, Dirk was disorganized. Often he would steam out to sea having forgotten to load some vital item.

Unlike his father, Dirk was often impatient. When he first took command of the *Northwind* he gave orders like Captain Bligh. The other boys resented it. They obeyed him, but grudgingly. Later, when Angel came aboard, she sometimes gave crisp orders too. The boys obeyed her too—again, grudgingly.

Although Dirk had been only nineteen—and Angel was much older—Fisher had made no effort to prevent or delay the wedding. Instead he had staged it. It took place at sunset outside on deck on the pirate galleon in front of two hundred guests and a minister from Vero Beach. The galleon's mainmast yardarm, on Fisher's orders, was lowered so that it formed a perfect cross against the most stunning sunset anyone could remember. The sunset billowed up beyond the galleon rigging until it had set fire to most of the sky.

After their wedding the young couple lived in what had been the supply houseboat. Fisher had had it towed in from the Marquesas and moored to the same embankment as his own. Fisher, even more than most men, wanted to keep his children close around him, and when his second son, Kim, got married, also at nineteen, Fisher acquired a third houseboat, and the three boats floated in a row, Fisher's slightly bigger, slightly shabbier houseboat in the middle—papa bear and the two baby bears.

Dirk had traveled some. He had been to Europe and parts of the Caribbean with his parents. But his formal education had stopped at high school, and his only serious interest was diving. His ambition was to go treasure hunting on his own. He had heard of a galleon off Colombia that was supposed to be one of the richest that ever sank. With the experience and money from the *Atocha* he would break away from his father and salvage that Colombian galleon.

First he wanted to become a completely schooled diver. Accordingly, the winter before, he and Angel had rented a small house in Vero Beach so that Dirk could attend the commercial deep-diving school near there. Dirk wanted to learn hard-hat diving, mixed gasses, underwater welding, and other such skills.

Dirk was not a success at the school. Most of what was taught he already knew. It irritated him to waste time. He was there to learn to work deeper and more efficiently for longer periods of time, but they were teaching scuba. He refused to study, though book learning would count 50 percent of final grades.

It also irritated him that none of the instructors seemed to know who he was. But he soon saw a way to straighten them out.

Each student was obliged to give a talk before the class. It was supposed to last ten minutes.

Dirk got up and began to talk about treasure hunting. His ten-minute talk lasted nearly an hour. From then on he was the star of the class; the instructors began to make up to him, and he began to enjoy himself. But his final grades were still poor.

Now, on a Sunday morning in July, Dirk dove deep under the *Northwind*. Down, down he swam. Reaching the bottom, he began to kick his way along, from time to time patting the ocean floor with his hand, testing its consistency—it was crusted mud here. He was searching only for yesterday's half-dug hole, but instead swam right into the most astonishing discovery of this or any other treasure hunt.

About a hundred feet off the tug's starboard bow he exploded screaming to the surface. He was screaming as loud as he could.

Aboard the *Northwind*, Angel rushed in panic to the rail. She thought he was being attacked by sharks. Then she made out Dirk's words, "We're rich. We're rich. Get a buoy quick!"

Then Dirk dove under again. Five of the *Atocha*'s cannons were down there. Down to the bottom he swam. At first he couldn't find them again. The water was murky. Visibility was about four feet. Then he saw them once more—first one, then all five. Bronze cannons.

He swam to the surface again hollering, "Five bronze cannons."

Angel later wrote in the log, "The day we've been waiting for."

Everybody was screaming. Everybody was in the water, free diving down to see the cannons. The cannons were great in themselves. But everybody was convinced that Dirk had found much more than cannons. The main portion of the galleon must be there too.

Angel, in the blue-and-white-stripped bikini she always wore, geared up and dove down with her Nikonos to photograph the cannons as they looked to Dirk, all in a tumble and partially covered with sand, for soon the landscape down there would be altered. Dirk wanted them dusted off so he could see them better.

It took nearly an hour to maneuver the *Northwind* into position exactly over the cannons. The water depth was measured: thirty-nine feet. Then the *Northwind's* engines were started up, the great props began to turn, and in a moment the mailboxes were thundering. For sixty seconds the Gulf of Mexico was turned against itself. The sea writhed as if being tortured, but at the end of that time, as if its resistance had at last been broken, this portion of the secret it had guarded so religiously for 353 years lay totally revealed: five bronze cannons. One by one, Angel and the nine divers all went down for another loving look.

Dirk couldn't get enough of his cannons. He had to touch each one. He swam around them in dazed circles. No treasure hunter had ever found five bronze cannons before. Bronze cannons in the past had hardly ever been found at all. They showed on no instrument. They had to be found with the eyes and the hands and the heart. In the treasure hunting business bronze cannons were legendary. Anybody could find gold, why not, there was so much of it down there. Bronze cannons were rarer than gold—the rarest prize of all. Bronze cannons were simply fabulous.

There was a good deal of ballast stone nearby, and Dirk, endlessly, happily circling, also found a copper ingot. His joy was indescribable. The entire galleon must be here. The cannons, the ballast stone, the copper—that's what it all added up to: the *Atocha*.

Angel had begun shouting the news into the radio.

"And guess who found them?" Dramatic pause. "Raddy!" Raddy was their pet name for each other, and the word was delivered in a kind of scream.

A crowd would be out from Key West soon, but in the meantime there was work to be done aboard the *Northwind*. One of the bow anchors was dragging. A new line had to be run out. A buoy had to be prepared and anchored firmly to those cannons.

This work progressed—except that every few minutes Dirk Fisher would stop what he was doing, stand up to his full height—he was six feet two—and let out a joyous yell. This yell Angel would answer by honking on the *Northwind's* foghorn.

The grin on Dirk's face would not go away. He wore it all day. He wore it from ear to ear. So did Angel. Every once in a while Dirk would plunge over the side and swim down to look at his cannons again.

The speedboats arrived from Key West. Mel Fisher brought steaks and champagne—and, inevitably, reporters. Mel Fisher went down to see the cannons himself. All the rest of the day he took down any visitor who wanted to see them. Aboard all the boats that had congregated there was a great deal of saluting, yelling, screaming, and honking. Cheers erupted for no reason. Champagne corks popped. Dirk Fisher was walking around in a dream. A TV news crew from Channel 4 Miami arrived, and the footage they made of Dirk and Angel was a record of happiness such as had seldom been filmed.

Across that day's calm sea the *Northwind's* celebration was audible for great distances. Shrimp boats came by to stare at all the crazy people aboard the old yellow tugboat. Pleasure boats came.

All day Angel kept announcing Dirk's cannons over the radio. She chirped and sang and wept.

Night came. The guests in their speedboats went back to port. Dirk and Angel were at last alone, but their happiness was as great as ever; and they got a dive light and swam down to look at the cannons one last time.

The next day everyone was up early. The seas were one to two feet. The wind blew at about fifteen knots, but it was steady. The water was exceptionally clear. Because they now lay totally exposed, and also because one now knew where to look, the cannons were visible from the surface. The *Northwind* had to be moved into a new position. But just after ten o'clock the mailboxes went down and the engines started a two-minute dig. A single cannonball was revealed and salvaged. Then came another two-minute dig. Dirk, Bouncy John, and a new diver named Rick Gage each found small bits of gold—buttons or heads. They were so small it seemed a miracle anyone had noticed them, but that day anything seemed possible, and divers on the bottom were all eyes. Rick Gage's piece of gold was about the size of a shirt button. He had only joined the crew a few days before, and for him too time was running out. He was as ecstatic as if he had found bullion. But as he climbed the dive ladder, the bit of gold fell from his grasp into the water. Dirk Fisher free dove down and found it immediately. Dirk was a superb free diver. He dove down thirty-nine feet, made a careful search, and emerged with a grin on his face, and the bit of gold between his fingers.

Digging soon stopped as the archeologist Duncan Mathewson, who had been preparing his quipment, plunged over the side, together with Don Kincaid and his cameras. On the bottom Mathewson began to take measurements and compass bearings, and to make drawings of how the cannons lay. A steel grid was laid out by Mathewson in sections, and Kincaid photographed each of the cannons in relation the the grid. Mathewson had been collecting data for a year and a half; with today's new data he would begin to form some new theories as to what exactly had happened to the *Atocha* on September 6, 1622.

The following day, Tuesday, Mathewson, and Kincaid were still down there. Above their heads, Dirk paced the deck restlessly. He wanted to dig. He still thought he had located the entire *Atocha*. A few blasts of the mailboxes would reveal it. The archeologist and the photographer were simply holding him up.

At noon Mathewson and Kincaid at last surfaced. Immediately Dirk ordered divers Jim Solanick and Pat Clyne over the side, and he turned the mailboxes on for a one-minute dig. But that first dig revealed nothing. Dirk thought about it for a moment, then ordered the tugboat's stern winched slightly south. A three-minute dig followed.

Both divers immediately surfaced shouting "Two more cannons!" Another three-minute dig revealed them more clearly. The divers surfaced again, and the news was shouted topside.

"Definitely bronze!"

Another three-minute dig. And still another triumphant shout from the surfacing divers, "Two more cannons!"

The hysteria of the first day was not repeated. Dirk Fisher was all business now. Nine cannons had been found. They weighed a total, probably, of fifteen tons.

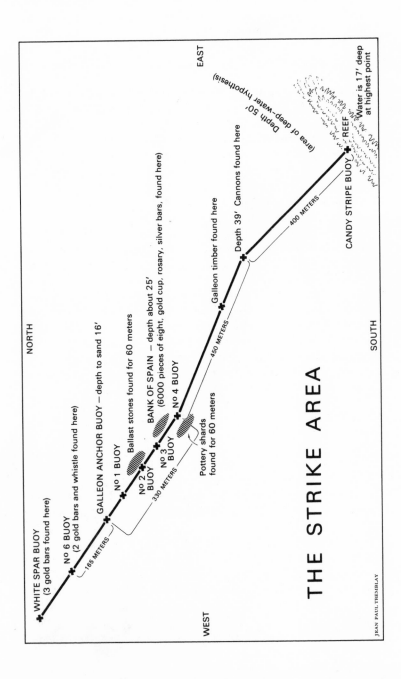

THE STRIKE AREA

WHITE SPAR BUOY
(3 gold bars found here)

Nº 6 BUOY
(2 gold bars and whistle found here)

165 METERS

GALLEON ANCHOR BUOY – depth to sand 16'

Nº 1 BUOY

Ballast stones found for 60 meters

Nº 2 BUOY

Nº 3 BUOY

330 METERS

BANK OF SPAIN – depth about 25'
(6000 pieces of eight, gold cup, rosary, silver bars, found here)

Nº 4 BUOY

Pottery shards
found for 60 meters

450 METERS

Galleon timber found here

Depth 39' Cannons found here

400 METERS

CANDY STRIPE BUOY

REEF

Depth 50'
(area of deep-water hypothesis)

Water is 17' deep
at highest point

NORTH

WEST

EAST

SOUTH

JEAN PAUL TREMBLAY

They could not have floated very far from where the *Atocha* sank. Any second Dirk Fisher expected to reveal the remaining nine cannons, and the sunken galleon's entire carcass.

The rest of the day was a series of short blasts down the mailboxes. A three-minute dig just before 1:00 P.M. revealed a bar shot and a musket ball. At 1:05 Dirk started a fifteen-minute dig. But it revealed nothing. At 1:35 a ten-minute dig was begun. But this hole was empty too. At 1:50 another ten-minute dig. Nothing.

Fretting, Dirk ordered the *Northwind* winched thirty feet to the southeast. Where were those other nine cannons? Any shifting of the clumsy tug usually took considerable time. Not today. The boys had her position in thirteen minutes, and the mailboxes began drilling a new hole. Five minutes deep into the sand a heavy incrusted object was revealed, probably a marlin spike. The engines were stopped while it was brought up, then started again. At 2:20 the divers found some broken pottery.

The missing nine cannons were not found that day, nor were any of the missing chests of coins or the silver bars. Nothing more was found that day at all, though Dirk kept winching the *Northwind* this way and that, and the anxious Angel kept noting each blast into the log: 2:36—10 minutes; 2:56—5 minutes; 3:24—5 minutes; 3:45—8 minutes; 3:58—5 minutes; 4:25—5 minutes; 4:54—5 minutes; 5:09—5 minutes; 5:25—5 minutes; 5:42—5 minutes; 6:10—5 minutes.

At 7:30 the mailboxes were raised, and it was over for the day.

The next day, Wednesday, dawned sunny but windy. The seas were running two to three feet. The mailboxes went down at nine in the morning, and during the day there were eleven moves. Eleven craters were blasted. But nothing was found.

The following day, with TV cameramen filming topside and below, and with Mel Fisher directing operations personally, two cannons were lifted off the ocean floor and swung aboard the. *Northwind.* It was a time-consuming and dangerous business, for each cannon weighed a ton and a half, and there was no way a secure line could be fastened to either of them. Instead, each had to be laid in a rope sling and guided up from the deep. If horizontal equilibrium were lost, the cannon would nose-dive out of the sling back to the bottom again, and its great weight would surely crush any person or thing in its way.

But the raising of the two cannons, though it took most of the day, was accomplished without incident. There they lay on deck exposed to sunshine again for the first time in 353 years. They were green and only slightly encrusted with marine growth. One bore plainly visible numbers, including the year it was cast: 1607; and its weight: 3,110 pounds. It was eight feet long and bore a shield or coat of arms as well. A few oysters and barnacles were stuck to the butt end, and a half inch thick crust circled the middle of the barrel near two graceful bronze dolphins which, curled as if to dive, formed handle loops. Dirk Fisher stared down at it with quit pride.

Duncan Mathewson, wearing blue denim shorts, his beard bleached by sun and salt, was crouched over this first cannon. He was comparing its numbers with those Lyon had found on the *Atocha's* manifest. This cannon was the twelfth one down on Lyon's list. The jubilant Mathewson cried, "This is positive identification! This cannon came from the *Atocha!*"

The second cannon bore no markings at all. Indeed, half its muzzle had been worn away, and it resembled nothing as much as the nose of a shark. Fisher, jumping down to the fantail as it was lifted on board, had cried, "That's the shark! I've been hunting for a bronze cannon for thirty years. These are the first I've found, and this one's mine."

When the reporters who had congregated on the *Northwind's* deck asked how much such cannons were worth, Fisher threw out a figure, "The going price for bronze cannons is $20,000 each."

Well, maybe. If he could find anyone who wanted one that badly.

Next a reporter wanted to know why one cannon was worn smooth.

Fisher's answer took its inspiration from the great sea turtle that the divers found nosing about the cannons that morning. Grabbing onto its carapace, Kim Fisher and Pat

Clyne had ridden the panicked creature toward daylight. When all three heads broke the water simultaneously, the crowd aboard the *Northwind* had broken into gales of laughter.

It was turtles such as this one, Fisher now confided to the reporters, that were responsible for the highly polished condition of cannon number two. "The turtles have been scratching their bellies against it for 350 years," he said, nodding sagaciously.

In fact it was Mathewson's opinion—and also Dr. Lyon's opinion later—that the polishing had been done not by turtles but by the tides, the currents, and the shifting sands. But Fisher liked his own romantic story better and went on repeating it. There was something about Fisher that militantly resisted ordinary explanations of anything. Other people in order to live needed principally food and clothing. Fisher needed hope and dreams. He needed drama. He was sustained by fantasy.

With two cannons on board, Dirk Fisher started back toward Key West, but the *Northwind* was so slow that he had to anchor for the night off the Marquesas. He continued into port the following day, where he off-loaded the cannons onto the deck of the pirate galleon amidst a second champagne celebration.

Fisher had promised a bonus of $2,000 to whoever should find one of the *Atocha*'s bronze cannons, and Dirk had found five in one day, and once the cannons were safely obscured under the sopping old mattresses, the proud father, who happened to be temporarily flush, handed his son a check for $10,000. This was enough money to keep the vessels at sea for three weeks or more, and it just about cleaned Fisher out.

Dirk rushed straight to the bank to get the check cashed. Drunk with success, the boy stared with glazed eyes at the money. He had $10,000 in cash in his straw hat. Then he and Angel flew to Miami. They came back that same night driving a new car that had cost more than $5,000.

In the morning Angel Fisher went grocery shopping for ten days' provisions for ten divers and herself, and then the *Northwind* set sail again. Dirk couldn't wait to get back to his remaining cannons, and to the *Atocha*'s main treasure mass, which he was sure lay so close. Mel Fisher on the pier watched with a benevolent smile as Dirk backed the *Northwind* into the harbor. With father and son waving to each other across the increasing distance, the decrepit yellow tug steamed out of Key West on what was to be its final voyage—and the final voyage for a number of those aboard, too.

The *Northwind's* crew was a confident and extremely happy one. The generous Fisher had distributed bonuses to everybody—$500 to each of the veteran divers, $100 to the new ones. A favored few, Bouncy John for one, had also received new wet suits.

At the wreck site forty miles away, the *Virgalona* was digging. The day's yield: a solid silver candlestick. No one knew it then, but this was the last treasure that would be recovered that year.

Demostines Molinar, captain of the *Virgalona*, reporting the find by radio, had reported also that one of his mailboxes was broken. He was steaming to the Marquesas for repairs. So as darkness fell the *Virgalona* lay at anchor there, and the divers aboard watched the *Northwind* approach.

Dirk Fisher had hoped to anchor over his seven remaining cannons by nightfall, but he had been slowed by rough seas. Now he decided to drop anchor where he was in the lee of the Marquesas. Everyone would sleep better and tomorrow would be a big working day.

The shallow draft *Virgalona* lay about two hundred yards off the island. The big yellow tugboat rode at anchor about a mile and a half farther out. The two boats were plainly visible to each other. The *Northwind* was brightly lit; it made a path like moonlight across the water. Being three stories high, it looked, from the *Virgalona*, as substantial as a building. It carried more of everything, especially beer, and presently divers dropped down into the *Virgalona's* little whaler, started the outboard, and headed toward the tug, climbing the ladder of moonbeams across the open sea.

On board the *Northwind*, a rather quiet party was in progress, for this was Angel Fisher's twenty-eighth birthday.

Angel was already twenty-six when Dirk met her.

Her maiden name was Curry. She came from one of the oldest and most important families in Florida history. One of her ancestors was William Curry, who reached Key West as a boy in 1837. Curry and Key West grew up together. Soon he was the wealthiest merchant in the town, and Key West was the richest and most populous city in the state. By the time Curry died in 1896 he was the richest man in Florida. He owned a solid gold dinner service, and even now, as Angel Fisher celebrated the last birthday of her life, that gold dinner service was on display in a downtown Key West bank.

When Angel and Dirk met she had been attending Florida Keys Community College, where she had taken courses in marine biology and also scuba diving. For some reason certification as a diver was being withheld, and she had come to the pirate galleon to get divers to sign her petition. She was trying to force the college to certify her.

Among those who signed was Dirk. He eyed her up and down and liked what he saw. She liked what she saw too. Dirk was a big, raw-boned blond. He wore a blond beard. He looked older than ninteen, and Angel looked younger than twenty-six. She stood about five feet five. She was slim. She had a small, neat bosom. She had blue eyes and blonde hair that hung to her waist.

Dirk and Angel began living together, and then very soon decided to get married.

After the wedding Angel usually went to sea when Dirk did. In between she worked in the office aboard the pirate galleon. She was an attractive girl, a sweet girl. She seemed to have only two interests. Finding the *Atocha's* treasure was one, and helping to manage the tangled affairs of Treasure Salvors, Inc., was the other. She was a much more organized and efficient person than any of the Fishers, a trait Dirk sometimes resented. At sea Angel kept the log books, she photographed recovered objects, and most often she did the cooking. The boys considered her a gourmet cook. At sea she tended to give orders. She organized things. She sometimes seemed more in charge than Dirk was. Dirk saw this too, and he didn't like it.

Before meeting Dirk, Angel had modeled clothes professionally. She had traveled with rock music groups, and she had dated at least two major rock figures.

After their marriage, Angel introduced Dirk to the rock world. They went to a number of concerts, a number of parties. The effect was to bring out jealousy in Dirk. He was jealous of the life his wife had once lived. He was jealous of the men she had allowed close to her. He was jealous of the glitter she had known.

From then on Dirk watched carefully even the way the other divers looked at Angel. Was there anything to note? Most divers were much younger. Although Angel most often wore only the same blue-and-white-striped bikini, her figure was unemphatic and she was no sex goddess. For many of the boys she was more a mother figure.

One to whom she was not a mother figure was Jim Solanick, twenty-six. Solanick had gone through the dive school with Dirk the previous winter—had in fact graduated first in the class. One night Solanick had phoned Dirk.

"He's gone to Key West," Angel said. "Come on over to the Driftwood and have a beer."

The Driftwood was a bar. They sat in the gloom and talked for a couple of hours. But when Angel, as they were leaving, stepped into the ladies' room, Solanick decided that he didn't want any problems. Dirk was his friend, he wanted to be trusted by his friends, and he made it a policy not to mess with any friend's woman. So he drifted out to the balcony where Angel wouldn't find him.

Later Angel asked Solanick where he had gone that night.

Solanick said, "I didn't want to be seen leaving with you and have anybody talk."

Angel thought about it. "Okay," she said.

Angel's birthday party was not boisterous. Rick Gage, the new diver, gave her a shell necklace he had made. Bouncy John's present was a painting of a seascape at sunset, with two water spouts in it. The seascape was beautifully drawn, with delicate and subtle colors.

The birthday party remained quiet, almost muted. Talk centered on tomorrow. Would they find the *Atocha's* strongroom tomorrow? How soon would they start bringing up the *Atocha's* bullion?

Shortly after nine o'clock, leaving behind Solanick, who

had just transferred to the doomed tug, the visiting divers prepared to leave. As they climbed down into the outboard cheerful bets were made as to which boat would be on the site first.

22

Mysticism

However assiduously he has sought gold down through the ages, man has always believed that it carried a curse. Gold was something men had bought women with and killed each other for since the dawn of time, and the curse of gold, it was said, had destroyed men wherever they touched it.

The young men who searched for the *Atocha's* gold were not the ignorant slaves who once dove for Melián. They were not notably religious. Superstition was not part of their lives. Yet they too began to believe that gold was cursed, or at least that the *Atocha's* gold was cursed. Too much had happened that was not explainable: disembodied laughter, dogs growling at nothing, voices in the night, accidents. They sought a supernatural explanation because they could not find a natural one.

Was there indeed a curse on the *Atocha?*

Maybe.

Too often, as soon as significant gold was brought aboard, a ferocious storm would come down on the boat. It was as if the sea was trying to take back its gold—and them with it.

The year before, Bouncy John had found the heaviest

and most beautiful gold chain yet. It had seventy-four links, each about five-eighths of an inch in diameter, and the gold was exquisitely worked.

Reaching the surface and handing it up, Bouncy said, "I'm going right back down and get some more."

But as he disappeared beneath the waves again, a storm arose that blotted out the horizon. The wind blew fiercely. Heavy seas crashed over the *Southwind.*

There was no radio communication then or ever with divers on the bottom. When you wanted the divers up, you banged on the mailboxes with a chunk of iron.

Bouncy heard the banging and swam to the surface.

The entire sky had disappeared. The wind was rocking the tugboat. The wind was already at thirty-five to forty knots.

Bouncy, clambering hurriedly aboard, muttered, "It's the ghost of the *Atocha.*"

By the middle of the night the seas were walls around them. The divers were working frantically to lash things down. The tug's anchor lines were chafing through. Dawn came. The seas were sixteen feet high, and the winds were fifty knots. The divers had been working all night trying to save the ship—and themselves.

The bilges were full of water. The anchor lines began snapping. Kim Fisher, eighteen, started the engines, but couldn't drive into the seas, because the wind was tipping the boat over. The tall tug lay at an astonishing list. Kim Fisher began driving in circles in a desperate attempt just to stay afloat. Orders were given to pump all the fuel to the opposite side to correct the list.

But the fuel transfer pump wouldn't work.

In the engine room Bouncy and Hugh Spinney, deathly seasick, were being thrown from one side to the other. There was oil and vomit all over the floor. Bouncy ripped a length of hose off the engine, attached it to a bilge pump, and jammed it down into the fuel. The bilge pump began to transfer two-thousand gallons of fuel while Kim Fisher continued to drive the tilted tug in circles.

"What do you think?" shouted Bouncy." "Do you think we ought to throw the thing back in the ocean and appease the gods?"

With two thousand gallons of fuel transferred, the tug

rode a little straighter, and the trip back to Key West began. It took thirteen ghastly hours.

The curse of the *Atocha?* When they had gold on board, the divers could not wait to get it off-loaded. All down through history man had sought gold at any cost, and they were doing the same thing—and were paying the same heavy price.

Having seen so much gold, the divers realized how different it was from other metals. For one thing, it was enormously heavy. Its specific gravity was 193, almost as heavy as lead. A cubit foot of gold would weigh 1,187 pounds. It was eight times as heavy as sand, two and a half times as heavy as iron.

Gold was beautiful. Even beneath the sea, in water so deep that much light and most color had been filtered out, gold had a twinkle to it, and on deck in the sun it was gorgeous.

Gold was rare. They understood that it did not occur in veins, like coal. An entire mountain might give up only a bag full. In most parts of the world gold did not exist at all.

Gold was permanent. There was no way to break a piece of gold in two. You could twist or bend a gold rod back and forth a thousand times, but it would never snap, nor even thin out, and flakes of it would never chip off. Although time tarnished everything, and the sea destroyed everything, yet three and a half centuries at the bottom of the Gulf of Mexico caused no chemical change in gold whatsoever. When found it did not even need to be polished. It already shone as brightly as if it had just come from Tiffany's window. It was the most permanent metal known.

Perhaps any curse attached to gold was permanent also.

It was not difficult for the divers to imagine the origins of this supposed curse of the *Atocha.* All had read Lyon's research. The gold aboard the *Atocha* had been mined in New Grenada by slaves, mostly Africans. The Peruvian silver had been mined by Mita Indians who, though technically Spanish citizens, had been worse off than slaves. The mint people, who were Spaniards, were allowed to place the Mitas into service, and to work them until they dropped. The Spaniards paid their Indians principally in coca leaves, the Peruvian chewing tobacco of those days. Coca is the base of cocaine, and on this powerful narcotic the Mitas could work long hours, and they required very little food.

A good deal of the gold and silver aboard the *Atocha* was Crown revenue from the sale of slave licenses, and a good deal belonged to Duarte de León Marquéz, a notorious slaver. Bar No. 4584, the first one found on the wreck site, appeared to be what Lyon called double blood money. The bar had been mined by slaves, and now it was going back to Spain as the Crown's tax on the Cartagena slave market.

The recovery of this bar had been followed almost immediately by the death of Nick Littlehales, churned to death in the *Southwind's* propellers. There had been other bad accidents, each usually following the recovery of important treasure. Hugh Spinney's hand had been mashed. Dave Hargreaves had been thrown into a winch; it caved in his cheekbone, and although his face was repaired by plastic surgery, permanent double vision remained. His ruined sinuses could not be fixed, and he could no longer dive.

Now the worst accident of all was about to follow the recovery of *Atocha's* cannons.

All along, other bizarre events had occured.

Aboard the *Southwind* as it had towed the *Northwind* from New Orleans to Florida, all three crewmen sat in the galley, talking. On the table stood a bottle of champagne to open when they reached Key West. All three men then went up to the wheelhouse. When they came back to the galley, the champagne was gone.

During the same trip, at a moment when everyone's location was known, one of the men, standing in the shower stall, heard laughter. He peered out, saw nothing, and closed himself back inside the shower. Then he heard more laughter. Drying himself off, he went in search of the other two, but they were asleep at the opposite end of the boat.

One day one of Fisher's supply boats, an eighteen-foot fiberglass outboard, sank in deep water in Boca Grande Channel when a patched hole in its hull opened up. There were two people aboard, John McGaughy and his wife,

Maria. Alone amid the waves, they had been traveling
nude. Then they were in the sea, three miles from land,
still nude. To the bottom went the boat, its engine, the
supplies, the couple's money, their bathing suits—
everything.

Another of Fisher's boats happened to come along immediately. It rescued the nude McGaughys, and three
months later the McGaughys and another couple were
anchored beside a small mangrove island picnicking when
a brightly colored object floated by and snagged on a
branch. The branch was right next to the boat. Maria took
the object into her hands. It was the bathing suit she had
lost three months before and fifteen miles away.

The people around Fisher hesitated to talk to strangers
about these things. They did not like to be considered
crazy.

Fisher apparently did not care whether anyone thought
him crazy or not. One day he brought a renowned
psychic, one Olaf Jonsson, out to the wreck site. Jonsson
was going to attempt to point to treasure like a bird dog.

Although Jonsson had never found treasure before, he
had often succeeded in predicting such historic events as
the divorces of film stars, and Fisher believed in him, or
pretended to, and the divers did not laugh. Too much of
the inexplicable had already happened here. All were willing to believe both that gold was a mystic metal, and that
certain men, possessing mystic powers, might be able to
receive messages gold sent out.

Jonsson soon convinced them he was such a man.

On the way out in the speedboat, Jonsson had hung on
tight, for the boat was shaking and shivering as it bounced
along. In a speedboat in the open sea the psychic was no
different from ordinary mortals. Jonsson had also remained silent and had kept his eyes closed. When questioned he said he was meditating, trying "to see."

At the wreck site Jonsson ordered the engines put on
idle, saying, "My mind has an adverse effect on electric
motors." At that precise instant one of the speedboat's
motors ceased to function. It simply cut out. Nor could it be
restarted until a mechanic, having taken it apart, had
found and replaced a burnt-out fuse.

The psychic stretched both his hands over the waves.

"What do you see?" asked Fisher, and all leaned breathlessly forward awaiting the great man's reply.

The psychic announced that he saw the shipwreck clearly, but that it was widely scattered and buried.

This Fisher knew already.

The human bird dog then pointed out eleven areas where Fisher should dig. Nine had already been dug. But two were new, and gesturing toward one of them, the psychic said smugly, "I can see it from here. You're going to find armament." The other hole, he promised, would contain gold.

The first spot coughed up an arquebus and some cannon balls. The second produced a six-foot length of gold chain.

Presently Fisher swam down to the bottom, bearing with him a sealed and signed deck of psychic cards. Though separated from the cards by thirty feet of water, the psychic proceeded to identify each card in order.

"He has a very brilliant mind," said Fisher, after surfacing.

If Fisher was truly impressed, he was the only one—so far. All of Jonsson's "feats" were easily explained. The psychic had studied the history of Fisher's search before proceeding to the wreck site. He knew in general where treasure had been found in the past, and the finding of additional treasure and artifacts in spots selected by him was perhaps coincidence or chance. And the rest, particularly the business with the cards, could be explained as a magician's trickery.

But now something happened which seemed to resist any reasonable explanation.

"What else do you see?" asked Fisher.

The psychic's eyes closed. He meditated hard. Again he stretched forth his arms over the sea. "I see a man dying here on his knees," he said. Leaving behind him a deck of soggy cards and this cryptic remark, the psychic went home.

At that moment, already in the mail to Fisher but not yet received in Key West, was a letter from Dr. Lyon that reported additional details from the sinking of the *Margarita*: in the darkness and terror below decks a priest leading

the faithful in prayer had pitched forward onto his face,
dead of a heart attack.

Was there really some sort of aura hanging over the
wreck site, one so strong that the psychic could read it?

Was this aura a curse, and had it somehow transferred
itself like an odor to Fisher personally and to the vessels
and people around him?

Fisher believed some people possessed mystical powers,
and that one such person was himself. He listened to
voices that told him where to position his mailboxes over
treasure, and he called this the Fisher Factor. He claimed
to have studied self-hypnosis, and that it worked. More
than once he offered to hypnotize guests who became
seasick at the wreck site, always assuring them that he
understood hypnosis, and that his technique was infallible.

Bob Moran, Fisher's vice-president, believed in previous
lives. He sometimes believed he had once been a pirate, or
a sea captain who had lost his ship in the Caribbean.
Moran was aware that one of Cadereita's captains had
been named Moran, but Bob Moran stopped short of
thinking himself the reincarnation of this Spaniard dead
three and a half centuries.

Dirk Fisher believed in mystic powers. For four days
before finding the cannons he had fasted, saying nothing
about it. At last his shipmates noticed that he was no
longer eating meals. "Are you feeling sick, Dirk?" one
asked him.

Dirk replied that he was trying to find the cannons. If
he maintained his fast, he would find the cannons.

Then he did find them. "See," he said mysteriously, "I
was right."

The tugs often sailed with animals aboard, particularly
Dirk and Angel's pale-eyed, silver-gray hunting dog,
which they called Admiral. At sea this dog—and other
dogs—occasionally started growling at some unknown
thing. At times Admiral would position himself against
this unseen enemy, as if attempting to protect Dirk and
Angel.

Anchored over the wreck site, various divers reported
hearing ghostly laughter or voices. Bouncy John was once
awakened in the night by a voice calling, "Help! Help!"
Jumping up, he trained his flashlight into all corners of

the decks, but saw nothing, though the voice continued to wheeze the one terrifying word, "Help."

Realizing that the voice came from the sea, Bouncy shined his light onto the black water, searching for the head of a swimmer, but the beam caught only the back of a turtle starting down. The cries for help stopped, and Bouncy went back to bed, though not to sleep. Was it the turtle he had heard? he asked himself. Or some tortured soul still down there? Were turtles capable of making sounds like that, or was it a spirit of some kind? No one aboard had answers for him, though they discussed Bouncy's "voices" all the next day. If a supernatural existed— and none of Fisher's divers was willing to deny this outright any more—and if it was possible to imagine that the *Atocha* had sailed under a curse, then this curse might still hold. A curse was perhaps as immune to the seas and tides of 350 years as gold itself.

Perhaps all these occult events were meant to be warnings.

If so, then there was to be one final warning, and because of it some of those aboard the *Northwind* on the night of Angel Fisher's twenty-eighth birthday would live. The warning came in the form of a hollow mournful voice calling, "Hey, look out up there," which awakened Don Kincaid.

23

The Curse
of the Atocha

Kincaid, the first to find treasure, was now twenty-nine, and the oldest of the divers, though he wasn't really a diver any more. The *National Geographic* had assigned him to the Fisher-*Atocha* story as a photographer. He was earning $500 a week, more money probably than Fisher.

Kincaid, a military brat, had started diving in the Philippines at the age of eight. His first camera was a Brownie, which he operated from inside a plastic bag. The son of an air force officer, Kincaid as a child had lived six years in Europe, three in the Orient, and other years in Virginia, Florida, California, Texas, and Georgia. Whenever he lived near water he dove. He took up photography because no one would believe the fantastic things he said he saw underwater. Later he took photojournalism courses at two colleges, and magazines began to buy his photos.

But his main interest was always underwater, and so, inevitably, he reached Key West, where, inevitably, he asked Mel Fisher for a job.

As the years passed, other divers came and went. Kincaid stayed. He was not married. He loved diving. He did not mind the financial insecurity. He lived in a broken-down rented trailer in a trailer park and drove a broken-down ten-year-old car. The security of himself and the other divers, he once said, was in their dream of the future and in their camaraderie and in their reliance on one another.

"It's all very romantic, he said. "But most people don't have the nerve to do it."

He was small, about five foot seven, but heavily muscled. He was considered the strongest swimmer among the divers and the best free diver. He gave the impression of absolute competence. He once remarked that he had a prethought-out, predetermined response to any given situation that might arise at sea.

"You cannot be on the sea without inherent risks," he explained. "You should be ready for shark attacks, for hurricanes, sinkings, water spouts, whatever. If you don't think it out ahead of time, then you shouldn't be on the water."

The *Northwind* was a diving platform, and that's all it was. It was filthy, rusted, and old. It was a river tugboat. The gunwales were a foot and a half above the waterline, and the superstructure rose up out of the deck in straight flat walls three stories high. The *Northwind* was a floating iron tenement with eleven people asleep in it.

It had never been designed to sleep eleven.

The top floor was the wheelhouse, around which ran an open gallery or balcony. On this gallery on mattresses slept three divers and a child: Bouncy John, Bob Reeves, Pete Van Westering, and Angel Fisher's twelve-year-old brother Keith, whom the boys called Sharkbait.

Kincaid was asleep on the level below that, the second floor, so to speak. Part of his mattress lay on the open deck, part extended into the dive locker.

"Hey, look out up there!"

Kincaid, awakened by the mysterious voice, imagined that perhaps some guys had come over from the *Virgalona* again, perhaps to borrow more beer. It was too late for social calls. It was five-thirty in the morning, but Kincaid didn't realize this.

Jumping up, he looked around the decks, and even

imagined he saw someone near the stern. The night was still very dark.

Ducking back into the dive locker, he felt around for his glasses, and as his fingers fumbled with folded stems he heard the voice a second time; it was as hollow and mournful as before. He heard it very clearly.

"Hey, look out up there."

He dashed outside, glasses in place on his nose.

There was no one there.

Other guys, he remembered with a kind of dread, had heard voices and had seen what they thought were people.

Now he noticed that the *Northwind* was listing. The list did not seem alarming. The *Northwind*—the *Southwind*, too—had listed worse than this plenty of times. But it did need to be corrected. Kincaid went down the ladder into the crew's quarters, two tiny cabins in the bow—the tug's normal crew must once have been four—where he woke up the eighteen-year-old Donny Jonas. Together Kincaid and Jonas hurried down into the engine room, which was below water level. The engine room had water in it.

We must get the bilge pumps working, Kincaid thought.

Now the tug lurched into a still steeper tilt. It didn't stop there. It lurched again. And then still again. The tug was heeled well over, and the list was still increasing. In seconds the list was so steep that the tug could not possibly ever straighten up again.

Kincaid thought, We're capsizing. To Jonas he shouted, "Get out of here!"

The engine room had three entrances. As Kincaid hesitated, two doors slammed shut. He heard them lock. The third door, which led into the galley, also slammed shut, and Kincaid heard the galley stove slide across in front of it jamming it there. Kincaid ran for this galley door. He had a flashlight. As he shouldered out of the engine room into the galley, the stove slammed the door shut again. There was no sound of Jonas behind him.

Kincaid thought, We're going over and Donny Jonas is locked in the engine room. But there was no time to save Donny. There was perhaps not time to save himself. He was running hard, trying to reach the open deck before the tug capsized.

Kincaid had his diving gear on the fantail. He knew

that the best he could hope for in the next few seconds was to be thrown into the sea in the night nearly naked, with no flotation apparatus. It was one of the crisis situations he had thought out in advance and he went for his diving gear. If a man had mask, fins, wet suit and snorkel, he could stay afloat for days, Kincaid had always told himself. A week if necessary, no problem. Plus he would have some form of transportation. Kincaid was sprinting for his diving gear. He never reached it.

From the rear deck a pair of two-hundred-pound anchors, each with eight hundred feet of line attached, plus hoses, air bottles, dive gear, and other paraphernalia came sliding at Kincaid. Line, hose, and gear knocked him down, knocked the flashlight out of his hand. It buried him. Then the *Northwind* flipped.

Donny Jonas, trapped in the engine room, was a tall skinny kid with crooked teeth and a bad case of acne. His pimples were a trial to him. He was still not shaving regulary. Supposedly he was the *Northwind's* engineer, though he was not a mechanic, plumber, or electrician; nor did he weld. He was "engineer" by default. Aboard Fisher's vessels everyone wanted to dive. But someone had to clean bilges and transfer fuel. Whoever did this was called engineer—invariably the title went to whichever boy was youngest, or newest, and he worked up in rank, if he could, to diver. Bouncy John had started as engineer. He was the one all engineers wanted to emulate. Donny Jonas, however, was so young and so new that he was proud of his title. He believed it described his true importance. When the *Northwind* came in from a cruise, Donny liked to brag, "As far as running the boat was concerned, me and Dirk done everything."

Donny Jonas had been to school, but had not been notably successful there. There were vast gaps in his education. Though he had lived in Key West from the age of six months, he had been born in the North. Asked where, he would reply, "Connecticut."

"Where in Connecticut?"

"Boston."

Donny Jonas had been sleeping soundly when Don Kincaid shook him and said, "The boat's listing."

To correct the list, fuel would have to be transferred from starboard to port, Transferring fuel was one of Donny's jobs.

Stepping down into the engine room, Jonas saw, as did Kincaid, that the deck plates were underwater. He also saw that the toilet hose had ruptured again; it was gushing fresh seawater. As the list increased, all the seawater was collecting on the side of the list, accentuating it. Between the starboard hull and the starboard fuel tank the water was knee-deep already, and deepening fast. Jonas saw that he had two immediate jobs. One was to shut off the toilet pump before it pumped the hull full; the other was to transfer fuel into the port tank so that the *Northwind* could straighten up.

A rubber toilet fitting had burst earlier in the day. Bouncy John, former engineer, had shown Donny Jonas how to fix it, and the repair job had held up fine all afternoon. The pump was a powerful one. It was designed to shut itself off at a pressure of eighty pounds per square inch; but if a hose burst, then it could not attain this pressure, and it would go on sucking up seawater until it had filled the entire ship. That was what it was trying to do at the moment.

Jonas might have shut the pump down first, but he was only eighteen, and so chose to busy himself with the fuel transfer system, a more complicated and satisfying job, and well worthy of the talents of an engineer. It didn't much matter. There were only a few seconds left to him anyway.

Something seemed to have burst in the fuel transfer system also. The two tanks were supposed to give up fuel in orderly amounts, maintaining the equilibrium of the boat, but now they had done the reverse. With all the water collecting on the starboard side, all the fuel had poured across to that side also.

Donny, trying to get the fuel pumping back to the port side, heard Don Kincaid shout, "Get out of here!"

After Kincaid had forced open the door into the galley and jumped out, the *Northwind* had lurched, slamming this door shut again, and Jonas was thrown up against the starboard generator, which caused violent pain in his knee. He was trying to fight his way up the stairs to the galley as Kincaid had done, but a wall of water poured down these stairs, pushing him back. He ran around to the other hatch door on the port side, but couldn't push it open. In his panic he no longer knew what was happening to him. The water knocked him flat. Steel deck plates rained down on him from what was first the wall and then the ceiling. Everything went black. He fell backwards and down, and as the *Northwind* toppled completely over, the water swirled up and covered him.

Jonas's roommate in one of the tiny cabins forward had been Kane Fisher, sixteen, an extremely tall, skinny boy with bright-red hair that hung to his shoulders. When Don Kincaid had come in to shake Jonas awake, Kane Fisher had sat up too. He heard them go down into the engine room. After a moment, Kane stepped out on deck and looked up at the stars. He yawned, wondered what time it was, and then he was in the water swimming. The wheelhouse was lying sideways flat on the water. The *Northwind* had capsized that quickly. Kane could hear the generator roaring, going really fast. The deck lights went super bright. The *Northwind* lay on its side another second or two. Then the wheelhouse dipped on under and continued down. All the lights were out, and Kane was swimming in darkness, alone as far as he knew, beside the upside-down hull.

In the starboard crew's cabin, which measured nine feet by five, slept the two new divers: Jim Solanick, twenty-six, a lumberjack's son from Tunkhannock, Pennsylvania; and Rick Gage, twenty-one, who was from Jamestown, New York. They had met at the diving school the previous winter and had traveled together since then. First they had driven to New Orleans hoping to find diving work on off-shore oil rigs. Both loved the water. But the oil companies, they found, did not love the water, and carelessly flushed pollutants into it. Wherever the oil companies worked, the marine plant life died, and the fish floated bellies up. So Solanick phoned their classmate Dirk Fisher for jobs, and they drove back to Florida to dive on the *Atocha*.

There was a big brother—little brother relationship between Solanick and Gage. Solanick was a college graduate in physical education. He understood machinery. Day by day he sought to impart his mechanical knowledge to Rick; in return, he once said, he was learning Rick's essence, Rick's love of all living things. Solanick stood five feet eight but weighed 165 pounds. Most of the weight was in his shoulders and arms. He was another of those who could lift the *Northwind's* 200-pound anchors out of the water by himself.

Rick Gage was a bit taller, but skinny, and not nearly as strong. However, when they ran along the beach together, Gage could leave Solanick behind. Gage was a long-distance runner.

Solanick had a superb body and was a card-carrying nudist. He played volleyball for a nudist camp team from Fort Lauderdale and was so good that the camp had accorded him free membership, a kind of athletic scholarship, in exchange for his ability to score goals. Nudism seemed natural to Solanick. He got to lie around in the sun, and to play volley ball, and to meet nude girls. He found nude girls more relaxed, more sure of themselves than girls with clothes on. There was less intrigue, he thought, when everyone was nude. A couple of these girls Solanick had made love to a number of times. Afterward, he found, he considered them almost like sisters.

Aboard the *Northwind* Solanick's great strength impressed everybody. Gage was impressive in a different way. There was no animosity in him at all. He didn't like any kind of brutality. He hated pollution too. Other divers casually tossed beer cans and Styrofoam plates over the side. Rick Gage kept his own trash in a garbage bag in his locker.

Gage was an intense young man. Dirk sometimes teased him. When the cannons had been hoisted on board the *Northwind*, everyone had rushed to admire them except Rick Gage. Gage's concern was for the 150-pound turtle ridden up from the depths by Kim Fisher and Pat Clyne. Gage was worried that it might die on the hot deck. He kept trying to cover the turtle with one of his wet shirts.

Dirk sidled over and murmured, "We're gonna make turtle soup out of that thing."

Gage was horrified. As soon as no one was looking, he tipped the turtle over the side, back into the sea.

Now, as the *Northwind* started to capsize, Solanick and Gage, in their tiny cabin forward, still slept.

It is of accidental decisions, millions every day, that life is composed.

Solanick, who should not have been aboard until the next day, had opted to transfer from the *Virgalona* that night, for this would mean an hour's extra sleep in the morning. Or an eternity's extra sleep. There had been, also, a second accidental decision. Solanick lay asleep in the lower bunk. Normally he slept on top, next to the porthole. Tonight Rick Gage had asked to switch. It was his turn at the fresh air, he said. Solanick had agreed.

As the *Northwind* pitched onto its starboard side it threw Solanick, sleeping nude, out of bed, and he fell on his hands and knees in pitch darkness on what had been the starboard side but was now the floor.

He had been in a deep sleep. Solanick had studied, among other subjects, sleep. He had been deep into the alpha sleep pattern at that hour, really dead asleep. Then he was awake, and had to move.

The open porthole was close beside his hands. Solanick was totally disoriented. The tug lay flat on the sea and the water was rushing up through the porthole in the floor. Solanick was immediately drenched. He could see nothing. The cabin door, swinging flat, must have hit him. In any case he found it. On his hands and knees he crawled out the cabin door onto the wall of the corridor outside. The boat was almost completely over. At the end of the corridor was the head, and inside the head was a porthole. Because the head door had swung all the way open, Solanick could see the porthole. Above it was the night sky, stars, air to breathe. The sky was brighter than the inside of the boat. Solanick moved along the walls toward the sky. He was not thinking, just moving. The sky was his only chance of escape.

With water rushing in behind him he scrabbled frantically towards it. But the porthole barred his way. It was no more than ten inches in diameter. Logically it was too small for a man to pass through, particularly a man with weight lifter's arms and shoulders.

In his panic Solanick tried to bull through head first.

His shoulders stuck. He couldn't move in or out. He wrenched savagely sideways. He was free, though still inside, an avalanche of water now beginning to pour into the porthole into his face. Backing off, trying to collect both his strength and his reason, he thrust his arms outside and, in the position of a swan dive tried to wriggle out of the boat. The edges of the porthole began to take the skin off his armpits and sides. Then he was far enough out to do a kind of pushup against the outside of the hull. He forced his hips through, just as the *Northwind* flipped completely over, its entire superstructure now beneath the surface of the sea. Solanick was still stuck in the porthole, and the sea, rushing into the porthole past his hips and legs, pinned him there, at the same time carrying him deep.

With a final effort he was through the porthole, free of the *Northwind's* superstructure and swimming for the surface. His head broke into the night air, and he gasped for breath.

Behind him, Rick Gage also had fallen out of bed. Like Solanick, Gage had found himself on his hands and knees beside a porthole through which poured, it seemed, half of the Gulf of Mexico. Gage too crawled towards the door, and in the hallway Gage spied the same porthole, and scrambled towards it. But he had awakened a second or more later than Solanick. He had reacted a second or so slower. As he reached the porthole through which Solanick had just escaped, the sea surged into it and beat him back in the direction from which he had come.

Bouncy John had been asleep on the gallery that ran around the wheelhouse. Before carrying his mattress up there, he had checked out the anchor lines and the bilge pumps, as was his custom. He had checked out the new toilet fitting, and it looked fine. The former hippie had become one of the most careful and responsible of Fisher's divers.

He did not even look like a hippie any more. His beard was gone and his hair was short.

Some months previously his air had run out on the bottom. Swimming up in the turbidity into the maze of lines under the tugboat, Bouncy had snagged his hair on an anchor chain. He was caught there just beneath the surface, and he had no more air. The divers on deck were pointing down at him, laughing at his frantic efforts to free himself. Because air tanks look the same empty as full, the divers on deck did not at first realize that Bouncy John was drowning. Suddenly comprehending, one of them loosened the anchor chain, and the red-faced Bouncy broke the surface and gulped in air.

After that he had cut off his hair and beard.

He was the most successful of Fisher's divers. Among his major finds had been three gold chains, a heavy silver pitcher, some silver candlesticks, some arquebuses and swords, and five to six hundred coins.

That night Bouncy John had lain on the gallery in the dark, watching the stars until he dozed off. Apparently it was the *Northwind's* sudden list that woke him up, for this list also woke up Reeves, Van Westering, and little Sharkbait. Bouncy stood up and looked down at the sea. The *Northwind* by then was tilted about fifteen degrees off center. Nothing too spectacular to Bouncy, though the water was coming up over the rail. He must have realized, for the others did, that something had to be done about the list. No one thought there was any immediate danger.

Suddenly things started rolling. Then everything was rolling. Things crashed into other things. Their ears were filled with a rumbling noise.

Spinning around, Bouncy looked straight at twelve-year-old Keith Curry, and then straight at Reeves. Bouncy was looking at both of them. Both started screaming. No one could remember afterwards whether Bouncy screamed or not.

The tall tug's list increased in a series of lurches. Only two or three seconds had passed, but the *Northwind*, toppling, was at an angle of fifty-five degrees.

Reeves, Van Westering, and Sharkbait were in the water so suddenly they had no recollection of how they got there.

Bouncy John Lewis was less lucky. Reeves saw Bouncy jump up onto the rail, but as the water rushed up to meet him, the iron wall of the wheelhouse gave him a terrific whack in the back, and as the wheelhouse dove toward the bottom it drove Bouncy deep beneath it.

Don Kincaid, buried under anchor lines and hoses, had

clawed his way free as the sea poured down on top of him. To him the *Northwind* now seemed to capsize with infinite slowness. The rail he clung to swung him slowly down into the water, and as the hull slowly exposed itself he climbed barefoot up the hull, using the barnacles for handholds, until he had reached the keel, and there he sat down and tried to comprehend what had happened.

The other heads surfaced one by one, some gasping, and he pulled them up onto the hull: Sharkbait, Kane Fisher, Reeves, Van Westering, and Solanick, who was stark naked. Counting himself, six out of eleven saved.

A final head, gulping air, broke the surface of the water.

"Who's that?" cried Kincaid.

The voice was almost a croke. "It's me, Bouncy John."

The former hippie was hauled aboard. The others pummeled and embraced him as they used to do when he had found treasure.

Then the brief celebration ended, and they huddled together on top of the hull of the *Northwind*, seven survivors out of eleven. The nude Solanick, squatting on his heels, could not even sit down until someone passed him a balled-up shirt to put between his bare buttocks and the barnacles.

Beneath them they had been conscious all along of the muffled, unending, bloodcurdling screams of eighteen-year-old Donny Jonas, trapped in the upside down engine room. They were crouched directly over him. He was only the thickness of a half-inch steel plate away—but that half inch represented the difference between living and dying. They knew that the hull they sat on was settling lower and lower into the water and would sink. They knew it would take Donny down with it.

"Open the hatch, open the hatch!" Donny screamed. Then he wasn't screaming words, just sounds. The screams would degenerate into a whimper, then become full-voiced again. The divers crouched on the hull knew he must have plenty of air for the moment. He must be standing on something, his chin above water. He whimpered and whimpered, screamed and screamed.

They tried to talk to him through the intervening steel plate. They urged him to calm down, to conserve his air.

Dawn was coming soon, they told him. They would get him out as soon as they themselves could see.

But he gave no sign of hearing any of this, much less understanding it. The screaming went on.

Bouncy John said, "I'm going down and get him out of there."

Kincaid had counted the dead or dying. It was bad enough already. He was the oldest diver and therefore the captain now, or so he thought himself. He could not bear the thought of losing any more men. "You'll only get killed yourself," said Kincaid.

Bouncy would have to plunge down more than ten feet just to get in under the rail—further if he was to reach any hatch giving access to the engine room. It could not be done in the dark, without gear. If Bouncy reached the hatch, he would not have enough air left to get up again. He would be moving underwater by feel alone, through absolute darkness. He would be totally disoriented because the tug was upside down. He would not be able to decide where he was. Lines and hoses would be dangling like webs to ensnare him.

"Don't go," Kincaid pleaded. "You can't reach him. It's suicide to go down there."

Bouncy John said, "He's going to die."

"I know," said Kincaid.

They listened to Donny Jonas, aged eighteen, whimpering for his mother.

"I've got to try," said Bouncy John.

Kincaid heard Bouncy scooping in air. Then the waves, for the second time that night, closed over the former hippie. The seconds passed. The minutes. Kincaid in alarm had jumped to his feet on the barnacles before Bouncy's head reappeared.

"It's crazy down there," gasped Bouncy. "You can't see a thing. I swam in under the rail to the deck. I couldn't find where anything is. I started working my way down the deck to find the engine room door. I ran out of air."

Kincaid said nothing.

Both heard Donny Jonas breathing. They also heard the noise of the sea bubbling into the upturned hull, and they felt or sensed the stern starting to tip down into the water. There was very little time left. Almost none.

Bouncy John sucked in air and plunged downwards, swimming hard. He was trying to see in the dark against the darkness of the capsized tugboat. It could not be done. There was no light except for a green phosphorescence that floated in the water. Again Bouncy saw in under the rail. A rope or hose snaked against him. He shrugged it off and kept swimming. He found one of the doors that gave into the engine room, and the phosphorescence showed him its handle, which he grasped. But the door would not open. It was frozen shut, presumably by the pressure vacuum inside. No matter how he tugged on it, it would not open He began trying to think where the other doors were, and how to find them. His air was gone. He began working his way out into the clear again, avoiding the maze of lines, the railing, remembering to swim still further down before he started up.

Again he broke the surface gasping for breath.

The next time he dove Kincaid followed him down. Kincaid was sure now the hull would sink within minutes. Kincaid was trying to find flotation gear. The currents here were strong and would carry them well away from the Marquesas. Without something to hold on to they might all die. They might all die anyway. All were cut and bleeding from the capsizing, and from the barnacles. Their blood would attract sharks.

And so Kincaid too swam deep into the darkness, into the snarled lines and hoses. His hand found a life ring, but it was wedged tight and though he jerked on it with all his strength, he could not free it. Though his air was exhausted, he stayed down, punishing his lungs, trying to find life jackets. He failed.

Close together, Bouncy John and Kincaid surfaced.

The curve of the upturned hull still showed above the water. Inside it Donny Jonas was still screaming.

Again and again Bouncy John dove. Then, his strength gone, he sat on top of the hull with his face in his hands. "I can't do nothing."

Below him Donny Jonas was still screaming.

Suddenly the screams ended. They could hear him breathing, as if he was thinking something over. The boys on the hull didn't know it, but in the total darkness inside the upturned engine room, something had just floated against Jonas. It had bumped him in the chest. It had seemed to nudge him, like an animal demanding attention. His blind hands felt for it, and sought to identify it. They closed around it: a flashlight.

The idea of a flashlight snuffed out his screams as instantaneously as the rising water was about to do.

Even in his terror it occurred to Donny that with a flashlight he might save himself, provided it still worked. Was it water soaked? Would it turn on?

He told himself to be calm, to screw the flashlight tightly together, before trying it. He did this. Then he hit the button.

The light came on. It seemed to him brighter than a flashbulb, brighter than the sun itself. It was so bright it made him blink.

With light in which to examine his tomb, sanity returned to Donny Jonas. The flashlight's beam raked the *Northwind's* ribs, it searched out the dimensions of the diminishing cavity of air around his face. He no longer screamed. In total silence, he searched the future for whatever possibilities might be left to him.

He became conscious of his shipmates tapping on the hull, evidently trying to signal him. He ignored them.

Above him in the night, with the waves now lapping at their feet, the others wondered why Donny no longer screamed. They could hear his every breath through the steel.

Donny was trying to orient himself. On the port side—the starboard side now that the *Northwind* was upside down—there was a ladder, and at the top of that ladder was the door that was the way out of this place. Donny worked it all out in his mind. To get to the top of that ladder, he would have to swim down, not up.

He did not dare immerse the flashlight in the water. Wedging it among the *Northwind's* ribs, he tried to feel the ladder all the way down. But his arms weren't long enough, and when he put his head under water he couldn't see. He came up for breath and thought about it. His eyes were burning from the diesel fuel and his face and hair were slick. Taking another deep breath, he again followed the ladder all the way down. But he was still disoriented. Nothing was where he thought it should be. Realizing that he was feeling for the exit door on the wrong side of the ladder, he came back up and tried to make himself calm down.

"I've got to think," he told himself. "I've got to get out of here."

He knew by now that no one could help him. He would have to get out on his own or not at all. He looked around, studying everything he could see. He decided exactly where he was, and where the exit door should be. Diving back down again, he found the door at last. He felt all around it. Then he tried pushing it open, but nothing happened. So he propped his back against the *Northwind*'s engine block and forced the door open with his bare feet. He kept pushing on it. As his air started to give out, it at last began to open. He forced it open wide enough for an eighteen-year-old boy to swim through.

For a moment absolute panic returned, and he almost plunged through the door then and there.

Just in time he regained control of himself. He was almost out of air, and once out that door it was going to be a long swim to the surface, so he floated back up into the now-tiny air pocket where his flashlight still shone. With his head against the ribs, the water was now up to his chin, and the remaining air was putrid with diesel fumes. Nonetheless, it was the only air he had, and he began to hyperventilate. Sucking in a last deep breath, enough air to last him for the entire journey, he hoped, he took the flashlight into his hands, hauled his way down the ladder and slipped out through the door. As he swam out of the *Northwind* he reminded himself that there was a railing, that anchor lines and hoses might be strewn about ready to entrap him. Holding the flashlight in front of him, he kicked his way down, down. Only when he judged he was deep enough, did he begin to swim away from the capsized tugboat. He swam until he was completely out of air. He was at least forty feet from the hull before he surfaced.

Crouched on the hull, all of the survivors saw the point of light moving deep away from the boat. No one knew who that light represented, only that it meant one additional survivor, and when it surfaced they began shouting, "Over here, over here!"

Bouncy John's hands were all cut. They were cut from the barnacles on the hull and from the effort he had made trying to open the vacuumed-shut engine room door. Now, though bleeding and nearly exhausted himself, he swam out towards the glowing flashlight, and when he got there he held Donny Jonas afloat.

Donny, sobbing, wore only cutoff blue jeans. His body was covered with grease. Bouncy John swam him back to the *Northwind*. On top of the hull, Bouncy sat holding Donny Jonas in his arms.

The hull of the *Northwind* sank ever deeper into the water.

Donny Jonas asked "Where is little Keith, man?"

"Keith's okay. Keith's here," soothed Bouncy John.

Donny Jonas asked, "Where's Dirk and Angel?"

For a moment no one answered. Then Don Kincaid said, "They're not here."

Solanick said, "Rick's not here, either."

No one spoke. After a moment, Donny Jonas said, "Dirk and Angel had them new dive tanks in their room. They was gonna try them out. Maybe they was able to get to them dive tanks."

Well, it was possible. They could be under there still breathing, working their way free.

Maybe even Rick Gage got out but drifted away from the hull. Maybe Rick Gage was safe some distance off. There was some discussion of this. Everyone tried to sound hopeful.

Dirk and Angel's room was in the exact center of the boat, but its starboard window was blocked by an air conditioner, and its port window was nailed shut. The door opened into a kind of narrow stairwell from which a ladder led up to the dive locker.

Kincaid thought, No one could have got out of that room.

Then he thought, Maybe we should have dived for Dirk and Angel, and for Rick. But if they didn't get out in forty-five seconds, we would have been too late, and now we would have their bodies to safeguard as well.

Kincaid had begun shining Donny's flashlight on the

water, which was glossy with oil, and littered with lines and other junk. Kincaid was searching for flotation devices, anything at all, for the bubbles were rushing out of the *Northwind* now. It was on its way down. Suddenly the flashlight beam shone on something that no one recognized. Bouncy John swam out to grab it.

Even as he started back, the *Northwind*'s hull slipped beneath the waves, and there was nothing to swim back to except heads bobbing in the sea.

Kincaid, treading water, shone the flashlight on Bouncy's prize. It was a small rubber life raft. When they blew it up it measured two feet by four. No one knew where it had come from. All were sure it had not come from the *Northwind*. No one had ever seen it before. They helped twelve-year-old Keith Curry into the raft, and the rest of them clung to its sides. Cold, exhausted, and scared, they drifted with the current.

Pete Van Westering said, "I won't be able to make it. I'm not a good enough swimmer."

Kane Fisher said not a word. He was always a quiet boy, and now, from the moment he had climbed onto the *Northwind*'s hull, he had not spoken. Donny Jonas had lapsed into a state of semishock. Sometimes, for no reason, he laughed strangely.

Kincaid began to talk about the currents. Alone of all those aboard he knew exactly where they were, and also where they were likely to be by dawn. The currents would take them swiftly away from the Marquesas. No one could swim against such currents. But perhaps they would drift close enough to the target ship *Patricia* to swim there. Or perhaps they would be spotted by the *Virgalona*. If it headed directly for the wreck site on a west-southwest course it might see them. If it headed directly west, it would not.

Their chances of being picked up depended upon two things: on the currents, and on the sharks. Even those like Kincaid, who had never worried about sharks before, worried about them now.

The *Northwind* had stayed afloat for approximately fifteen minutes. It must have sunk, Kincaid judged, at about quarter to six. Now he watched the dawn begin to come. The day got lighter. Soon he could see the trees on the

Marquesas. At first he thought he might be wrong about the current—the trees seemed to be getting nearer. But then he realized they were only getting lighter.

And so the little raft drifted on the open sea. The small boy sat in it. The seven divers, each alone with his own thoughts, clung to it, and waited.

24

Survivors

Demostines Molinar was awake each morning with the first light, and when Mo woke up, everybody woke up. The *Virgalona* was known to the divers as an early boat—under Mo the working day started at seven o'clock, or before. The *Northwind* was a late boat, for Dirk Fisher liked to sleep late. The *Northwind* rarely had divers in the water before nine in the morning, and sometimes later.

Therefore it was a surprise to Mo when, stretching and yawning in the clean fresh light of dawn, he glanced off toward where the *Northwind* should be and found the sea empty.

Only one explanation occurred to Mo. Dirk Fisher must be terrifically eager to get back to his cannons. He must have hauled up his anchors in the dark. He must be almost to the wreck site now.

Some of Mo's divers, lying on their mattresses on deck, had begun to stir. Those that hadn't, Mo nudged with his foot, calling, "Everybody up!"

The divers too peered off to the southwest and were surprised. Spencer Wickens and Tim March began to rag Mo.

"Let's go, man."

"Let's get out there, Mo."

"They're going to beat us to the wreck site, man."

The sea was glossy. The low sun bounced directly into a man's eyes. It was going to be another fine day.

Mo started the engines. As they hauled in the anchor rope, the boys were in good humor. Today might be the big day. In a few hours they might be diving on the main treasure. Mo spun the helm, and the *Virgalona* joined what everyone supposed was a race to the wreck site.

Mo at this time was forty-three years old, a chunky brown man with the start, now, of a considerable potbelly. The divers all liked him. Everyone liked him. He was known to be a rough man in a barroom brawl, but at sea he had an easygoing manner and an infectious grin. The divers obeyed his orders not so much because he was captain, but because they wanted to please him. Also, they trusted him absolutely. Mo seemed to understand everything about the sea. He was as at home on the sea as in his own skin, and Mo seemed in no way defensive about his color. He seemed to believe himself not so much a black man as a foreigner. Being a foreigner his achievement was considerable—he had made good in someone else's country. He was at ease in a language not his own.

He had been born in a slum in Colón. At fifteen he had left school and gone to work on a banana boat sailing between Darien and Panama. After that he became a mechanic; he never earned more than fifteen dollars a week. On Sundays he went spearfishing for food for the table. He knew nothing about sophisticated diving, but he owned a pair of goggles and he could hold his breath two minutes or more. He had no equipment except a crude spear gun propelled by rubber slings, but he knew how to use it.

Sometimes he dreamed about going to the United States. "It was a dream to keep life from being so bad," he said once. "You keep it in your secret heart to use when you need it. If it was an easy dream, it wouldn't be any good."

When Mo was twenty-eight, the *Golden Doubloon* put into Panama for repairs on its diesels. Mo was the mechanic assigned to the job. Mel Fisher watched his every move. Did Mo know where galleon cannons lay on the bottom, Fisher asked. Sure, said Mo, and led him there. The black man was a natural treasure hunter, Fisher decided, and when the *Golden Doubloon* left Panama, Fisher took Mo with him. Upon their return to Panama, Fisher gave Mo one thousand dollars to get his papers in order. Mo reached California aboard the *Golden Doubloon,* and from then on shared all of Fisher's adventures. Fisher taught him scuba diving. Fisher sent him to school for six months to learn English. Fisher made him a founding partner in Treasure Salvors, Inc.

Many times during Fisher's early expeditions to the Caribbean Mo had surfaced clutching a chunk of brass, "Is this gold, Mel?"

"No, Mo, it's brass."

Again and again this dialogue was repeated.

But it was never gold.

Like Fisher, Mo sold everything he owned in California and joined the search for the 1715 plate fleet off Vero Beach. The day came when Mo surfaced clutching gold ingots in each hand, and with an impish grin asked, "Is this brass, Mel?"

Mo personally found so much treasure there that he became the subject of an eight-page article in *Ebony* magazine that began this way: "Demostines Molinar is the kind of a guy who thinks nothing of jumping into Caribbean waters boiling with maddened sharks to rescue his white diving buddy."

It happened off Silver Shoals. A sudden storm had snapped Fisher's anchor lines. When dawn came, Fisher and Mo in a small skiff went looking for the anchors, peering down at the bottom through a glass-bottom bucket. At last they found one. But about fifty sharks of all sizes were swimming around it.

Armed only with a sharp-pointed wooden pole, Mo jumped into the water; Fisher followed. The sharks trailed the two men down. On the bottom Fisher carefully attached his flotation bags to the anchor while Mo jabbed his stick at sharks that came too close. By the time Fisher was ready to inflate the gear with air from his scuba tank, the water was so thick with sharks that the American white man and the Panamanian black man could not see the surface above their heads.

When the anchor at last started to rise, one of its flukes got caught on a coral ledge. To free the anchor cost ten more minutes. The sharks swirled around. As the anchor started up, the two men clung to it, and it dragged them toward the surface through the sharks.

But they broke the water well away from their boat. The sharks were still circling, and there was nothing to fend them off with, for Mo's shark stick lay forgotten on the bottom. Mo decided he had to have that shark stick. Abruptly, he dived down to get it. Most of the sharks went down with him. Four extremely big and aggressive ones remained just under Fisher, for he could see their fins and backs, and they began to rise and come in at him, scraping him with their flanks, butting him with their noses. Fisher, dodging around the suspended anchor, kept trying to paddle it toward the boat. By the time he reached the boat he was nearly exhausted. Unable to climb into it, he struggled to slip out of his tank. But a six-foot shark swam in and fastened its jaws on Fisher's arm. Fisher spun sharply, banging the shark on the head with his tank, and it let go. Hurriedly he tried to clamber onto the boat, but another shark sped forward, clamped its teeth on one of Fisher's swim fins and jerked him back into the water. Fisher had no strength left, his heart was booming and leaping, and the shark was dragging him down, shaking itself and him furiously as it sought to chew through the swim fin. Then Demostines Molinar arrived. He beat the shark off, grabbed Fisher, and swam him to the surface, jabbing sharks with his stick with the other hand all the way.

From then on the relationship between Fisher and Mo was an extraordinarily close one.

As a sea captain Mo had a number of attributes, one of which was unusual vision, as had been demonstrated one day when both the *Northwind* and the *Virgalona* had been retreating from the wreck site because of storm winds and heavy seas. The *Northwind* was towing a whaler, and when this threatened to smash itself to pieces on the *Northwind*'s stern, Dirk Fisher dropped two divers down into it, told them to drive it to Key West, and set it adrift. It would be a five-or six-hour trip through murderous ten-foot seas with only a compass to guide them; but than Dirk Fisher did not fear the sea, and neither did any of the other boys.

In such high seas there was no way to keep visual contact with the whaler, though Dirk Fisher tried. When hours passed with no sight of it, even Dirk became alarmed. Was the *Virgalona* able to see the whaler, he asked by radio.

Mo, who would never have cast two boys loose in a whaler in seas like this, climbed up onto the *Virgalona*'s superstructure and began scanning. At length he spied the whaler, a miniscule dot riding high on distant mountainous waves and then plunging down again. Mo also was able to determine that the whaler was not under power. It lay dead in the water.

Turning the *Virgalona* about, Mo fought his way back there, where he rescued two frightened, drenched boys, and took the whaler, which had run out of gas, under tow.

Mo was more than twenty years older than most of the divers. He was the only solid adult citizen who regularly went to sea for Fisher. He was the only one, including Fisher himself, who always accorded the sea all the respect it deserved.

Now as he steered the *Virgalona* toward the wreck site, his eyes scanned the horizon ceaselessly, partly because he was looking for the *Northwind,* and partly because one always scanned ceaselessly at sea. But he couldn't find the tall yellow tugboat, and he was surprised.

What he did discern was a low small object way off to the west. Fishermen? Tourists? More likely some sort of flotsam, which did not concern him—except that at sea everything concerned everybody. Mo turned the *Virgalona* toward this flotsam, whatever it was. The more he stared, the more he could see. Something was moving. And then—somebody was moving. It was twelve-year-old Keith Curry standing up in the tiny raft waving, trying to attract his attention.

When he came nearer, Mo began to see faces, and then to recognize them, and he was filled with dread.

As the survivors were helped on board, Mo asked, "What happened?" But he knew the answer already. He had counted heads.

Kincaid said, "Well, the *Northwind* sank."

Mo asked, "Where's Dirk? Where's Angel? Where's the new guy?"

After a moment, Kincaid said, "We don't know."

Mo again scanned the seas, and about half a mile away something was floating. It was not any kind of boat. It was not a raft. Mo knew, even as he pointed the *Virgalona* toward it and opened his engines full speed, that it was nothing to interest him—floating junk, nothing more—but he refused to believe this. Clinging to that debris over there would be the three victims, who had survived. He would find them just over there.

The junk, when it came up close to the bow, was only junk.

Mo spun the wheel and headed back toward the Marquesas.

Now he was looking for an oil slick in the approximate place where the *Northwind* had gone down. He soon found it. Then he spied the *Northwind's* anchor buoys, which were white Styrofoam balls attached to light line. They would ride directly above where the anchors must be. The sinking of the vessel would not have disturbed its anchors.

Mo called to the divers he wanted: Spencer Wickens, Tim March, John Brandon, Tom Ford. With the survivors exhausted, and huddled together in a state of shock, these four were the strongest divers on board.

"Gear up," Mo told them.

Mo sent Tim March over the side first. March followed a buoy line down, found the anchor chain, and began to haul himself along it until he reached the carcass of the sunken tug. The depth was about forty feet. The *Northwind* lay on its starboard side. March could see the drag marks where, upside down, it had bounced along the bottom.

Surfacing, March called out, "Here it is! It's right under me."

At the dive ladder, with March in the water and the other three on the steps, Mo gave firm orders. "You go down in twos, and you stay in twos. We don't want to lose any more." His face was grim, but he bit his lip and added, "Be—careful."

The four divers descended onto the *Northwind*. The water was murky. The *Northwind* on its side was a big target, and painted yellow, and the sun was coming down through the water, which refracted it into billions of particles.

The *Northwind* could not be seen from the surface, but when they had swum down deep enough its color began to materialize, and after that its details: railings, a mooring bollard, a ladder, the painted lettering on its side: Treasure Salvors, Inc.

They swam along the sunken tug until they came to the nailed shut window of Dirk and Angel's cabin. They got the first of their answers there: Dirk had not escaped. Through the glass they could see a man's hand, with rings on it. They recognized the hand as Dirk's by his coin ring.

It would be no easy job to reach Dirk's cabin, for they would have to swim into the interior of the vessel, and the tanks on their backs would make every passageway a tight squeeze. Also it would be dark in there.

They had with them one dive light. They switched it on and, in single file, threaded their way clumsily inside the tug.

Dirk and Angel's cabin door was in a kind of alcove at the bottom of the steep steel stairs from the dive locker above. They entered the dive locker and pulled their way along the steps, which were running sideways.

The dive light then illuminated Angel. She was at the bottom of the steps. Her long blond hair was sprayed out in all directions. The cabin door was open, and she floated half in, half out of the cabin.

So she had been awake, and had tried to escape, but had made it no farther than here. She did not look dead. She had all her usual coloring—her deep tan. She wore a beige nightgown and coin rings on many fingers, and her wedding ring.

Because he had done more cave diving than the others, Tom Ford had been leading. It was not true to say he had been in love with Angel, or even that all the divers were slightly in love with her, the principal woman in their lives. Ford was new this season, and had hardly known her. But he was in love with her at that moment, and as he took her into his arms for the first time, tears came to his eyes behind his face mask, and when hands reached to help him, he shrugged them off. Gently, as if fearing to hurt her, he moved Angel in her beige nightgown through the doorway, along the staircase and out of the dive locker into open water, where he swam up with her toward the sun.

As Mo lifted Angel aboard, the nightgown clung to her, seeming more transparent than it was, and Mo sent for a sheet to cover her with. The sheet that was brought was one that various boys had been sleeping under for days, if not weeks, and it was none too clean, but it was the best they had. Mo wrapped Angel in it, and laid her down close to the fantail.

Inside the *Northwind*, the other three boys had pressed backwards to let Ford and Angel pass. With the dive light in front, they then swam up to the cabin door and peered in. Spencer Wickens swam into the room. John Brandon and Tim March waited in the doorway. Dirk still lay in his bunk. His face was the face of a man sleeping, and he still held the treasure book in his hand. Tim March pulled Dirk out of bed by his heel. Dirk was wearing red diving shorts. They paused a moment while Spencer wrapped Dirk in a sheet off the bed he had died in, and then they swam him toward the surface.

Until Tom Ford had reached the dive ladder with Angel, there had been some hope, however slim, that the *Northwind* was empty, that their missing shipmates had got out. The sight of Angel's long blonde hair, trailing in the water, had ended this hope, and no one wanted to watch as Mo laid the second shrouded body out along the fantail. There were tears in Mo's eyes too. There were tears in everybody's eyes.

The grim business continued. Don Kincaid, the only one of the *Northwind's* survivors still able to act rationally, put diving gear on and went down with Tom Ford and Spencer Wickens to find Rick Gage. They had to swim for a considerable distance inside the *Northwind*, turning corners, following corridors. It was a tricky and dangerous swim. They found Gage wedged in the shower room, a few feet from the porthole Solanick had escaped out of.

He was wearing gym trunks and a T-shirt. They wrapped him in a sheet off one of the beds, edged him back along the corridor, and then up toward the dive ladder.

It had taken about thirty minutes to extricate the bodies. This soothed Kincaid's conscience. We never could have helped them last night, he told himself. I was right not to try. It would have been suicide to try.

Still, he wished he had tried.

With the shrouded bodies at the stern, Kincaid dove again on the *Northwind*. So did certain of the others. Kincaid's camera gear, with the exception of instruments designed to operate underwater, was no doubt ruined, but he salvaged it all. A good deal of diving equipment was salvaged also, including the two new tanks in Dirk's room. They had not been used.

During the more than two hours that the survivors had drifted with the currents, twelve-year-old Keith Curry had borne up well. He had never whimpered. He pretended to be cheerful. But as his sister's body was lifted aboard, the child had started to cry, and he went up to the bow of the boat and sat there by himself weeping. After a moment Jim Solanick sat down beside him, put his arm around him, and held the little boy close.

Later Solanick sat beside the body of Rick Gage. He put his hand on Rick's shoulder thinking, He was my little brother. He was teaching me his essence, his love of all living things. My little brother is dead.

It was a long silent ride back to Key West.

At the pier a crowd was waiting: the sheriff's men, ambulances, the medical examiner, reporters, and Mel and Dolores Fisher. The distraught Fisher said, "It's a powerful ocean. It takes people and ships."

But the next day Fisher sent another boat out to the wreck site, and when asked why, he replied, "Dirk would have wanted us to go on."

A double funeral was held at Vero Beach where Dirk and Angel had grown up. The coffins and most of the mourners reached there on a DC–3 that Fisher chartered from Air Sunshine Airlines. Dirk was buried in the flaming Hawaiian shirt, and Angel in the two piece white sarong in which they had been married less than two years before, and twelve of their shipmates, also wearing the flaming Hawaiian shirts of the wedding, bore the coffins to the graves in the junglelike cemetery that lay between Indian River and the Atlantic Ocean. While Fisher wiped his eyes and Deo sobbed, the Reverend Arville Remer, the same minister who had performed Dirk and Angel's marriage ceremony, read the burial service over them. "On the sea they met," he said. "On the bosom of the sea they married. It was the sea that covered them with the blanket of death, but their love story is still going on."

Rick Gage's father had come down from Jamestown, New York, to claim his son's body. With Solanick, he went through Rick's things in the room that Solanick and Rick had rented together, but never lived in.

"Listen," Mr. Gage said. "If you want to come up to Rick's funeral, I'll fly you up. I really would like to have you there."

Rick's funeral took place the same day as Dirk and Angel's and among the divers only Solanick was in attendance. Solanick had never seen so many flowers, or such quiet grief. It was the first time he ever realized how much a son could mean to his parents, he said.

In the aftermath of the tragedy Donny Jonas suffered from nightmares. Repeatedly he dreamed that he was trapped in the dark in water up to his neck. Night after night the air pocket got smaller and smaller and smaller and he woke up stiffling, soaked in sweat.

Demostines Molinar found that he was unable to talk of recovering the bodies at all. Reporters would question him, and he would answer with his usual charm, but at a certain point in the narrative his face would stiffen, his voice would choke up, and he would break off the interview and bolt from the room.

Kim Fisher, nineteen, decided abruptly to go to college, and he chose one in Michigan, far from the sea; presently he was gone, together with his young wife Jo, and to either side of Papa Bear's shabby houseboat, the two smaller houseboats now rode empty.

And Fisher, as if to protect himself from any further temptation, ordered the *Southwind*'s deflector dismantled and removed. The sole surviving Mississippi tugboat would never again go to sea as a diving vessel.

25

Aftermath

Then, for more than a month, the sea was empty over the *Atocha*'s grave except for the scattered pencil buoys bobbing mindlessly in the swells. The remaining seven cannons still lay on the bottom. Fisher no longer wanted to bring them up. He wanted to leave them there as a memorial to his slain son.

Bob Moran remonstrated with him, "That's foolish, Mel. Someone will only go out and steal them."

Fisher's eyes blinked behind his glasses, and he nodded soberly. After a while he said he'd have a bronze plaque made. He would bring a preacher out, and they would have a memorial service at sea. Then Fisher and Deo would swim down and plant the plaque on the ocean floor at the spot where Dirk had spied the first of the cannons. This plaque would memorialize Dirk forever. Until the plaque was ready, Fisher did not want the cannons raised.

Moran took over the running of the company. Fisher seemed unable to focus his mind on it. Their desks stood side by side in the sterncastle of the pirate galleon. It was a low-ceilinged, windowless little room with a canted floor. The chairs slanted downhill; the desks were level only because their front legs rested on blocks. The air conditioning was out, and only the bilge pumps hummed. Fisher looked the same; he sat naked to the waist, the sweat running down his breastbone under the gold doubloon.

But it was Moran who answered the phones, Moran who made the decisions.

"Isn't that right, Mel?"

"Did you say something, Bob?"

Reporters came, drawn by the tragedy, and when they asked about treasure, Fisher's answers were sometimes too effusive. "Next week we may cut into ten or twenty or fifty million dollars," he told one reporter cheerfully, "and I don't know what we're going to do with all the stuff when we bring it up. All our banks are full." Clearly he enjoyed talking of banks overflowing with fresh treasure. But also the reporter thought, it was as if he imagined that Dirk could hear him, as if with talk of so many millions, he could bribe Dirk's shade to leave him in peace.

Fisher's thought had drifted off on a tangent. "It really gripes me," he said pleasantly, "all our beautiful and fascinating things locked up in banks. I'd like to put it all on display in a glass vault in the middle of a parking lot some place so that people could drive up at any time of the day or night and admire it."

The idea pleased him, and he pursued it. The vault would be bulletproof and bombproof of course, he said. And it would be floodlit at night so that people who couldn't sleep could see inside it.

"A vault like that would be a real challenge to a super thief though. I guess we'd have to have about six different security systems to outwit the super thief."

Super thieves would come from all over, he seemed to think, drawn to his mythical vault not so much because of the value of the treasure inside, as by the wonder of it and by the fame of Fisher himself. The thieves would be giants in their field, as he was in his, and would want to match his achievements with one of their own.

Fisher had been the most pragmatic of men; now his ideas were often as fanciful as this one, which, as if loathe to return to reality, he followed to the end. "Whatever security measures we might devise, the super thief would figure out a way to get around them. We'd have to learn to stay a step ahead of the super thief." And he nodded sagaciously several times.

As a husband Fisher seemed still able to function—when Dolores was nearby his eyes narrowed, and he watched her carefully. It was clear to everyone that she was on the edge, likely to begin shrieking or weeping on any provocation, or none. Deo herself seemed able to sense an outburst coming.

Sometimes, apparently trying to forestall her own hysteria, Dolores would cry sharply, "Mel!"

Fisher would step to her side, perhaps draw her off into a corner. Sometimes she clung to him. Always he talked softly to her until, temporarily, she was calm again. Other times he did not get there soon enough and, aboard the pirate galleon, or in the Chart Room bar where the treasure salvors gathered each evening, there was a scene. She was drinking too much. So was Fisher. So were all of them.

The courage that had carried Deo this far was, for the moment, gone.

She was only thirty-nine. As a girl she had been a beauty, but she seemed to have aged ten years in the last few days. She had always been conscious of her appearance. Although she owned very few clothes—for years a new dress had been for Deo an event—still she had always been careful to make up her face and to groom her thick lustrous red hair. Now in her grief she was less careful, sometimes looked dowdy, and she cried so much that her face was often streaked with eye makeup. Fisher arranged for her to spend much time in the company of Angel's mother, an older woman, and an exceptionally calm one, and this helped somewhat, but more than a month would pass before Deo was herself again.

In the meantime Fisher couldn't leave her, though he had to, and at length did.

If the search for the *Atocha* was to continue he desperately needed an influx of capital. He had paid out too many bonuses, had chartered an airliner, and had paid funeral expenses. He was broke. So he went north to try to coax more money out of more investors, or perhaps the same ones.

He showed his coins and bars. He tweeted on his new

bosun's whistle. He was still trying to sell "points." A point cost $50,000. But he would take whatever he could get. One investor that month bought in for $2,400, the price of the new sub-bottom profiler that the next stage of the search required.

But bad luck haunted him. Less than three weeks after Dirk's death, Fisher was mugged in the street outside the Tallyho Hotel in Willmington, Delaware, at three o'clock in the morning. He was a big man, but fifty-two. The muggers were younger, and there were three of them. Fisher had gone to meet with Mel Joseph and other possible investors in an attempt to raise immediate money. The muggers beat him severely, threw him to the ground and ran off with his watch and $600 in cash. Among Fisher's injuries was a six-inch gash down one shin which, perhaps because of his emotional state during that period, did not heal for weeks. When he had returned to Key West it showed beneath his Bermuda shorts and drew questions. These Fisher answered cheerfully. The muggers had bungled the job, he would say, giving a pleased laugh. The doubloon around his neck was worth about $8,000 but they had missed it.

"I guess they thought it was a religious medal," Fisher added with amusement. "They didn't want it." If the Delaware street muggers had recognized Fisher's doubloon as a religious medal, they were not alone. Its significance to Fisher seemed entirely that. It had no other.

It was six weeks after Dirk's death before enough money had come in for serious diving to resume. Fisher sent the *Virgalona* and two speedboats to sea, and he rode one of the speedboats out himself, bringing along his new gold dectector. All day he supervised this instrument as it was moved about the bottom by a diver, and buoys got thrown overboard where Fisher decided. All day the other divers and vessels waited. "Mel doesn't get out here very often," Don Kincaid said, "so when he does, we humor him. We let him throw buoys in wherever he feels like it." But Kincaid, standing inactive on the *Virgalona*'s tossing deck, fretted all day, and so did the others. The payroll for the day would come to about $500, and Fisher was wasting it.

At last Fisher fixed on one particular spot. That was the

hot spot, he shouted across to the other boats. If the divers dug there tomorrow, they would find gold.

The Fisher Factor had worked before, and would again.

Fisher seemed happy. He went back to Key West in his speedboat to await the good news.

While waiting, he went out and contracted to buy four and a half acres of Key West waterfront property at a price of $275,000. He had beaten the price down from $350,000, he bragged. Now he would be able to consolidate all his boats and gear, his offices, his machine shop, his preservation laboratory—everything. Perhaps he was thinking of his transparent glass vault as well. Where he would get the money for the down payment no one knew. Fisher himself seemed confident. He had always been able to raise money in the past. What was another $275,000?

The divers, when they began excavating Fisher's hot spot found no gold, no solid metal at all. What had Fisher's instrument detected then? Traces of iron, apparently. Iron that may have come from the *Atocha*; or that may have been an old fish trap—there was no way of telling. Iron so rusted away that it had spread through the sands leaving behind only a vast stain. Well, it wasn't the first time this had happened.

November came, a kind of anniversary. Fisher had now been looking for the *Atocha* eleven years. "I never dreamed it would be this hard to find," he said.

26

The Deep-Water Hypothesis

The search now moved into deep water between the reef and the cannons, because Fisher's advisors said that was where the *Atocha's* carcass surely lay. The move was against Fisher's better judgment. He had no faith in the deep water. He had never yet dug there.

Instead Fisher's instinct told him that there must be other treasure and certainly other cannons close to the ones Dirk had found. But the scholars and scientists he had hired were not interested in the area around Dirk's cannons, and they had reasons.

All treasure and artifacts salvaged so far had been found inside the straight corridor between the patch reef that had staved in the *Atocha's* hull, and the galleon's anchor.

From reef to anchor the corridor measured about 1,100 yards, and it was defined by buoys floating about 100 yards apart. The so-called Bank of Spain, which had held the richest concentration of treasure so far, lay about 350 yards from the galleon anchor, about 750 yards from the reef. The cannons were about midway between the Bank of

Spain and the reef along the same line. Between Dirk's cannons and the reef the water was deep—fifty feet or so everywhere.

The scholars and scientists were telling Fisher that if he searched in the fifty-foot water he would find what he called the mother lode—what they always referred to as the primary cultural deposit. Fisher had no faith in their theories. Fisher did not want to do it, but at last decided to let them have their try.

The deep-water hypothesis was chiefly the work of Duncan Mathewson, the thirty-eight-year-old marine archeologist. Mathewson, who did not yet have a Ph.D. degree, had done his undergraduate work at Dartmouth, and postgraduate work at the universities of London, Edinburgh, and Florida Atlantic. He had previously worked six years as director of archeological excavations for the University of Ghana; and he had worked on the sunken city of Port Royal as archeologist and director of excavations for the Institute of Jamaica.

Though he had not dived until he came to work for Fisher, he had since spent a great deal of time on the bottom, where he had tried—sometimes with success—to make Fisher's operation conform to archeological method. In any case, he was the only one of the *Atocha* scholars and scientists with firsthand experience beneath the waves.

Having collected and collated data for almost two years, Mathewson now concluded that everything Fisher had salvaged so far represented what archeologists call a secondary scatter pattern. It did not represent the whole ship. Nor did it represent the spot where the *Atocha* sank. That spot was somewhere else. Mathewson's reasons were these:

1. The *Atocha*'s ballast stones, totaling about two hundred tons, had ranged from fist size to about one hundred pounds. So far Fisher's divers had found about eighty tons of stones, Mathewson guessed. The stones had not been brought up. The biggest weighed about eighty-five pounds. But if the main body of the *Atocha* had sunk here, there should have been more ballast, and especially more big ballast.

2. The divers had not recovered any real ceramics. They

had found only fifteen olive jar fragments—other wrecks, Mathewson knew, had produced upwards of a thousand.

3. The divers had found no ship's rigging, no completely articulated hull structure.

Mathewson did not mean to denigrate the *Atocha* as an archeological achievement. More artifacts had been recovered than from any other wreck in Florida's waters, and to Mathewson the *Atocha* already constituted one of the most important artifact assemblages in the world. But so far the wreck site had not produced either the types or numbers of artifacts that one would expect if dealing with the remains of a complete vessel. It was clear to Mathewson that there had been impact along the corridor between the reef and the galleon anchor. That accounted for a part of the vessel, but not the complete vessel. The Bank of Spain seemed the center of this impact, and as one moved away from it, either in toward the cannons or out toward the anchor, the material recovered became thinner and thinner, more and more scattered.

In addition to his own data, Mathewson was studying Commander Cryer's data. The U.S. Navy meteorologist, working principally with details Lyon had amassed, had recreated the 1622 storm and had plotted its devastating course.

Cryer had had to start by assuming that certain factors had remained stable during the past 350 years—that the Gulf Stream had run in the same place then and at the same speed, that local tides and currents had not changed significantly. Then, working from Cadereita's report to the king, Cryer was able to fix many ships into specific positions in the line that left Havana at dawn on September 4, and to judge how much distance they had covered before the storm struck. Lyon's research also told Cryer which ships had returned to Havana and in what condition, and by determining where these ships had been placed in the line, Cryer was able to measure the size of the eye of the storm. He was working with a great many clues, some of which were quite specific. For instance Admiral Larraspuru's galleon, the *San Juan Baptista*, had been at the head of the column, and it returned to Havana with all its masts and rigging more or less intact. Whereas the *Atocha* and the *Margarita*, both at the tail of the column, had gone to the bottom. The eye of the storm therefore could not have been very large.

Cryer came to the conclusion that the storm had not been tremendously powerful. It may have been barely of hurricane intensity, or not even of hurricane intensity—something, say, in the order of sixty-five to seventy-five knot winds. It had been, in any case, strong enough.

Lyon had found a document describing how ships en route to Havana had hit bad weather north of Santo Domingo. It was this document that enabled Cryer to guess that the storm had come down north of Haiti, north of Puerto Rico, and along the north coast of Cuba, and it seemed to him to resemble the 1926 Miami hurricane, and the 1935 Florida Keys hurricane, both before his time, but well documented.

And so Cryer prepared for Fisher a report such as Cardereita might have written 350 years before.

The flagship, showing the signal to reduce sail, was sailing southeast from a position close to the keys, trying to get back into deeper water. Then the whole formation broke up. One group of ships went scuttling to the west with a northeast wind behind it, and this group was fantastically lucky, for every ship in it, though battered, remained afloat. The *Atocha* group continued on the southeast course, trying to sail across the storm to gain the deeper water. The lead ship on this tack, Larraspuru's, made it all the way across the storm and out the other side. Other ships in the group, the *Atocha* and the *Margarita* among them, did not make it across. The eye of the hurricane passed directly over them, and when, after the lull, the wind suddenly struck them from the exact opposite direction, it pushed these ships north onto the reefs and keys.

By working out the average speed and leeway of the entire fleet on the known courses, and allowing for the set and drift of today's Gulf Stream, Cryer was able to plot the progress of the *Atocha* as the oncoming hurricane carried it to destruction. As he worked, Cryer had no accurate knowledge of the latitude and longitude of Fisher's wreck site. Nonetheless, his own computations led him to place the *Atocha* only about one mile west of the galleon anchor Fisher had found. It had struck the reef, he guessed, stern first.

Cryer's single most valuable contribution was perhaps only now coming into play. According to Cryer, the *Atocha* had approached the wreck site from the south and on this tremendous detail Mathewson was basing his current hypothesis as to where the mother lode lay.

Mathewson built his hypothesis this way: (1) Directional approach from the south; (2) Point of impact on the reef; (3) Immediate sinking in the fifty-foot deep water just beyond the reef itself, well in front of the Bank of Spain; (4) Breakup and secondary dispersal on the edge of this vast underwater sand dune; and (5) Further spread toward the northwest.

A month later had followed the second hurricane, and this one had been, possibly, even wilder than the first. Unfortunately, it sank no capital ships, and therefore left behind it almost no recorded data. There was no way today for Cryer or anyone to determine where it came from, or where it went, or what it might have done to the sunken *Atocha*. Since the galleon was apparently standing upright on the bottom on its keel, the top of the sterncastle must have lain only fifteen or so feet underwater. In any case, when Vargas came back to that spot, the *Atocha's* mizzenmast was gone, and the surface of the sea was smooth once again.

It was the second storm that, three and a half centuries later, was so perplexing to everyone. Where had it left the *Atocha's* treasure? One could only guess.

Mathewson was guessing that the treasure had not budged at all, that it was still close to the reef in deep water. Deep water was the place to look.

And so the work began. There were innumerable delays.

The *Virgalona* reached the wreck site only to find that it had sailed with the wrong diameter coupling for a vital water hose. It radioed the base for the correct size, and a new coupling was sent out by speedboat. The speedboat belonged to a free lance named Spider Snyder, who had hired out to Fisher for the day. The boat's name was *JFL* which, Snyder reported proudly, stood for Just Fucking Lovely. The *JFL* was not new either, and during the ride out Snyder had trouble with his throttles, trouble shifting his engines into reverse, and trouble with his engines over-heating. Finally they seized, and stopped. While the *JFL* wallowed and pitched in three-foot seas that were rapidly increasing in size and violence, Snyder waited for his engines to cool down. During the next hour he tried repeatedly to restart. Finally he decided to change the starter motor—fortunately he had a spare with him—and this he accomplished during an additional hour, working with wrenches under the floorboards while the *JFL* bounced crazily in worsening seas.

But now his batteries were dead. All this time the *Virgalona*, lacking the proper coupling, was inactive. Snyder radioed across to it for help. He needed a battery and some jumper cable. The decision was made to send John Brandon across the five or six miles of intervening ocean in the tiny whaler, even though Snyder's boat was not visible from the *Virgalona*. Snyder was to wait twenty minutes, then fire a flare. This would give Brandon, low in the water in the whaler a fix on Snyder's position.

The seas were running six feet high now, and the crossing by Brandon consumed another hour or more. But his outboard motor did not fail, he did not lose his bearings, he arrived safely, and the JFL was at last restarted.

By the time it reached the *Virgalona*, it was too late and too rough to dive, and in any case, the coupling, which Snyder had come all that way with, did not fit the pump either.

Possibly in revenge, Snyder was handed a fresh battery and the job of installing this battery and a flashing light in Fisher's latest theodolite tower two miles away. Crashing from wave top to wave top, the *JFL* reached the tower without difficulty, but then Snyder faced the job of transferring the strobe light, which weighed nothing, and the automobile battery, which weighed plenty, from speed-boat to tower.

This tower, like most of the others, had been made by welding pieces of angle-iron junk together. It stood on a sand bar into which it had been sinking for months, and the platform rose only about six feet out of the water. During those same months the tower had remained unlighted, another navigation hazard of course. But Fisher had always meant to rectify this before the Coast Guard found out, and was doing so today.

The tower was rusty and sharp-edged, the seas were crashing over it, and Snyder, as he approached, could not count on his throttle—he might or might not be able to throw the boat into reverse.

The tower's platform was also a bird roost of course, and was as slippery as wet chalk. The cowling of the *JFL*, being plastic or fiberglass, was slippery too, but on it crouched Snyder's passengers, a diver and a reporter, the battery in a sling between them. As Snyder nosed close to the tower the diver made a lunge for it, and as the waves splashed over him, he hauled himself on to the platform. The *JFL*, having successfully backed off, now made a second approach, pitching and diving in the tumultuous seas, while the reporter, with his footing slippery and nothing to hold on to, tried to extend the car battery at arm's length to the diver. As he managed to hand the battery across, Snyder, for the second time, successfully jammed his engines into reverse.

A third approach was made to take the diver off the tower. But the diver's shoes had become slick from seas and bird excrement, and what all had feared now occurred. The diver lost his footing, slid down the rusty tower and clung there waiting to be crushed by the oncoming *JFL*. Snyder banged the lever hard toward reverse. Again the lever slid home. Snyder's props bit, and the tragedy was averted. A fourth pass was made, and the diver leaped off.

It was not a day to be reported in the newspapers. The *Virgalona* reached the Marquesas, safely. The *JFL* reached Key West, safely. Nothing had occurred all day to merit a headline. No gold or silver had been found, or even looked for. No diver had died, or even been hurt. Fisher had spent a lot of money and used up a lot of luck, perhaps. That was all—an ordinary day in the search for the treasure of the *Atocha*. There had been hundreds like it.

Fisher's only diving vessel was now the *Virgalona*. Although the exmackerel boat was equipped with mailboxes, its engines were not powerful enough to dig in water fifty feet deep, especially since the composition of the ocean floor had changed too. The sub-bottom was now soft mud, but there was a solid crust on top, and this crust proved impervious to any mailbox blast from the *Virgalona*.

So Fisher devised a new technique. He equipped the *Virgalona* with a water pump that operated a fire hose under tremendous pressure. Divers on the bottom could ram the fire nozzle through the mud crust, and the powerful jet of water, expanding underneath, would break the crust up. Used in conjunction with the mailboxes, this method worked well enough for a time. Chunks of mud would break loose, and the mailboxes would blow them away. But it was slow and also dangerous work. Because the fire hose became stiff as a flagpole, its nozzle had to be heavily weighted if the boys were to have any chance of holding it pointed straight down. In addition, since they were now standing on the bottom instead of hovering above it, they found that it was impossible to work in swim fins. They began to go down wearing rubber socks instead, surrendering almost all mobility. One day, when Tim March ran out of air on the bottom, they learned how dangerous lack of mobility could be. March was not at first alarmed. This had happened plenty of times in the past. He merely let go of the hose and tried to kick himself to the surface. But he was deeper than ever before, his feet were mired in mud, and he wore no fins. He did wear weights, and a heavy tank, and although he swam mightily, he saw he was not going to reach the surface in time. So he began trying to shed his lead belt, and his tank. But his fingers failed to work properly. The lead belt fell, but it is almost impossible for a diver to shuck a tank unaided at the bottom of the sea, particularly in a state of panic. March ran out of breath. He was drowning. But other divers grabbed him, gave him air, swam him to the surface, and so saved his life.

The bad weather of autumn had settled in over the keys. The *Virgalona* alternately plummeted and soared as it rode the tumultuous seas. If it rose too high, its anchor lines jerked it back down with a smack. Its mailboxes caught the sea full in their open mouths, they were pounded and finally broken by the perpetual surge, and each time the *Virgalona* had to sail to Key West for repairs two working days would be lost in transit.

The weeks passed, and nothing was found.

At last the *Arbutus,* a steel-hulled, 187-foot, former Coast Guard buoy tender, was ready to be towed to the wreck site. Fisher had bought the engineless derelict for $17,000 at auction and had made elaborate plans to turn it into the definitive salvage vessel, a bigger and better version of Cousteau's *Calypso.* He would paint her up, put engines back in and . . .

In Key West Fisher had assigned half his crew to refit her, but there wasn't enough money for paint or engines. Sometimes there wasn't any money at all, and Fisher ordered all her portholes unscrewed and sold as brass. Squares of plywood were bolted over the absent portholes so that rainstorms and high seas could not get in. Of course light and air could not get in either. Nor, in case of emergency, could anybody very easily get out.

On an exceptionally calm autumn day the *Arbutus* was towed to the wreck site. On its front deck it bore an enormous air compressor of the type that usually powered jackhammers in the street. In the engine room in place of the vessel's nonexistent engines, an electric generating plant had been installed. Because this generator filled portions of the ship with foul fumes, and because it made a harsh groaning noise, it was always shut down at night at which time dim battery-powered lights came on. These lights and most others hung inside lampshades that had formerly been coffee cans.

There were no tide tables aboard. Nor was there any compass. The type compass that would give accurate readings amidst all that steel would have been expensive.

The *Arbutus'* rudder was fixed in a hard-to-starboard position and bolted there, lest it start flapping in rough seas and tear the stern to pieces. Of course that made it almost impossible to tow the ship in a straight line.

The *Arbutus* had only one working toilet, beside which stood a bucket on a rope. The bucket, replenished over the side, was what flushed this toilet, meaning that the floor around the toilet was perpetually awash.

On the other hand, the *Arbutus* had been constructed, as were most buoy tenders, to provide maximum stability. A kind of great iron flange surrounded its hull, and this tended to smother all but the roughest seas.

It had also been furnished with a number of second-hand refrigerators, freezers, and stoves, and with a revolving television antenna that brought in color pictures—though weak ones—from Miami and Tampa. The color TV stood on a shelf in the former wardroom, which was also furnished with plenty of crotch books, a dart game, and some ruined leather sofas.

There were more than enough cabins to go around, and some divers had even decorated them. Bouncy John, the former art student, had turned his walls into futuristic paintings. The pipe frame bunks were fitted with former doors instead of inner springs. On top of the doors lay foam-rubber mattresses, and the sheets and pillows were as filthy as always.

Most of the door handles had been sold for brass at the same time as the portholes, and loops of rope hung out of the holes in their place.

Now at last watches were kept every night, two hours per diver, and each was supposed to tour the ship, checking all bilges, every twenty minutes. Each diver was also supposed to sleep with a working flashlight beside his pillow. There even was an occasional bilge alarm drill, though the first of them was not very encouraging.

At three-thirty in the morning the captain, who was Hugh Spinney that week, sounded the engine-room siren. Spinney later noted in the *Arbutus'* log the results of this drill.

> Don Jonas, first one to the engine room. Pants in hand. Dropped his life jacket on the way. Flashlight didn't work.
>
> Dave Hargreaves, second one to engine room. Pants on, no life jacket, no flashlight.
>
> Pat Clyne, third one to engine room. Pants on, no life jacket, no flashlight.
>
> Steve Middleton, fourth one to engine room. Pants on, no life jacket, no flashlight.
>
> Steve Wickens checked all aft quarters to see that everyone was up. No life jacket, flashlight didn't work.
>
> Charlie Clyne went straight to the forward hold. Life jacket on, flashlight working.
>
> Bleth McHaley (who was on board that week as

cook) slept right through everything. Didn't hear alarms. No one woke her where she was sleeping in the forward cabin.

Recommend we take steps to see this type of unorganized drill does not happen again.

The *Arbutus* had probably been built before World War II. It had not been painted in decades. The hull had once been black. Most of the rest of it had once been painted alternately salmon and white. It needed to be chipped and painted in the most desperate way, but of course Fisher had no money for that. The *Arbutus* was incredibly rusty.

One of the things Mathewson had learned, he once noted, was that treasure hunters had difficulty developing any sort of logical reasoning. Fisher believed in hunches, not evidence. He didn't want to search close to the reef, he would have preferred to go on bombarding the ocean floor close to the cannons, some three hundred yards away.

But with the *Arbutus* immovably anchored in the deep-water area, Fisher was committed to Mathewson's hypothesis, at least for a time. The archeologist swam down to the bottom and placed cinder blocks there, delimiting an area that measured about nine hundred feet by six hundred feet, and further sectioning this area into a grid, each square measuring about a hundred feet square. A chart was then hung on the wall of the pirate galleon, and each square as it was probed would be crossed off. But there were more than fifty squares, and it was going to take time.

The *Arbutus* had no mailboxes. Its principal diving tools, were a number of eight-inch airlifts and one set of two such airlifts mounted in tandem. These things could dig narrow deep holes rather quickly, but they did not expose very much bedrock at one time, hardly enough to stand up on. They were not going to lay bare the bones of the *Atocha* all in one day, if ever.

And so the divers began crisscrossing each square of Mathewson's grid, boring new holes every twelve feet. This made for about twenty holes per square, and in the rough seas of late autumn and early winter divers were lucky to drill four or five a day. For one thing the water was now so deep that only two dives a day per man were permitted, a total of only 130 minutes. Otherwise long decompression periods underwater would have been necessary, and if someone got the bends, there was no emergency decompression chamber aboard.

At first the divers drilled holes to bedrock. Then Mathewson took core samples and had them tested by a marine sedimentologist. It was this expert's opinion that the mud there had been forming, much like mud in the Florida Bay area, at a rate of only about one millimeter per year. In 350 years, this added up to thirty-five centimeters of mud, about a foot and a half. About eighteen inches down, Mathewson told the divers, they could expect to find the top of the *Atocha's* ballast pile. Henceforth they should dig no deeper than five feet. The upper five feet of mud would contain all they were looking for. The job was predictable now, Mathewson said. The days of digging like hell on big hits—which usually turned out to be fish traps or some such thing—were over. He had systematized the work of Fisher's divers, and even Fisher himself seemed to be impressed. They would have the *Atocha's* treasure by spring, Mathewson promised.

With that Fisher became cheerful, and started an office lottery. He began to sell the squares on the chart beside his desk. Which square would the treasure be found in? He sold squares to Bleth McHaley, to Bob Moran, to Don Kincaid, to Lyon, to Mathewson, to various divers, and he also bought one himself. The price was one week's pay, and although one week's pay on Fisher's payroll was not necessarily very much—Moran as vice-president was earning only $10,000 a year plus stock—still, to these people, it represented a good deal of money.

The digging was arduous and slow. It was like boring holes through a tree.

Inevitably efforts were made to shorten the job.

A new gold detector was brought out and tried. Very strong readings were recorded, and the next day Don Kincaid and Bob Moran took the detector to the bottom to confirm them. To their great excitement the readings persisted in four directional passes. The area covered measured about a hundred feet square, and it pegged the meter throughout. Had the *Atocha's* bullion at last been pin-pointed? Moran, who was captain that week, expected to know within minutes. However, before divers could be put in the water, the *Arbutus'* air compressor broke down. Hurriedly the compressor was dismantled. While this was being done, Moran ordered bow and stern anchors raised, and he drifted the *Arbutus* backwards on the current until she was positioned directly over the hot readings.

The next morning a spare compressor was jury-rigged to a bilge pump motor, but this proved too weak to work an eight-inch airlight. So on the third day, with no ability to dig at all, Moran ordered a visual search of the bottom, and for hours divers clung to an underwater sled—it was a plywood board with handholds—and were towed by the whaler back and forth across the bottom of the sea. Visibility was about four feet. They saw no more cannons, or any other treasure either.

It was not until a mechanic was sent out from Key West by speedboat that the air compressor was made to work again, after which it was possible at last to dig on the peg readings. Surely these would prove to be bullion, and while divers dug down into the bottom, everyone topside hung over the railing to await the thrilling report.

But the reading wasn't bullion at all. It was beer cans. The "gold" detector had proven as indiscriminate as that other great prostitute, the sea itself. It would swallow anything fed to it. Hundreds of beer cans had gone over the side in this spot over the last five years. Such careless pollution of the sea had not seemed costly then, but Fisher and his divers were paying for it now. Beer cans had rendered the gold detector useless.

Back to crisscrossing squares in the grid. One by one the corresponding square on Fisher's chart was crossed off and somebody said good-bye to any chance of winning the lottery. A few ballast stones were discovered in a few of the holes. Each such discovery caused a flurry of excitement—the big pile must be near. But it wasn't near. It didn't seem to be anywhere. A quarter of the squares on Fisher's chart had been marked off, and no gold or silver had come to light.

The days passed, and the weeks. The water jet broke and had to be back-flushed. The main generator blew. The water dredge jammed and had to be taken apart; a shell was found in the discharge end. A new mag survey was attempted, but the mag failed; it would not zero out. The electric water pump motor burned up due to seaweed clogging up the intake; the divers switched over to a gasoline-driven pump, and the diving continued. Another new gold detector was brought out and swum down to the bottom. But it uncovered only more beer cans.

The *Southwind* arrived with fuel and water, but broke down when it got there, its rudder arm broken. For two days divers worked to fix it, and there was no diving for treasure. The weather then blew up, and the *Southwind* was being swamped by seas that it could not position itself against. But it survived; when the weather moderated, it staggered back to Key West.

One night both of the *Arbutus'* engine room bilge pumps were found to be inoperative.

Soon half the squares were gone. Mathewson encouraged Fisher and the divers to be patient and to continue their slow methodical work. "The cannons have told us what direction they came from and where to dig for the main cultural deposit," he kept saying. "We must listen to the message the cannons are trying to give us."

Fisher was restless. He wanted to go back to the cannons or back to the underwater Bank of Spain. He was convinced that the cannons could not have floated that far away from where the *Atocha* sank.

The *Arbutus* was supposed to make radio contact with Fisher's office in the pirate galleon any time treasure was found, and a system of code words was ready in case the next report should be the mother lode itself—a treasure so fabulous that an army might be needed to defend it. The image of a bunch of boys in bathing suits standing guard over tens of millions of dollars was frightening to all. Silver bars were to be referred to as conch shells, coins as small conch shells, gold as coral, cannons as jewfish, copper as sharks. There were three separate code words for describing the wreck site itself: Reno, Diamond Head, Stingray. However, no need to use this code ever arose. A few pottery shards were found, a few encrusted objects, nothing more. These grubby trophies lay on a shelf in the captain's cabin. They looked like nothing so much as a permanent reproach.

The sea continued to delay and destroy. Each transfer of stores from the *Virgalona* to the *Arbutus* was an exploit. Fuel was shipped out in fifty-five gallon drums, and these were thrown over the *Virgalona's* side and swum to the *Arbutus'* dive ladder, after which divers attempted to fit a sling under them so they could be hoisted on board. Sometimes the sea was so rough that the divers lost control of individual barrels and ended up swimming after them hundreds of yards away from the ship.

Other times no one wanted to risk winching the barrels on board at all, and a garden hose was stretched between the *Virgalona* and the *Arbutus*; each drum was pumped out individually, while the garden hose alternately sagged into the sea or was stretched almost to the breaking point.

Fresh water reached the *Arbutus* in waterbeds, which made an enormous amorphus weight. Fisher liked waterbeds. He and Deo slept on one. But there was no convenient way to lift the waterbed from one vessel to the other, and usually the same garden hose, having been flushed out with sea water and attached to a different pump, siphoned the fresh water up into the *Arbutus'* tanks. However, after that the water no longer tasted quite so sweet. A better container than waterbeds might have been devised for transporting fresh water, but what? Eventually the fresh water tanks aboard the *Arbutus* went rusty anyway, and from then on were used only to provide showers. Drinking water began to arrive in plastic milk bottles, one gallon at a time.

Christmas neared. A Christmas tree was brought out; it was set up on a hatch cover on the topmost deck with a coffee can for a stand and ropes holding it upright against the worsening winds.

27

Winter Dreams

To Key West the Christmas season brought a thirty-year-old West German. He did not speak English. He had a dictionary, but did not seem to know how to work it. Fisher understood that the German's father was rich and owned a factory; the young man might want to buy an investment contract in the *Atocha*.

Deciding that the best sales talk was a visit to the *Arbutus*, Fisher sent the German out there in a twenty-one-foot speedboat despite bad weather and tremendous seas. The seas were ten feet high, with waves coming down on top of the speedboat. The buffeting was so severe that the boat's fiberglass hull split open, and by the time it reached the *Arbutus* it was sinking.

The speedboat was lashed to the *Arbutus*, and its diver and the potential investor were taken aboard. Both men were soaked and exhausted, so they were wrapped in blankets, and the German kept repeating the one English word he was sure of: "Rum."

That night the weather worsened. The *Arbutus* was anchored sideways to the wind, and given the intensity of the storm, it could not be turned. It was rolling so far in both directions that its scuppers were sometimes under water. During one roll it came down on top of the speed-boat and sank it.

The storm lasted three days. The *Arbutus* kept rolling to the scuppers. All on board wore life jackets and were at all times prepared to abandon ship.

The German wandered around hanging on to things, muttering, "Rum."

On Christmas Eve the weather eased. Fisher was able to send a boat out for the seasick German. The potential investor did not invest. Once ashore he said *danke schön* to everybody, and hurriedly left town.

The Christmas season ended. The tree was dropped overboard, and it drifted away.

When the weather was good enough the divers continued to carve down through the mud with their airlifts, opening up—and eliminating—new squares in Duncan Mathewson's grid. But the weather was seldom good enough. The Key West area was experiencing its worst winter since 1918. During one storm the seas bent the dive ladder. Another lasted so long that the divers ran out of food, and Bouncy John and Tom Ford, wearing tanks and carrying spear guns, dove into ten-foot seas to try to shoot some fish. They found nothing, and Bouncy John, having run out of air, was forced to the surface a hundred yards from the Arbutus and down current. With a tank on his back he could never swim to the ship on the surface, and the seas were too rough to launch a whaler to pick him up. Ford, who still had air, might swim back submerged, but not Bouncy. The current was moving him farther away each second.

Ford helped Bouncy shed tank and belt, and Bouncy, swimming hard, managed to reach the lee of the *Arbustus*, where he was thrown a rope. He then swam the rope back to Ford. Both were rescued. They did not even lose a tank.

Still another storm arose. The *Arbustus* was again smashed by tremendous seas. Rain and waves beat against the plywood portholes. Dragging its enormous anchors, the *Arbustus* was driven hundreds of yards away from the grid area. Obviously it could not be moved back under its own power—it had no power. One could only wait—and this might take days, or even weeks—for winds and currents to shift into the opposite direction, at which point one could lift anchors, and the *Arbutus* might drift back to the desired spot. Or Fisher could send the *Southwind* to sea to take the *Arbutus* under tow. But Fisher was afraid to send the *Southwind* to sea ever again.

Or Fisher could hire somebody else's vessel to do the towing; however, Fisher had no money.

Fisher took this as a sign from the gods: the deep-water area must be empty. He wasn't meant to search there, and the reason must be the *Atocha* was somewhere else.

Though it had not been entirely searched, the deep-water area was abandoned.

The *Virgalona* went out with stores and a change of crew. Two crews had been alternating aboard the *Arbutus*, one commanded by Hugh Spinney, the other by Bob Moran. The seas were still high. Only a portion of the stores could be transferred at all, and the difficulty of transferring people was extreme. The *Virgalona* could not approach close enough. The arriving crew had to strip naked and swim over, gauging the waves carefully so as not to be dashed against the dive ladder. Their clothes, rolled into balls and stuffed into a box, followed them over on a jury-rigged breach's buoy.

Aboard the *Arbutus* the divers waited for the few good days. Bouncy John wove mats out of disused rope. Bob Moran rigged beer cans or clothesline, hoping this would keep the sea gulls off. When it did not, he got out his stainless steel Smith and Wesson .38, and began shooting at them.

One fine day the *Virgalona* magged still again, trying to find some anomalies half a mile to the west that Don Kincaid remembered from some years before. These big hits had never been checked out; there had been so many hits in the area that it had always been impossible to check them all. Kincaid now was searching well outside the corridor buoys, but the hits he was looking for suddenly registered on the mag, and he began to make repeated passes, defining the area closely. The depth, as measured on the *Virgalona*'s fathometer, was fifty feet—and as he noted this Kincaid began to believe in the readings he was getting. Did not the depth accord with Gaspar de Vargas's measurements?

Furthermore, as Kincaid continued to define the hot
area, he discovered that it measured about a hundred feet
in length, the *Atocha's* exact length—a hundred feet of
dense hits, with lesser hits extending outwards from either
end so that the whole area was three hundred feet long.
Kincaid was elated; so was Molinar, who was again driving the *Virgalona*, and their enthusiasm convinced Moran.
These people were like alcoholics. A single sip of hope
and they would go on a bender.

When the next day dawned flat calm, an extremely
rare condition in winter, Moran ordered the *Arbutus'* anchors hauled up—they weighed up to five tons, and it was
no easy thing to lift them—and the *Virgalona* began trying
to tow the *Arbutus* over the new site. But the tide was
wrong, and the *Arbutus* rudder was still warped hard
right. Although the little *Virgalona* tugged mightily in one
direction, the *Arbutus* continued to turn in another. Presently the *Virgalona* came around to the *Arbutus'* stern, and
a new tow was attached. In this ignominious fashion—stern
first—the *Arbutus* approached what was perhaps the final
resting place of *Nuestra Señora de Atocha*. The tow job
took all of this beautifully calm day; the only calm day,
most likely, for months. The day had been used up moving,
not diving. It was gone.

Fisher himself had come out in a speedboat, and he
stood with Moran on the bridge through the lunch hour.
But it was clear that he had no faith in this new site. "It's
probably another bomb," he said.

In a short while he signaled his speedboat to approach,
handed the mag gear down into it, and jumped down himself. All the rest of the day he could be seen off in the
distance, magging back and forth near the buoy that
floated over the cannons. From time to time Moran
watched him. To Moran there was something forlorn
about the distant figure. The activity was here, not there.
A new element had been added to Fisher's search for the
Atocha, Moran thought. Fisher didn't want the galleon
found over here. He wanted it found near the cannons. He
wanted Dirk to have found the *Atocha*, the beloved son's
final triumph.

But as darkness approached, Fisher had recorded not a
single hit. The *Arbutus* was now in position. There was

still time to send a single diver down, and Tom Ford, the supposed security guard, put his gear on: full wet suit, fins, and respirator. He took the enormous airlift down to the bottom and in fifty feet of water began digging. A vast gray bubble erupted on the surface, a miniature atomic cloud.

Ford had time to dig two holes, and then it was dark. There was a hard sand crust down there, he reported when he had come up. Underneath the crust was mud. The two holes had yielded no evidence of any kind.

Everyone aboard the *Arbutus* had hoped to see him surface clutching a bar of bullion, so disappointment was already strong.

"Well," said Moran, "it's a big area. Tomorrow we'll start a systematic search."

Over the next weeks that area was thoroughly probed. Divers began to bring to the surfaces chunks of bombs. Then a car engine block was discovered, and after that a long length of iron cable.

So the *Arbutus*, one day when wind and tide were right, was drifted back to the cannons, and Fisher was happy, even if no one else was.

One day when Bouncy John was digging on the bottom he became conscious of some heavy presence in the water near him. He sensed that something or someone was close by, and his first thought was that another diver must have come down. The water was always murky here, and visibility was about four feet, as usual. Glancing around for this other diver, Bouncy made out a faint dark shape close by. It was as big as a diver, bigger probably.

That night a shark line was put out.

But when morning came, the divers found that the shark line would not haul in—the hook must have snagged on the anchor chain.

So they began to winch up the anchor.

Suddenly a twelve-foot tiger shark, hooked through the jaw and through the chain, began to rise toward the hawsehole. The winch was shut down, and they tried to decide how they were going to get the shark unhooked from the chain. They concluded that someone—but who?—would have to go into the water and attach a rope to that shark's tail.

Pat Clyne, the formerly fearless shark butcher, flatly refused.

Jim Solanick said he didn't mind. So he plunged in and did it.

The shark, hoisted tail first above the deck, began to regurgitate. Out came an incredible variety of treasure: the remains of a turtle whose shell measured four feet in length; a coil of wire; a conch shell; the four-foot torso of fellow shark, minus its head; part of a fish trap; an entire cormorant. Jokes were made: that must have been one helluva surprised sitting duck.

The shark also had bad breath. A most atrocious odor now added itself to the charms of the *Arbutus*.

With hammers and knives they boys began to attack the shark's jaws for teeth to wear around their necks. Not until the brute was nearly toothless did they worry about getting rid of the carcass. The shark weighed about 1,200 pounds. They couldn't just push it over the side, for it might attract relatives. Already much of its vomit had leaked overboard, and a surface stain was spreading outwards. There would be no diving that day, that was for sure.

The whaler was dropped into the water, with Bouncy John to drive it, and with a running start Bouncy yanked the dead shark tail first off the deck into the water, where it landed with a tremendous slap.

Tom Ford beside him was ready with a sharp knife should the shark sink, and start to pull the whaler down with it, but this did not happen. The two divers towed the shark a mile away, same as they did kitchen garbage, and cut it loose there.

Fisher could not pay his divers. He had not paid them in weeks now, and so some drifted away. Though he could not afford it, he was obliged to keep a minimum of four divers at sea even when it was too rough to dive, just to make sure the *Arbutus* did not sink. The *Arbutus'* generator broke down—now there was no television, no refrigeration, and no lights at night. The boys regularly ran out of beer, but most often Fisher was too poor to send any out. Not surprisingly, morale was extremely low.

A former lawyer of his was dunning Fisher for $87,000 in fees.

No investor would invest. The Justice Department was still claiming ownership of the *Atocha*. Invest in winter in an already speculative wreck Fisher perhaps didn't own? Not likely.

At last the ownership case came to trial. The judge ruled resoundingly in favor of Fisher, and he also awarded Fisher jurisdiction over the *Atocha*—this meant that Berrier, Webber, and other rival treasure hunters could no longer poach. If their boats came out and found treasure, this treasure belonged to Fisher. So that threat was ended; as for the government lawyers, they said they would appeal. The one thing certain for Fisher was more legal bills.

Needing cash, he sold the *Southwind*; he didn't dare send it to sea any more anyway. To replace it he needed a big new digging vessel, and his mind teemed with ideas. He would buy a disused submarine, submerge its hind end, and its props would clear vast tracts of ocean floor. It would probably turn up the treasure within a week.

Bob Moran said, "Individuals are not allowed to own submarines, Mel."

Bouncy John said, "You're not getting me down inside any submarine."

Or Fisher would acquire the *Glomar Explorer*, that notorious salvage vessel owned either by the Central Intelligence Agency or by Howard Hughes, or both, which had raised part of a Russian submarine—the sub was steel and had rung on mags—in water thousands of feet deep. Did not Congress want to scrap the *Glomar Explorer*? Perhaps the University of Florida could buy it for a dollar and then lend it to Treasure Salvors, Inc. In exchange Fisher would lend the university a treasure exhibit, and he would let their marine archeology students do field study on his wreck site. But nothing came of this plan.

At last Fisher decided to raise Dirk's seven remaining cannons using a salvage barge borrowed for the occasion. Dr. Eugene Lyon was once more driven out in a speedboat to provide positive identification.

Lyon, in a state of repressed excitement, held a copy of a document 355 years old that listed the serial numbers of the *Atocha*'s cannons. One of the first two cannons that had been raised eight months ago had matched this list. Would these?

Lyon's document was dated September 1621, which was when the *Atocha* had been armed in Spain. At that time the *Atocha* had already been designated vice-flagship of the Mainland Fleet, and so it had received a vice-flagship's complement of guns. However, much might have changed in the intervening year before it sank. For instance two fleet galleons were lost at the Sanlúcar sand bar as they left Spain; their thirty-six guns were salvaged and redistributed among the remaining ships, which took them in ballast to Havana where two new ships were waiting. But the *Atocha* might have kept some of the ballast guns or switched them with its own. Anything could have happened in a year, and the scholar had been unable to find any document dated later.

Maybe the guns beneath the barge were not the *Atocha*'s at all. What if the numbers didn't match?

It was not easy to raise those cannons, but one by one they emerged from the sea, dripping, and were laid out like dead men upon the deck. In one barrel something rattled, and when Don Kincaid with a flashlight peered inside he saw that it was cannonball. So the *Atocha* had sailed and sunk with its guns primed.

In his excitement Lyon was scampering about underneath the 3000-pound guns, trying to read their numbers while they were still in the air, and there was some danger that one would break loose and fall on him.

But he was able to read nothing in the air, and when he crouched over each barrel in turn, he saw that four of the seven were eroded smooth and bore no serial numbers, or markings or decorations of any kind.

What about the other three?

They had crests, diving dolphins for decoration, and their numbers matched numbers on the list in Lyon's hand; they were the *Atocha*'s.

28

More Silver Bars

Spring. The months became warmer, the seas calmer. Summer. Still the mother lode was not found.

Dr. Lyon was in the position of a football coach on the eve of the championship game. He had drilled his team superbly. He had diagramed all their plays. But if his team should fail to score, then he was a loser too. So he took on the added role of cheerleader. He wrote letters to everybody, seeking to encourage continuation of the work. The worst danger was the flagging of desire, the historian wrote, and he appended a description from the archives of the breakup of the vice-flagship of the 1715 fleet. That galleon, after striking a reef, had broken into several parts. The hull sunk at once; the poop and bow separated and floated toward shore. Lyon believed the same thing had happened to the *Atocha*. If anyone thought that the *Atocha's* upper works and gun deck could not have floated Dirk's nine cannons, Lyon pointed out that the deck beams and planking made a massive and heavy raft. "Best, Gene Lyon."

To most of those involved, the search for the *Atocha*

had passed far beyond greed. No one was thinking any more about becoming rich. The search had become a vast intellectual puzzle. One was obsessed not with gold but with unanswered questions. Where could the *Atocha* be? And how did it get there? Nothing added up. How could nine cannons be found, but not the other nine? How could three silver bars lie all alone in the Quicksands, when according to Lyon's research, the bars had been packed in boxes, four to a box?

During slack hours, particularly at night, everyone speculated. In the Chart Room bar at the Pier House hotel, Fisher and his office staff drank and speculated. Aboard the *Arbutus* the divers speculated. One night during his watch, Bouncy John wrote out his own two-page hypothesis. Bouncy had begun to wonder if Cadereita's report—if any of the documents—could be believed. Were not all these people, as they wrote to their king, attempting mainly to save their own skin? A man who is powerful enough—and Cadereita was very powerful—could write what he pleased. No one would dare contradict him. There was no way the king could check up. And who had verified what Vargas had seen or done out on the open sea? Some or all of the documents might merely be self-serving. Even if the documents were honest, the details could be completely wrong. As everyone knew, three survivors of the same car crash would describe it in three different ways. Why should we attribute better accuracy to the Spaniards, merely because they had committed their testimony to documents?

Everybody had his own idea of where and how to search.

Bouncy John wanted to make additional visual surveys of the bottom. He wasn't satisfied with those done so far. Don Kincaid wanted to do pinpoint magging outside the corridor. Lyon and Mathewson still believed in the deep-water hypothesis. Fisher still believed the treasure was close by the cannons, and sometimes he told of an incident that had occurred two years before.

It had been a summer day, and the *Virgalona* was bringing up so much treasure that Fisher, having rushed out in a speedboat, had put on a tank and swum down. The hole the *Virgalona* had just opened up was about twenty feet wide at the top, about eight feet at the bottom, and about ten feet deep—and bedrock was simply thick with coins.

There must be ten thousand coins here, Fisher had thought. At the edge of the hole was the fused together mass of still another chest of coins.

Fisher, dazzled by the sight, hovered, staring. Suddenly above his head the *Virgalona* engines stopped, and the walls of the crater began to cave in over the coins.

There had been a coral head in the hole as well, and Fisher had grabbed it up, and as the hole filled Fisher had kept pulling the coral head free. Finally, when the hole was completely full, he had deposited the coral head on top as a landmark, and had swum to the surface to demand why Mo had shut down the engines.

But so much treasure had been found that day that Fisher was unable to bawl out his friend. Instead he said, "There were ten thousand coins down there."

Mo laughed and pointed to the disappearing sun. "It's late, man. Those coins ain't going nowhere. They still be here tomorrow. We'll be anchored right over them."

As a precaution Fisher got a concrete block and a buoy, and he swam down and planted the block firmly beside the coral head. Tomorrow that buoy would lead him to the exact spot.

The *Virgalona* had four anchors out, but about four in the morning such a fierce storm arose that the vessel could not hold station over the treasure.

When the storm lifted and the *Virgalona* sailed back, the buoy was gone. Divers were sent down, but the coral head and the concrete block were not to be seen, and the sand was smooth for hundreds of yards in all directions.

The spot had lain only about fifty yards outside the corridor. Sometimes now Fisher would gaze off in that direction saying, "It's just over there. We've looked many times, but we've never been able to find it again."

Bedrock strewn so deep with coins that a man could shuffle them with his swim fins—perhaps it was this fabulous vision that still riveted Fisher to his search. He had seen Eldorado with his own eyes. He knew absolutely that treasure was still down there.

The divers took their faith from Fisher—their hope too, and the search continued.

Meanwhile, in the Cape Coral Bank, Fisher put on display the most beautiful of the cannons, together with a mass of other treasure and artifacts, and the public response astonished him. The lines were around the block. People waited up to ninety minutes to get in. In four days some twenty thousand people, far more than the population of that sleepy little town, filed past the Atocha's gold and silver, her ornaments, her ancient articles of war.

The awe and delight of all these people affected even Fisher, who stood beaming with pride. For the first time he ceased to fret over the 898 missing silver bars, and he saw, instead, the magnificence of that treasure which, forty miles out into the open sea, he had found and brought up from the depths again after three and a half centuries.

It wasn't all on display here of course, but the list was long: almost 7,000 hand-stuck silver coins, and dozens of gold ones; 10 gold bars and 1 six-pound gold disc; 1 golden chalice with an emerald setting; several gold rings, one a reliquary; a heavy silver pitcher; a gold and coral rosary; 3 silver ingots, each weighing approximately sixty-five pounds; some bar copper; 37 swords and daggers; 37 arquebuses and muskets; a rare, immensely valuable sixteenth-century astrolabe; 8 quartzite cannonballs and 105 of iron; a bosun's gorgeous gold whistle on a double strand gold necklace; 42 silver candlesticks; 38 gold chains of varying lengths and weight; 9 bronze cannons. It was the greatest hoard of treasure ever found in modern times.

In June the treasure was transported under guard to Washington where it went on exhibition at Explorer's Hall. As the show opened, Fisher, though as broke as always, threw a champagne reception to which he invited hundreds of people, including fifteen of his divers whom he brought up from Key West by train. The divers stood by the floodlit show cases: Bouncy John, Pat Clyne, Spencer Wickens, Jim Solanick, Tim March, Tom Ford, Joe Spangler, and all the rest, and they called out to one another and the the crowds:

"See that gold rosary? I found that gold rosary."

"That bar of gold is the one I brought up."

The show would last until September, and approximately a million people would see it: entire classes of school children would come, and busloads of tourists visiting the capital, and government workers on their lunch hours.

But that night was the divers' show, and Fisher's show. A reception line formed. The smiling Deo looked regal in a long gown, with a diver on either arm. There stood Fisher, who greeted his guests—backers, reporters, and government officials for the most part—with a kind of euphoric grin on his face.

The compliments were as banal as always at such events, but their effect on Fisher was a moving thing to watch.

"It's a beautiful exhibition, Mel."

"Thank you."

"Gorgeous, Mel."

"Thank you."

"You must be very proud, Mel."

"I am. I am."

As people filed by congratulating him, Fisher seemed to be experiencing a kind of ecstacy such as few men know.

The queen of Spain came, and after he had greeted her Fisher acted out the most grandiose gesture of the entire adventure—he asked Queen Sofia to accept on behalf of the Spanish people the most beautiful of Dirk's recovered cannons. He wanted the cannon, 354 years late, to return to Spain.

There, it was out, a gift to a nation from a man who lived in a houseboat.

There were those who watched and thought the gesture not out of keeping with the magnificence of Fisher's achievement.

Queen Sofia accepted, and once she had done so Fisher told her where he thought the richly decorated bronze cannon ought to be displayed. The queen should order it set up in the marble rotunda of the Archive of the Indies in Seville, for there it would serve as a monument to Dr. Lyon's search, as well as to his own.

The queen smiled. It was certainly the proper place for

such a beautiful cannon, she said, and she shook hands with him and with Deo and then, accompanied by her security guards, swept from the hall.

Fisher, beaming, watched her go.

The glorious night ended, and Fisher returned to Key West to confront the question that had not changed. What if he already owned all the treasure that the *Atocha* was to give him? What if there was no more for him, no mother lode, nothing? He could live with that now, he decided. He was seeing it clearly at last. He had found the *Atocha*. He had reached the most important of his goals already. He felt purified.

Of course he did not mean to stop searching yet for the hundreds of silver bars still down there, and he sent the boats back to sea.

New finds seemed to point off toward the deep water on a new trail. Pat Clyne found a fourth silver bar sitting alone atop a rocky patch of bottom. It weighed sixty-four pounds and was encrusted with marine life, encrustations that seemed so natural and so beautiful that they were not removed. Bouncy John and Ron Bennett, diving as a team, found a fifth bar, the heaviest yet, seventy-seven pounds. Bouncy said he could hear Ron screaming under the water from ten feet away.

Barrel hoops and cannonballs were found. An eighteen-inch, heavy gold chain was found, first gold in a year. Dr. Harold Edgerton, a Massachusetts Institute of Technology scientist, brought a new sub-bottom scanner out to the wreck site, and this instrument delimited a number of areas where the bottom seemed to conform to the approximate shape of a sunken galleon. Each such formation could turn out to be geological, Dr. Edgerton cautioned. But he failed to dampen the eagerness of Fisher and the divers. It took a long time to dig all the new areas out, and geological was what each of them proved to be. No matter, the instrument clearly worked and would pinpoint new places to dig, and the barrel hoops and cannonballs seemed to be pointing in a specific direction also. Fisher came out with a new hydro-flo digging machine, a kind of flexible mailbox, and it became possible to move sand fast again. Everyone felt that the *Atocha's* carcass could not elude them much longer.

The search goes on. The 896 silver bars, the 78 chests of coins, the 9 remaining cannons, the fortune in gold bullion—all of it is still down there somewhere, washed every day by the currents and men's dreams.

About the Author

ROBERT DALEY is the author of twelve previous books, five of them novels, three of them picture books containing the author's own photos. His articles, photos, and short stories have appeared in most major magazines including *Esquire, Vogue, Playboy, Life, Reader's Digest, New York, The New York Times Magazine,* and abroad, in *Paris Match.* His photos have been exhibited in the Baltimore Museum, the Art Institute of Chicago, and other galleries. His work has been translated into many languages including Japanese, Portuguese, and Dutch. Certain of his books have grown out of personal experience. His six years with the New York Football Giants resulted in *Only A Game,* the first serious pro football novel; and his six years as a *New York Times* foreign correspondent resulted in another novel, *The Whole Truth.* In 1971 and 1972 he served as a New York City deputy police commissioner; the best-selling nonfiction *Target Blue* followed in 1973, and the novel *To Kill a Cop* in 1976.

To write *Treasure* Mr. Daley joined the divers on the floor of the Gulf of Mexico hunting with them both for treasure and for food; he also found and studied the original Spanish documents in the archive in Seville.

Mr. Daley and his French-born wife have three daughters and live in Connecticut.